TRADING OPTIONS WITH PURPOSE

# *The* GITA *of* OPTION TRADING

TRADING OPTIONS WITH PURPOSE

# The GITA of OPTION TRADING

RAJIV L B ROY

PRABHAT PRAKASHAN

*Published by*
**PRABHAT PRAKASHAN PVT. LTD.**
4/19 Asaf Ali Road,
New Delhi-110 002 (INDIA)
e-mail: prabhatbooks@gmail.com

ISBN 978-93-5562-990-6
**THE GITA OF OPTION TRADING**
*by* Rajiv L B Roy



*Edition*
First, 2024

*Price*
₹ 350 (Rupees Three Hundred Fifty Only)

*Printed at*
E.B. Print & Pack, Greater Noida

## Dedication

*This book is dedicated to my father, Late Krishna Kanta Roy, for your love, blessings and upbringing, which taught me how to persevere in difficult circumstances.*

# Author's Note

You may wonder why 'The Gita' is mentioned in this book. Let me explain why. In the ancient Hindu classic known as the Bhagavad Gita, Lord Krishna and Arjuna have a conversation. Lord Krishna teaches Arjuna how to live a moral life and fulfil his military duties. The wisdom and insights from the Bhagavad Gita are widely respected.

The title of this book, 'The Gita of Option Trading: Trading Options With Purpose' highlights the idea that option trading, like life itself, requires purpose, discipline, and a deep understanding of the underlying principles. This book draws inspiration from the Bhagavad Gita to provide traders with a framework for approaching option trading with clarity and a sense of purpose.

The Bhagavad Gita is known for teaching balance and detachment. Similarly, successful option trading involves a balanced strategy where traders carefully weigh the risks and benefits of each trade while keeping emotions in check. The concepts from the Bhagavad Gita can help traders develop the balance and impartiality needed to thrive in the fast-paced world of option trading.

*karmanye vadhikaraste maa phaleshu kadachana,*
*maa karmaphalaheturbhurma te sangostvakarmani*

The Bhagavad Gita says in Chapter 2, Verse 47: “You have the right to work but never to its fruits.” (Do not be motivated by the fruits of action, nor be attached to inaction.)

The phrase emphasises the need to remain unattached from the outcome of one’s activities. This means that while trading options, traders should focus on their trading strategies and tactics rather than becoming overly attached to particular transaction results.

This is crucial because emotions can cloud judgement and lead to poor trading decisions. If a trader becomes too attached to the outcome of a trade, they may hold onto a losing position instead of cutting losses and moving on to the next opportunity. This can result in increased losses and negatively impact overall trading success.

By focusing on the process rather than the outcome, traders can maintain discipline in their trading strategy and avoid irrational judgements. This means adhering to a set of rules for trading regardless of how individual trades turn out. This disciplined approach can ultimately improve traders’ consistency and performance in the market.

The saying—You have the right to work, but never to the fruits of work—underscores the importance of focusing on the trading process rather than fixating on the outcome of any one trade. By remaining disciplined and objective, traders can enhance their chances of long-term success in the field of option trading.

*The Gita of Option Trading: Trading Options With Purpose* aims to provide traders with a comprehensive guide to understanding the basics of option trading, analysing the option chain, interpreting FII, DII, and Pro traders’ data, developing option trading strategies, and adjusting those strategies using real-world examples.

The book starts by teaching the foundations of option trading, including terminology, option types, option Greeks, and other variables that impact option prices. It then moves on to option chain analysis, which involves studying the information in option chains to identify profitable trades. An important part of the book is the study of FII, DII, and Pro Trader data and how it helps in spotting market trends.

Additionally, the book covers various option strategies such as bullish, bearish and neutral strategies, explaining when to use each strategy based on the current market conditions. Real-world examples are provided to illustrate how these strategies can be successfully applied.

Finally, the book discusses how to manage existing option holdings, including strategies to minimise risk and maximise returns in different market scenarios. Adjusting option strategies is a key aspect of successful option trading. We will explore how to modify your strategy if the market doesn't move as expected or goes in the opposite direction.

Throughout the book, I emphasise the importance of having a purpose for each trade. In my opinion, effective option trading requires a solid understanding of the market and a well-defined strategy to achieve specific goals.

This book covers everything you need to know about buying and selling options. Whether you are a novice or an experienced trader, it will help you grasp the fundamentals of options and navigate complex option strategy adjustments. After reading this book, you will be able to identify market trends and adapt your strategy effectively when the market doesn't move as predicted.

I believe this book will be a valuable resource for traders at all levels who want to trade options with purpose and confidence.

❑

# Acknowledgements

To God for your blessings and for inspiring me to write a book.

To my wife, thank you for your support during the writing process and for showing me love and care.

To my family, especially my brother-in-law Dr R C Roy, for fostering me in pursuing my passion and believing in me.

❑

# Contents

# Options: An Introduction

Options are versatile trading tools that can be used in any market condition, whether it's bullish, bearish, or even range-bound. While options were once considered risky and suitable only for experienced investors with significant capital, they have now become increasingly popular and accessible to traders of all levels.

Options offer unique advantages, such as leveraging your investments and turning small capital into substantial gains. They can also serve as a form of insurance to protect your investments in case of market downturns. Therefore, it is essential for every trader and investor to understand and utilise options effectively.

In this book, you will learn about various aspects of options trading, starting from basic calls and puts to more complex option spreads. You will gain a comprehensive understanding of index options and stock options. Additionally, you will discover how to assess the market using data from foreign institutional investors (FIIs), domestic institutional investors (DIIs), and open interest build-ups on option chains.

By the end of this book, you will have a thorough knowledge of option trading. You will be able to execute basic strategies and explore advanced techniques like straddles and spreads. Importantly, you will also learn how to adjust your option strategy based on real-life scenarios when the market doesn't go in your favour.

Whether you are a beginner, intermediate trader, veteran, or professional money manager, this book will equip you with the necessary knowledge and skills to navigate the world of option trading successfully.

## WHAT IS AN OPTION?

An option is a contract between a buyer and a seller that grants the buyer the right, but not the obligation, to buy or sell an underlying asset at a specific price (known as the exercise price or strike price) on or before a predetermined date. It is considered a derivative because its value is derived from the underlying asset, which can be a stock, index, commodity, or other financial instrument.

To better understand the concept of an option, let's use the example of buying an apartment. Suppose you find an apartment in your desired neighbourhood that costs ₹1 crore, but you don't currently have enough funds to purchase it. However, you don't want to miss out on the opportunity, so you negotiate with the builder for an option contract.

In this scenario, you pay an upfront fee of ₹1 lakh to the builder for the option to buy the apartment for ₹1 crore within a six-month period. Now, consider two possible outcomes:

a. The market value of the apartment increases: If, within the six months, the apartment's market value rises to ₹1.10 crore, you can exercise your option and buy the apartment for ₹1 crore. Since the builder is obligated to honour the option contract, you can sell the apartment immediately for ₹1.10 crore, resulting in a profit of ₹9 lakhs (1.10 crore – 1.00 crore =1 lakh).

b. The market value of the apartment decreases: Conversely, if the market value of the apartment drops to ₹90 lakhs, you have the choice to not exercise your option. In this case, you would not proceed with the purchase and would only lose the upfront fee of ₹1 lakh paid for the option. Thus, you avoid incurring a loss of ₹10 lakhs (the difference between the option price of ₹1 crore and the reduced market value of ₹90 lakhs).

From this example, two key points about options become evident. First, purchasing an option grants you the right to enter into a contract but not the obligation. You can choose whether or not to exercise the option based on market conditions and your desired outcome. Second, options are contracts based on underlying assets, which explains why they are considered derivatives. The underlying asset in the apartment example is the flat itself. In the financial market, underlying assets are typically stocks or indices.

When a buyer purchases an option, they pay the seller a fee known as the premium. The premium is the price negotiated and established when options are traded on various exchanges. For instance, if you want to purchase an ITC 350 call option with an August expiration date for ₹5, you have the choice (but not the obligation) to buy 1,600 shares of ITC (the lot size of ITC is 1,600 shares) at ₹350 per share before the option expires. In this case, the premium would be ₹5, and ₹350 would be the exercise price or strike price.

## TYPES OF OPTIONS

Indeed, call options and put options are the two main types of option contracts. Let's further explore these types:

*1.* ***Call option:*** A call option provides the buyer with the right, but not the obligation, to purchase an underlying asset at a specified price (strike price) within a predetermined timeframe. The buyer pays a premium to the seller for this privilege. By holding a call option, the buyer anticipates that the price of the underlying asset will rise. If the price of the asset increases above the strike price, the buyer can exercise the option and profit from the price difference. However, if the price remains below the strike price or the option expires, the buyer may choose not to exercise the option and will only lose the premium paid.

*2.* ***Put option*:** A put option grants the buyer the right, but not the obligation, to sell an underlying asset at a predetermined price (strike price) within a specific time period. Similar to call options, put options also involve the payment of a premium by the buyer to the seller. The buyer of a put option expects the price of the underlying asset to decrease. If the price falls below the strike price, the buyer can exercise the option and sell the asset at a higher price, thus generating a profit. However, if the price remains above the strike price or the option expires, the buyer can choose not to exercise the option and will only lose the premium paid.

In the options market, there are four types of participants based on the positions they take:

*i.* ***Call buyers*:** These are individuals or entities who purchase call options, acquiring the right to buy the underlying asset at the specified price within the designated timeframe.

*ii.* ***Call sellers*:** Also known as call writers, they are the sellers of call options. They receive the premium from the buyer in exchange for the obligation to sell the underlying asset if *the buyer exercises the option.*

*iii.* ***Put buyers*:** Put buyers are those who purchase put options, granting them the right to sell the underlying asset at the predetermined price within the specified timeframe.

*iv.* ***Put sellers*:** Put sellers, or put writers, sell put options to buyers. They receive the premium and take on the obligation to purchase the underlying asset if the buyer exercises the option.

It is important to note that while option buyers have the right to exercise their options, option sellers (writers) are obligated to fulfil the terms of the contract. The distinction between buyers and sellers is crucial in understanding the rights and obligations associated with options contracts.

## STYLES OF OPTIONS

Options can be categorised into two main styles: American options and European options. Here's an overview of each style:

***American options***: American options provide the holder with the right to exercise the option at any time before its expiration date, or on the expiration date itself. The flexibility of American options allows the holder to choose the most favourable time to exercise the option, depending on market conditions. American options are commonly traded for equities and indices. The majority of options traded on US exchanges are of the American style.

***European options***: European options, on the other hand, can only be exercised on the expiration date of the contract. Unlike American options, they do not allow early exercise. The exercise of European options can only occur at the end of the option's lifespan. These options are frequently traded in the over-the-counter (OTC) market and are commonly found in European markets.

It's worth noting that the exercise style of options can vary depending on the underlying asset and the market in which they are traded. In the Indian market, for example, all equities and index options are exercised as European options. Weekly options in India expire on Thursdays, while monthly options expire on the final Thursday of each month.

Understanding the distinction between American and European options is crucial for options traders, as it affects the flexibility and timing of exercising the options.

# USES OF OPTIONS

Investors and traders utilise options primarily for two reasons:

i. Speculation

ii. Hedging

***Speculation:*** Speculation is the practise of buying and selling stocks for short periods of time in order to outperform long-term investors. Speculators take risks in anticipation of future market movement in the hope of making large rewards that exceed their risk. Speculators seek to benefit by forecasting the price movement of securities in the near future.

Because the option is an incredibly versatile trading tool, speculators never fall behind in using its adaptability. The main advantage of trading options is that you are not limited to benefitting from rising market moves. You can earn even if the market is heading downward or sideways.

Option trading allows you to make a lot of money rapidly. However, if your estimate is inaccurate, you might lose a large quantity of money. If you are an option buyer, you must precisely estimate not just the direction of the security's price movement, but also its magnitude and timing. To succeed, you must predict accurately whether the price will go up or decrease, as well as how much it will vary over time.

The finest component of option speculating is the use of leverage. A single contract might provide you ownership over hundreds of shares. On the other hand, this is why it is dangerous too. A considerable movement is required for the security to produce a profit.

For instance, if you wanted to acquire stocks in firm ABC at the current share price of ₹100 and you had ₹1,00,000 to invest, you could buy 1,000 shares. You might sell the stock and make a profit of ₹10,000 (10% return on your initial investment) if the stock price increases by ₹10.

On the other hand, your profit might have been far bigger if you had used leverage to purchase the stock option. You may purchase 20,000 quantities of a call option on the aforementioned stock with a strike price of ₹100 for each option, allowing you to purchase 2,000 shares of stock (taking a lot size of 1,000 shares into account). You may use your option to acquire shares at ₹50 and then immediately sell them for ₹60 if the price increases to ₹110. Your profit in this scenario would be ₹2,00,000. The return on your initial investment of ₹1,00,000 would have been 100% this time.

That is the power of leverage. When employing options, a trader may trade with little capital and control more shares with a lower investment. However, if your guess is wrong, you might lose a lot of money. To succeed in option trading, you must make very precise stock movement predictions.

***Hedging:*** People use options as a secondary way to hedge their assets. It is a great investment hedging tool. This option is comparable to an insurance policy. Unlike our vehicle or house, we insure our assets to protect against unforeseen disasters; our portfolios may also be protected against a downturn. If you are dubious about your stock picks, you should either hedge your position or avoid investing. Options are routinely used by large financial institutions to safeguard their interests. Individual investors might benefit from it as well. Assume you want to invest in the chemical industry as a result of the Chinese industrial crisis in order to profit from the stock's rise. However, you also want to keep your losses to a minimum. Therefore, buying options allows you to cost-effectively reduce the downside risk while still taking full advantage of the upward movement.

Let's look at an illustration of how options-based hedging works to control portfolio risk. Consider that you have 1,000 shares of the stock ABC and are concerned about a decline in value. Therefore, you want to use options to hedge your portfolio. If you wish to sell that stock at the specified strike price regardless of how much the market price of the stock declines, you could purchase a put option on it. As a result, by paying a premium, you have protected yourself from any more losses below the strike price. This is how using this conservative method, you can reduce your potential market losses.

❑

# Some Terminologies

The realms of investing and trading are packed with numerous sophisticated jargon to give the impression that only professionals or specialists can handle equities. Despite their frightening and confusing look, they are only a few simple ideas expressed creatively. Given the unique nature of option trading within the financial business, it is important to become familiar with the language used in option trading. Before beginning to trade options, it is critical to understand and be comfortable with the terminology. In the following portions of the book, the terminology will be discussed one at a time.

## OPTION PREMIUM

The option premium is the fee that an option buyer pays to an option seller in exchange for the right to purchase (in the case of a call option) or sell (in the case of a put option) an underlying asset at a certain price (strike price) within a specified time period. In other terms, the option premium is the price of an option contract on the open market. The premium is basically the option's cost, and it is decided by a variety of criteria, including the underlying asset's current price, the strike price, the time to expiry, and the projected volatility of the underlying asset. The premiums for out-of-the-money (OTM) options are made up entirely of extrinsic value, while those for in-the-money (ITM) options include intrinsic as well as extrinsic value.

The premium may be thought of as insurance since it protects the buyer from negative fluctuations in the price of the underlying asset. The seller, on the other hand, receives the premium and bears the risk that the buyer would exercise the option, resulting in a loss for the seller.

## LOT SIZE

In general, lot size refers to the quantity of an item purchased for delivery on a given date. A lot size is the number of stocks purchased in a single trading transaction. A lot is the smallest number of units of securities that may be acquired or sold in an option trading transaction. SEBI (Securities and Exchange Board of India) determines the lot size for F&O traders. It regulates market price quotations by using lot size. Because the lot size is fixed, traders are constantly aware of the cost of each unit. There will be no price standardisation or bulk uniformity if no specified lots are used.

To better understand lot size, consider the following example.

A lot for ITC is 1,600 shares. As a result, traders may only buy it in multiples of 1,600. The value of the option contract is determined by the product of the number of units and their respective prices. As a consequence, if the ITC option price is 10 and a 1,600-lot amount is purchased, the transaction is worth 10 × 1,600, or ₹16,000.

SEBI determines the lot size for each stock and index that is allowed for derivative trading. It is crucial to recognise that lot sizes vary. Shares come in a variety of lot sizes.

## INTRINSIC VALUE

In finance, intrinsic value is the actual value of an asset determined by its basic characteristics and underlying cash flows. In the case of a stock, the intrinsic value would represent the current value of the company's expected future profits and cash flows.

The intrinsic value of an option is what the option would be worth if it were exercised immediately. In other words, it is the difference between the current market price of the underlying asset and the strike price of the option. The intrinsic value of any stock is always positive and can never be negative.

The intrinsic value of an option acts as a minimum value or floor since the option price should never be less than its intrinsic value. The remaining value of the option, if any, is known as the time value, and it indicates the potential rise in value if the price of the underlying asset changes before the option expires.

## EXTRINSIC VALUE

Extrinsic value, often known as time value, is the portion of an option's premium that is due to variables other than intrinsic value. In other words, it is the premium that an option buyer is ready to pay in return for the possibility that the option could change in their favour before it expires.

The time remaining before expiry, the predicted volatility of the underlying asset, and the level of interest rates all have an impact on extrinsic value. Changes in market conditions, such as changes in supply and demand for the option, shifts in market sentiment, or changes in the degree of implied volatility, can all have an effect on the extrinsic value of an option.

Extrinsic value is a variable amount that can change over time, as opposed to intrinsic value, which is a fixed amount based on the current market price of the underlying asset and the option's strike price. All else being equal, an option's extrinsic value tends to decline as it approaches expiration. This is because there is less time for the option to benefit the buyer and, as a consequence, less ambiguity about its potential value.

## STRIKE PRICE

The strike price, also known as the exercise price, is the price at which the holder of an option can purchase or sell the underlying asset before or on the expiration date of the option, depending on the kind of option. A call option's strike price is the amount at which the holder has the right but not the obligation to buy the underlying asset. The strike price of a put option is the price at which the holder has the right but not the obligation to sell the underlying asset.

A variety of factors, including the strike price, affect the intrinsic value of an option, which is the difference between the current market price of the underlying asset and the strike price. If the option is in-the-money (ITM), suggesting that it has intrinsic value, the option buyer might exercise it to profit. If the option was out-of-the-money (OTM), the buyer would not exercise it since it has no intrinsic value and would result in a loss.

The strike price is often specified when the option is issued, and it is one of the elements that determines the option's premium, along with the current market price of the underlying asset, the time to expiry, and the predicted volatility of the underlying asset.

## SPOT PRICE

The word 'spot price' refers to the asset's current market value at the time of the trade, such as the price of a commodity or financial instrument. The spot price, as opposed to the future price, is the price at which an asset can be acquired or sold for delivery at a later date.

In the context of equities, for example, the spot price of SBIN is the current market price of SBI share price that may be purchased or sold for immediate delivery, in contrast to a futures price, which is the price at which the stock can be bought or sold for delivery at a future date.

Numerous factors, including supply and demand dynamics, geopolitical happenings, changes in interest rates or currency rates, and the overall state of the economy, can influence spot pricing. Spot pricing may be used as a benchmark or point of reference to determine the worth of other financial instruments or contracts on occasion.

## BID AND ASK PRICE

The bid price and ask price are two important prices mentioned in financial markets for assets such as stocks, bonds, derivatives and currencies. These prices reflect the most recent highest asking price (bid price) a buyer is prepared to pay for an asset, as well as the most recent lowest offering price (ask price) a seller is willing to accept for the same item.

At any given time, the bid price is the highest price that a buyer is willing to pay for a security. It shows the market price at which a buyer can sell the securities. In other terms, it is the amount of money a buyer is willing to pay to obtain an asset from a seller.

In contrast, the ask price is the lowest price at which a seller is willing to sell the asset at any particular moment. It shows the market price at which a seller may purchase the security. In other terms, it is the amount of money that a seller is ready to take in order to sell an item to a buyer.

The bid-ask spread, defined as the difference between the ask and bid prices, defines how much it costs to buy or sell an item in the market. The quantity of supply and demand for the item, as well as other market conditions, may all influence the bid-ask spread. Assets with higher levels of liquidity typically have bid-ask spreads that are closer together, whereas assets with lower levels of liquidity typically have wider spreads.

## MONEYNESS

Moneyness is the current price of an underlying asset in relation to the strike price of a derivative contract. It exposes the intrinsic value of a particular choice in the present. It notifies the option buyer whether or not exercising the contract will result in a profit or loss. Moneyness is classified into three categories based on where the spot price is in reference to the strike price. As an example:

***In-the-money (ITM):*** If the option has a positive intrinsic value and the contract is set to expire today, it is referred to as an in-the-money or ITM option. It is referred to as an ITM option for a call option if the underlying price is above the strike price, and a put option if the underlying price is below the strike price.

***Out-of-the-money (OTM):*** A contract is considered out-of-the-money (OTM) if the intrinsic value of the option is less than the market price and the contract expires at that price. The spot price is lower than the strike price for call options and higher than the strike price for put options.

***At-the-money (ATM):*** An option is at-the-money (ATM) if the strike price and current market price are the same. The same is true for call and put options.

## OPEN INTEREST

Open interest refers to the total number of contracts for a certain futures or options contract that are still open and have not yet been resolved by delivery, offset or expiration. In other words, it represents all open contracts that have yet to be closed or completed. Open interest is a helpful statistic for determining the degree of activity and liquidity in a certain futures or options market. It may provide traders and analysts with insights into market mood and trends, as well as assist them in evaluating the level of interest in a certain asset or contract.

When numerous market players are actively trading an asset or contract, it has a high open interest. This can increase liquidity while also making it easier for traders to initiate and exit positions. Conversely, low open interest may indicate that there is less interest in the asset or contract, making it more difficult to find counterparties to trade with and potentially leading to larger bid-ask spreads and less attractive pricing.

Furthermore, open interest might disclose information about potential future price movements. Increases in open interest, for example, may suggest higher interest in the asset or contract and a potential price increase, while decreases in open interest may signal declining interest and a potential price reduction. However, open interest alone cannot be used to anticipate price changes since it overlooks other elements that may influence market pricing, such as supply and demand dynamics, current economic circumstances, and geopolitical events.

## OPTION CHAIN

A table or matrix that shows all available options for a certain underlying asset, such as a stock, index or commodity, is known as an option chain. It gives a detailed breakdown of the various option contracts available for that asset, including strike prices, expiration dates, and option premiums. Option chains often comprise information such as the underlying asset's symbol or ticker, the date of the option contract, the option type (call or put), the strike price, the option premium or price, and the option's implied volatility. Other information, such as open interest and volume for each option contract, may also be included.

Option chains are a significant tool for options traders and investors due to their ability to quickly compare and analyse various options contracts based on characteristics such as strike price, expiration date, and implied volatility. Use these tools to identify potential trading opportunities, balance risk and return, and develop trading strategies.

Option chains are available on the majority of financial and trading platforms. As new options contracts are issued and existing contracts expire or are settled, these chains are updated in real time. The option chain is provided free of charge by the National Stock Exchange (NSE). However, users must refresh the page to obtain real-time data.

## TIME DECAY

Time decay, also known as theta decay, is the progressive decrease in the value of an option contract as its expiration date approaches. It indicates how rapidly the extrinsic value or time value of an option depreciates as the option approaches its expiration date. Time decay happens because options have a finite lifespan, and as the expiry date approaches, there is less time for the underlying asset to move in a positive direction for the option to be lucrative. This decrease in time to expiry decreases the amount of time value left in the option, lowering the option's total value.

The rate of time decay is affected by the time till expiry, implied volatility, strike price, and current value of the underlying asset. Options with more time left before expiry frequently have a higher time value and, as a result, a slower rate of time decay, whereas options with less time remaining before expiration have a lower time value and a quicker rate of decay.

Time decay is an essential issue for options traders to grasp since it affects the profitability of options positions as well as trade timing. The impact of time decay on positions must be addressed when traders develop trading strategies in order to profit from a change in the underlying asset's price.

## VOLATILITY

Volatility means how much a price changes over time. It helps us understand how risky or uncertain an investment is. We measure volatility by looking at how much an investment's price has gone up and down in the past. If volatility is low, it means the price is more stable and won't change a lot. But if volatility is high, the price is more likely to go up or down quickly.

Many things can cause volatility, like changes in how people think about the market, the economy, or important events happening around the world. Volatility can be both good and bad for investors. It can be risky because it's hard to predict what will happen, but it can also create opportunities to make money.

Investors and traders use volatility to understand how much risk there is and to make trading plans. They look at volatility to figure out how risky an investment is. They might also use it to find times when the price is low and buy, and times when it's high and sell.

There are two types of volatility: historical and implied. Historical volatility looks at how the price has changed in the past. Implied volatility (IV) tries to predict how much the price might change in the near future.

## LEGS

In options trading, the term 'legs' means the different parts of a strategy that use multiple options contracts. For example, when you do a spread strategy, you buy one call option with a lower price and sell another call option with a higher price. This strategy has two legs: buying the cheaper call option is one leg, and selling the more expensive call option is the other leg.

Another strategy is called a straddle. It involves buying both a call option and a put option with the same price and expiration date for a particular asset. This strategy also has two legs: buying the call option is one leg, and buying the put option is the other leg.

By looking at the legs of a strategy separately, traders can quickly understand the possible risks and rewards. They can make changes to their investments as needed to get the desired outcome.

# SPREAD

A spread is a multi-leg option strategy that includes simultaneously buying and selling two or more option contracts on the same underlying asset. A spread is employed to possibly improve a trader's potential profits while lowering their risk exposure.

Options spreads can take several forms, including:

***Vertical spreads*:** These include the purchase and sale of option contracts with the same expiration date but differing strike prices. A bullish vertical spread is formed by purchasing a lower strike price call option and selling a higher strike price call option, whereas a bearish vertical spread is formed by purchasing a higher strike price put option and selling a lower strike price put option.

***Horizontal spread**:* This is the purchase and sale of option contracts with the same strike price but separate expiration dates. A horizontal spread can be used to profit from differences in implied volatility across option contracts with different expiry dates.

***Diagonal spread:*** This involves buying and selling options contracts with different strike prices and expiration dates. A diagonal spread can be used to create a risk/reward profile tailored to the trader's specific objectives.

❑

# Option Greeks

Option Greeks are a set of elements that help us understand the different risks involved in trading options. They are named after Greek symbols and are important for option traders. The Greeks, like Delta, Vega and Theta, are used to figure out how risky a portfolio is. They help traders calculate the potential profit or loss of a trade when the price of the underlying asset changes, which helps them manage risk.

The Greeks measure how sensitive the price of an option is to different factors that affect its value. The Black Scholes Model is a popular mathematical model used to price options.

There are five main option Greeks: Delta, Gamma, Vega, Theta and Rho. Each Greek is sensitive to different parameters and helps calculate the price of an option. In the upcoming parts of this book, we will learn more about each of these Greeks and how they work.

## DELTA

Among all the Greeks used by options traders, the delta is the most common one. Delta measures how quickly the price of an option changes when the price of the underlying asset moves. It tells us how sensitive the option price is to changes in the stock price.

If the market goes up or down by a point, delta measures how much the option premium will change. For both call and put options with the same strike price, we calculate delta separately. Call options have a positive delta value, while put options have a negative delta value. The value of delta for call options ranges from 0 to 1, while the value for put options ranges from 1 to 0.

Let's use an example to better understand the Greek delta. Assume that the current market price of a stock, let's say XYZ, is ₹100. The table below shows the various delta values for call options. The values in the table are speculative. It is prepared purely as an example.

| Call option | | | | | | | | | |
|---|---|---|---|---|---|---|---|---|---|
| **Strike price** | 80 | 85 | 90 | 95 | 100 | 105 | 110 | 115 | 120 |
| **Call premium** | 25 | 20 | 15 | 10 | 5 | 4 | 3 | 2 | 1 |
| **Delta** | 0.9 | 0.8 | 0.7 | 0.6 | 0.5 | 0.4 | 0.3 | 0.2 | 0.1 |

The values of delta for call options are higher for in-the-money (ITM) strikes than out-of-the-money (OTM) strikes, according to the above table. Consider an ITM option with a strike price of 90. The delta is worth ₹0.70, and the premium is 15. In other words, if the price of the underlying, XYZ, goes to ₹101, the new premium of the 90 strike will increase to ₹15.70 (₹15.00 + 0.70), taking other aspects into consideration. On the contrary, the option price will instead drop to ₹14.30 if the stock price drops to ₹99. (₹15.00 – 0.70).

Take yet another put option example for the same stock. At various strike prices, the accompanying table includes possible values for the option price and delta. In this case, the ITM put option's delta value bears move values, but it does so negatively. It indicates that delta has a negative correlation with option premium for put options. It is evident from the table that option prices are more sensitive to price at ITM strikes than at OTM strikes.

| Put option | | | | | | | | | |
|---|---|---|---|---|---|---|---|---|---|
| **Strike price** | 80 | 85 | 90 | 95 | 100 | 105 | 110 | 115 | 120 |
| **Put premium** | 1 | 2 | 3 | 4 | 5 | 10 | 15 | 20 | 25 |
| **Delta** | -0.1 | -0.2 | -0.3 | -0.4 | -0.5 | -0.6 | -0.7 | -0.8 | -0.9 |

For demonstration purposes, we'll use the same strike price, 90, which is now an OTM option. It states that the premium is ₹3.00 and that the delta is just ₹0.30. According to the definition of delta, if the stock price rises to ₹101, the price of the ₹90 strike will reduce by ₹0.30 and the new price will be ₹2.70. (₹3.00 – 0.30). But, if the underlying price drops to ₹99, the option price will rise by ₹0.30.

Also, it can be seen from the aforementioned table that the value of delta for a call option is almost 0.50 for at-the-money (ATM) options, less than 0.50 for out-of-the-money (OTM) options, and greater than 0.50 for in-the-money (ITM) options. The value of a put option, on the other hand, is - 0.50 for ATM strikes, larger than - 0.50 for ITM strikes, and less than - 0.50 for OTM strikes. The graph below will give you an idea of how the delta values for call and put options change depending on the spot price.

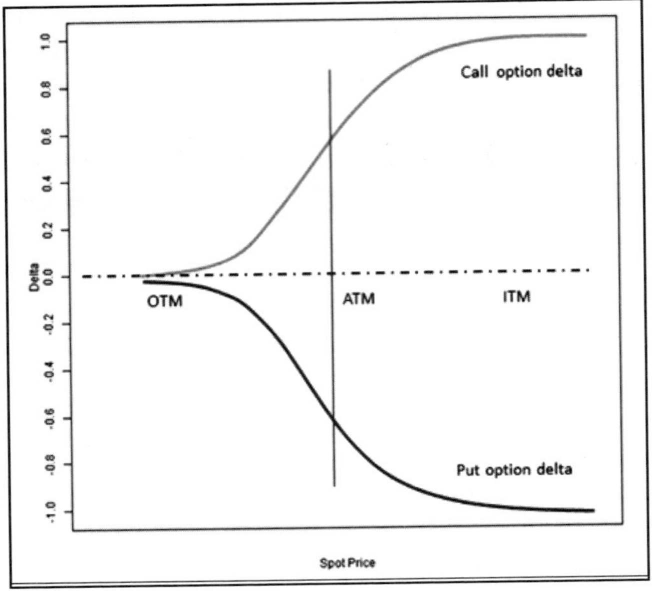


## GAMMA

The option Greek gamma is the rate of change of Greek delta. A call option's gamma, which is always reported in percentage terms, shows how the delta changes as the underlying asset moves by one point. Its basic definition is the rate of change of delta. Gamma can be thought of as acceleration if delta is the speed at which the option premium changes. It serves as a gauge for the stability of delta.

Let's use an illustration.

Suppose that ABC Company's stock is currently trading at ₹100. Assume the following hypothetical values for the various variables for the ₹100 call option:

| Stock price | Delta | Gamma | Option premium |
|---|---|---|---|
| 100 | 0.50 | 0.1 | 0.60 |

According to the definition of gamma, a change of one rupee in the underlying asset will cause a change in delta of ₹0.10. The values of the various variables will be as per the following table if the stock has now moved to ₹101.

| Stock price | Delta | Gamma | Option premium |
|---|---|---|---|
| 101 | 0.60 (0.50 + 0.10) | 0.09 (say) | 10.60 (10 + 0.60) |

The gamma values are influenced by the proximity of the strike prices and the expiration time. When comparing at-the-money options to out-of-the-money and in-the-money options, the value is significant for at-the-money options and gradually declines. In addition, the gamma value is greater for contracts with near-term expiration and decreases for those with far-term expiration. The accompanying graph demonstrates the relation among the gamma value, strike price, and time to expiry.

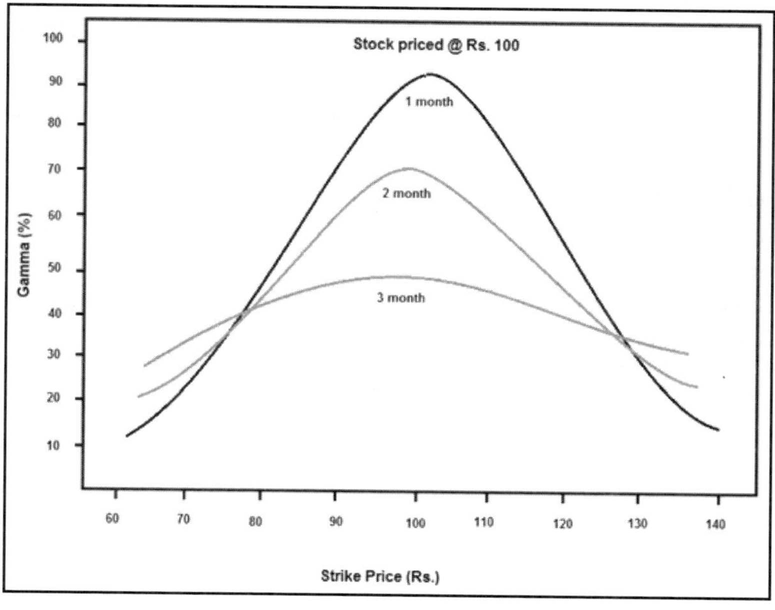

## VEGA

Vega is the change in option price for every 1% change in implied volatility (IV). Implied volatility is the market's prediction of a potential movement in the price of an asset. Vega affects the time value but not the intrinsic value of the option. Implied volatility and it are positively correlated. This implies that vega rises in parallel with an increase in the expected volatility of a security. Also, whereas the value of vega is negative for short option positions, it is positive for long option positions. The table that follows demonstrates how implied volatility and consequently, the option price affect the vega value.

| Initial option price | Vega | Final option price | |
|---|---|---|---|
| | | For 1% increase in IV | For 1% decrease in IV |
| 50 | 0.30 | 50.30 | 49.70 |
| 25 | 0.10 | 25.10 | 24.90 |

Moreover, unlike gamma, the Greek vega option's value peaks for at-the-money options while steadily decreasing for both in-the-money and out-of-the-money options. However, the value of vega is also influenced by the period of expiration. The vega has more value for long-term expiry than for short-term expiry. To better understand their relationship, look at the chart below.

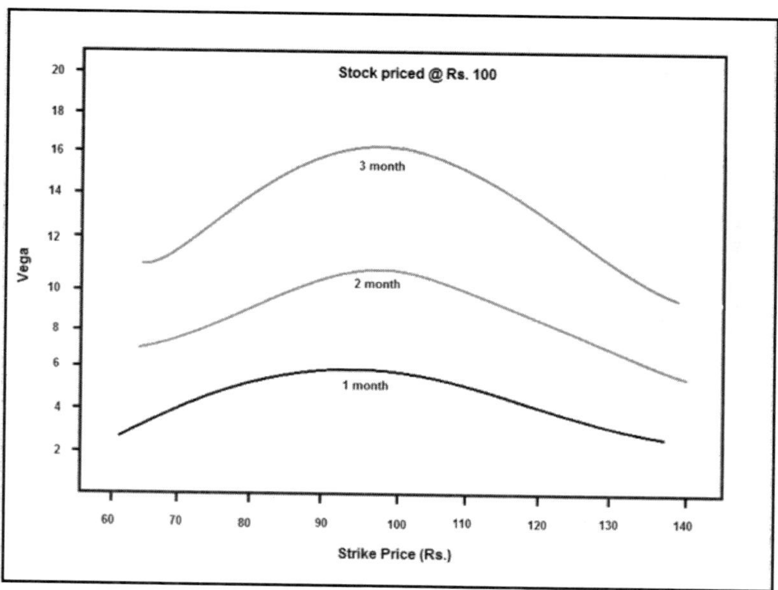


## THETA

Even while all other factors remain constant until the contract's maturity, the price of an option depreciates. Theta is the measure of how much an option's value declines. Hence, the Greek theta is the amount of decline in call and put option prices for a change of one day in the maturity time. It is also known as time decay and is expressed as a negative number. Due to its negative value, theta, also known as time decay, is the number one enemy of option buyers. Instead, it is the best buddy of option writers.

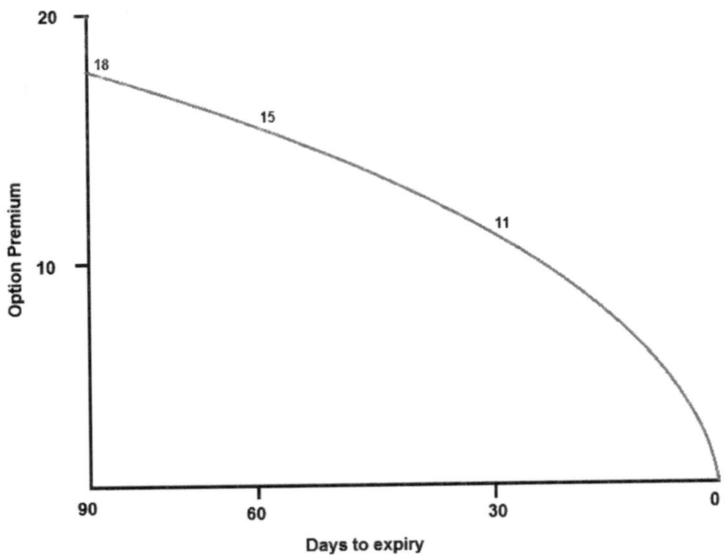


An at-the-money option premium decay is displayed in the graph above with more than three months to maturity. When ₹4 declined for the following 30 days while other factors remained constant, the option value only depreciated by ₹3 from 90 to 60 days. The value of the premium decline rate for the final 30 days before expiration drops to zero from ₹11. As the time value nears its expiration, it falls more quickly. This sensation is comparable to the hot summer sun on an ice cube. The temporal value of an option diminishes with each passing second. Moreover, the loss of time value happens more quickly close to maturation.

The value of theta also relies on the strike price. Theta has a high time value for at-the-money strikes but has a lower value for in-the-money and out-of-the-money strike prices. This indicates that OTM options are least sensitive to the theta value while ATM options are more sensitive to time value decay than ITM options. However, keep in mind that theta's value is always negative.

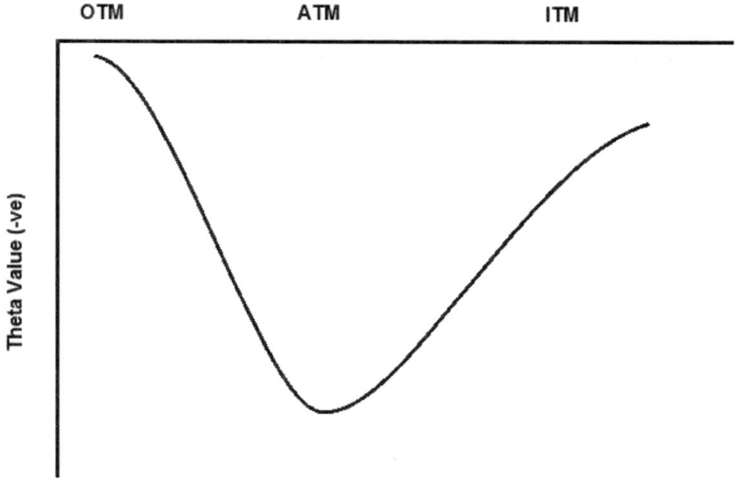


## RHO

Rho is an option Greek that measures how an option's price changes when there are changes in interest rates. It tells us the expected price change of an option for a 1% increase in interest rates. Rho is usually positive for call options, which means the price of the option will go up when interest rates rise. On the other hand, rho is often negative for put options, indicating that the price of the option will decrease when interest rates go up.

This relationship exists because interest rates affect the cost of carrying an asset over time. The cost of carry includes things like interest rates, storage costs, and insurance fees. When interest rates go up, the cost of carrying an asset also increases, which can lead to higher prices for the underlying asset. As a result, call options on the underlying asset may become more expensive.

It's important to note that rho is usually only meaningful for longer-term options because short-term interest rate changes don't have a significant impact on option prices. Longer-term options that are 'in-the-money' are more sensitive to changes in interest rates. Short-term options are less affected because interest rates don't fluctuate frequently. However, for long-term options, the cost of carrying can have a big impact on their value.

It's worth mentioning that rho is not always a major factor in option pricing, especially for options on stocks. This is because interest rates often have a smaller effect on stock prices compared to other factors like company earnings, market sentiment, and overall economic conditions. However, rho can be more important for options on assets that are sensitive to interest rates, such as bonds or currencies.

❑

# Option Chain Analysis

## WHAT IS OPEN INTEREST?

Open interest refers to the total number of options or futures contracts that are still active and have not been closed, expired or exercised. It shows how many contracts are currently being traded. Open interest is also sometimes abbreviated as OI.

When a buyer and a seller come together to open a new contract, the open interest increases by one contract. On the other hand, if both the buyer and the seller close their contract position, the open interest decreases by one contract.

However, if a buyer or a seller transfers their position to another buyer or seller, the open interest does not change.

In summary, open interest tells us how many contracts are still active and being traded, and it changes when new contracts are opened or existing contracts are closed.

It appears that the concept of open is simple but puzzling. Don't worry; the following example will clear up any confusion you may have regarding open interest.

| Day | Activity | Open Interest | Change in OI |
|---|---|---|---|
| Day1 | 'A' buys 1 option and 'B' sells 1 option contract | 1 | 1 |
| Day2 | 'C' buys 3 options and 'D' sells 3 option contracts | 4 | 3 |
| Day3 | 'A' sells his 1 option and 'D' buys 1 option contract | 3 | -1 |
| Day4 | 'E' buys 3 options from 'C', who sells his 3 option contracts | 3 | 0 |

The table above depicts both 'A' and 'B' establishing fresh positions on the first day, resulting in the creation of one open interest. In other words, 'B' writes a contract, and 'A' purchases it. Both 'C' and 'D' created three additional positions on the second day. As a result, open interest climbs to four contracts, and the change in open interest is three (three new positions established today). Look at the trades on the third day: 'A' and 'D' both squared off their previous holdings. As a result, open interest will be reduced by one contract. Finally, on the fourth day, 'C' exits his positions by transferring his three contracts to a new trader, 'E'. As a result, there will be no change in open interest, and the total outstanding open interest will stay the same, i.e., three contracts.

## WHAT IS VOLUME?

Volume is the total number of shares or contracts traded during a single trading session. Volume simply refers to the quantity of transactions. It also displays how active an option or futures contract is. Volume is occasionally used by traders to gauge the strength of a price shift. More volume in the derivative contract suggests more liquidity. It means that there are enough buyers and sellers in the market. Before making any trading choice in the near term, it is usually essential to examine the contract's liquidity.

Anyway, volume appears to be very straightforward, right? Please be patient! Most new traders get confused by open interest and volume. Let us first explain this topic. Look at the analogous scenario below:

| Day | Activity | Open Interest | Volume |
|---|---|---|---|
| Day1 | 'A' buys 1 option and 'B' sells 1 option contract | 1 | 1 |
| Day2 | 'C' buys 3 options and 'D' sells 3 option contracts | 4 | 4 |
| Day3 | 'A' sells his 1 option and 'D' buys 1 option contract | 3 | 5 |
| Day4 | 'E' buys 3 options from 'C', who sells his 3 option contracts | 3 | 8 |

At first, both 'A' and 'B' establish a new position, and so open interest and volume become one. Similarly, on the second day, 'C' and 'D' make additional deals, bringing total open interest and volume to four. On the third day, both 'A' and 'D' square off their previous positions, reducing open interest to three. However, since transactions occur between them, the total volume equals five. Finally, 'C' exits the market by selling three contracts to a new trader, 'E'. As a result, while open interest remains constant, the final volume increases to eight since three transactions occurred between them.

## IMPORTANT LESSONS

We have already covered open interest and volume with examples. The following points will help you differentiate open interest from volume.

- In contrast to open positions, volume represents the number of transactions.
- Volume always rises, although OI can rise or fall.
- Open interest reveals a contract's level of activity.
- Volume indicates how liquid a specific contract is.
- Professional traders use volume to determine a trend's underlying strength.

## INTERPRETATION OF OPEN INTEREST DATA

Open interest is a measure of the total number of outstanding contracts for a particular futures or options contract. It indicates the total number of contracts that have been bought or sold but not yet settled by delivery or an equal-and-opposite trade. Following are some uses of open interest:

1. ***Trend analysis:*** A specific futures or options contract's trend can be examined using open interest. In general, it is regarded as an upward trend when open interest rises along with prices. On the other hand, if open interest is falling while prices are rising, this can be a sign of a possible price reversal.
2. ***Liquidity***: A market that has a lot of buyers and sellers is said to be liquid when there is a high level of open interest. It is simpler for traders to enter and exit positions in a market that is liquid since it typically has narrow bid-ask spreads and cheap transaction costs.
3. ***Support and resistance***: Open interest can also be used to identify potential support and resistance levels for a particular futures or options contract. For instance, if open interest is high at a certain price level, it can mean that traders are making purchases or sales at that level aggressively, making it a possible support or resistance level.
4. ***Option trading:*** Since it indicates the number of outstanding option contracts that could potentially be exercised, open interest is particularly crucial in trading options. When an

option contract has a high open interest, it may be a sign that there is substantial interest in that contract, making it a potentially appealing alternative for trading.

You studied open interest and volume in the previous chapter. It's time to examine open interest in order to determine the current state of the market. It is a very useful tool for determining how prices are moving. For a better approximation of the derivative market's price movement, one should take into account data from both futures and options contracts. As a result, we will first talk about how to understand futures OI data, then options OI data, and lastly, how to combine them to determine the market trend.

## Interpretation of Futures Open Interest Data

While examining the futures open interest data, four situations can be visualised. These are:

### *1. Price increase + Rise in open interest*

There is potential for price rise. More traders enter long positions as the price rises, increasing open interest. It suggests a ***bullish trend***.

### *2. Price decline + Development in open interest*

There is potential for price decline. More traders enter short positions when the price declines, increasing open interest. It suggests a ***bearish sentiment***.

### *3. Rise in price + Drop in open interest*

There is a weakness in pushing the price higher. When prices rise, short sellers believe that the price will rise further and quit their positions, which causes open interest to decline. It denotes either a ***bullish reversal*** or a ***short covering***.

### *4. Price decrease + Fall in open interest*

There is a weakness in the price decline. When prices drop, buyers fear that the price will fall further and sell their positions, which reduces open interest. It denotes a ***bearish reversal*** or ***long unwinding***.

## Interpretation of Options Open Interest Data

Futures open interest may be easily and quickly analysed. However, it can be challenging to understand options open interest. Let's attempt to provide a clear and concise explanation of the interpreting process. I'll go over the reasoning behind this interpretation as well. Let's first analyse the call and open interest separately before combining them to forecast the price movement.

First, let's examine the call open interest statistics. The interpretation is quite similar to that of futures OI. While assessing the call OI data, you will also obtain four scenarios below.

### *1. Rise in CE + Rise in OI*

The rationale for raising the call premium is strong. More traders enter the trading floor as the call premium rises, increasing the build-ups of open interest. It suggests a build-up of ***long calls*** or ***bullish sentiment***.

### *2. Drop in CE+ Increase in OI*

There is potential for lowering the price of call premium. Open interest rises as additional option sellers enter the market to implement trades and desire that the price to drop even further as the call option's premium decreases. It alludes to what is known as ***short build-up*** or ***bearish sentiment***.

### *3. Increasing CE+ OI decline*

There is resistance to raising the call price. When the call premium rises, the call writers cover their positions out of fear of raising the price, which results in a decline in open interest. It denotes ***call short covering*** or a ***bullish reversal***.

### *4. Drop in CE+ OI decline*

There is a vulnerability in lowering the call premium. As the price of a call option declines, buyers reduce their open interest because they decide to sell their positions out of worry that the price will continue to fall. It signifies a ***bearish reversal*** or ***call long unwinding***.

It appears simple and engaging to analyse call open interest. Given that they are identical, if you enjoyed it, you will love the interpretation of put open interest as well. Let's look at it.

## *1. Increase in PE + Rise in OI*

There is support for raising the put premium. More traders enter the trading floor when the put premium rises, which results in the building of open interest. It indicates ***put long build-ups*** or a ***bearish sentiment***.

## *2. Drop in PE+ Increase in OI*

There is strength in lowering the put premium lower. Open interest rises as more option writers make trades and expect the price to continue falling as the put option's premium decreases. It indicates ***put short build-up or bullish sentiment.***

## *3. Increase in PE+ Reduction in OI*

The upward movement of the put option price is weak. Put writers cover their positions when the put premium rises out of fear that the price will rise, which reduces open interest. It alludes to ***put short covering*** or a ***bearish reversal***.

## *4. Drop in PE+ OI decline*

There is a weakness in lowering the put price. Put option buyers quit their positions as the price of the option drops out of fear that it may fall even further, which reduces open interest. It suggests a ***bullish reversal*** or ***put long unwinding***.

The interpretation of open interest appears fantastic. To assess the total market sentiment, we will now merge the call and put OI. Only the market sentiment will be confirmed if both options reflect the same market emotion, such as bullish or bearish. Did I confuse you? Not to worry! To avoid confusing you any further, let me blend the two interpretations first. If you have any questions, the following example can help you to understand them.

### *1. Call long build-up + Put short build-up*

The price can be moved higher. The put writers simultaneously push the price upward while the call buyers want the market to rise. It alludes to the ***bullish sentiment***.

### *2. Put long build-up + Call short build-up*

The price can be moved down with some force. Put purchasers want the market to decline, and call writers want the price to decline even further. It suggests a ***bearish sentiment***.

### *3. Call short build-up + Put short build-up*

There is limited room for price movement in either direction. The put writers support the price falling while the call writers prevent the price from rising. This is a market that is completely ***range-bound*** or ***sideways***.

### *4. Put short build-up + Call long liquidation*

There is less force in moving the price upward. The call buyers' decision to book profits could cause a slight correction, but the put writers will prevent the price from dropping. It signifies a ***sideways market with a positive tilt***.

### *5. Call short build-up + Put long liquidation*

There is less intensity in moving the price downward. The price does increase because of put long unwinding, but the call writers suppress this increase. It represents a ***sideways market with a negative bias***.

These five types of emotions are typically displayed by the market. Additionally, the market can occasionally become quite volatile. A volatile market is one that has abrupt price changes, which can go both up and down. Markets typically experience this type of movement because of quick news events, such as elections, budget sessions, and sudden announcements of significant government policies, among others. An index called India VIX is used to measure the market's level of volatility. Market volatility is anticipated to remain high if the index value is high, and vice versa.

In this manner, the intraday market trend can be determined by examining futures or options open interest. You can also predict the short-term trend if you routinely monitor the OI building on a given security. When futures and options data show a bullish attitude, go for opening a long position; if both interpretations point to a bearish emotion, open a short position. Avoid trading in a sideways market unless you have a sound sideways market approach. It is sometimes better to wait for an opportunity than to enter a bad trade.

## Identification of Support and Resistances Using Open Interest Data

So far, the interpretation of futures open interest and options open interest has been done in a methodical manner. But did you know that? Options open interest is a fantastic tool for identifying support and resistance. To determine this, look for a high level of open interest on both the call and put sides. The highest call OI implies a strong resistance for that expiry, while the biggest change in OI is thought to constitute intraday resistance. Otherwise, take the biggest change in call OI to be resistance1, and the highest outstanding OI to be resistance2. Similarly, the biggest OI on the put arm may work as expiration support, while the highest shift in OI may act as intraday support. Furthermore, the biggest change and remarkable OI might be considered for support1 and support2, respectively. When the peak and change in OI coincide, it is considered to be a strong support or resistance.

Now, you may be wondering why the highest call and put OI are regarded as strong resistance and support. Let me explain why. Consider maximum call OI initially. The call sellers took positions on a specific strike because they anticipated the price would not rise over that level. As a result, it will function as a barrier until the holdings are liquidated. The same argument may be employed on the put side as well. The put writers believe that the price will remain above that level until their bets are covered.

Support and resistance, however, may also break. Let's look at an example to understand how a support or resistance breaks. Consider that the Nifty is trading at 17,700 and that the highest call OI is at 18000 strikes, while the greatest put OI is at 17500. The Nifty will therefore encounter resistance above 18,000 and find support at 17,500 levels, according to this. Let's say the cost of 17500 put option is ₹60 at the start of the expiration. This implies that the put writers will lose money if the Nifty drops below 17,440 (17,500 – 60). The index will fall around 17,400 levels as a result of the put sellers being forced to square off their bets.

The highest positions, however, were taken by call sellers at the 18000 strike. If the call premium is ₹40 for 18000 strikes at the beginning of the expiry, the call writers will be at breakeven when the index reaches 18,040 (18,000 + 40). Beyond that point, option sellers who are short covering will push the Nifty higher to 18,100 or more. Supports and resistances are thought to break in this manner over time.

## Few examples

The interpretation of open interest for futures and options appears to be quite simple and exciting on paper. But is it really that simple in the market? Let's examine a few instances. Real option chain data for several market conditions are shown here.

### *Example 1*

It is a chain of Nifty options with a 2 March 2023 expiration date. The screenshot was taken during the market hour on 27 February 2023. At that moment, the index's spot price was 17,310 (rounded off). To determine the direction of the market, first consider the call OI, then the put OI, and then combine the two.

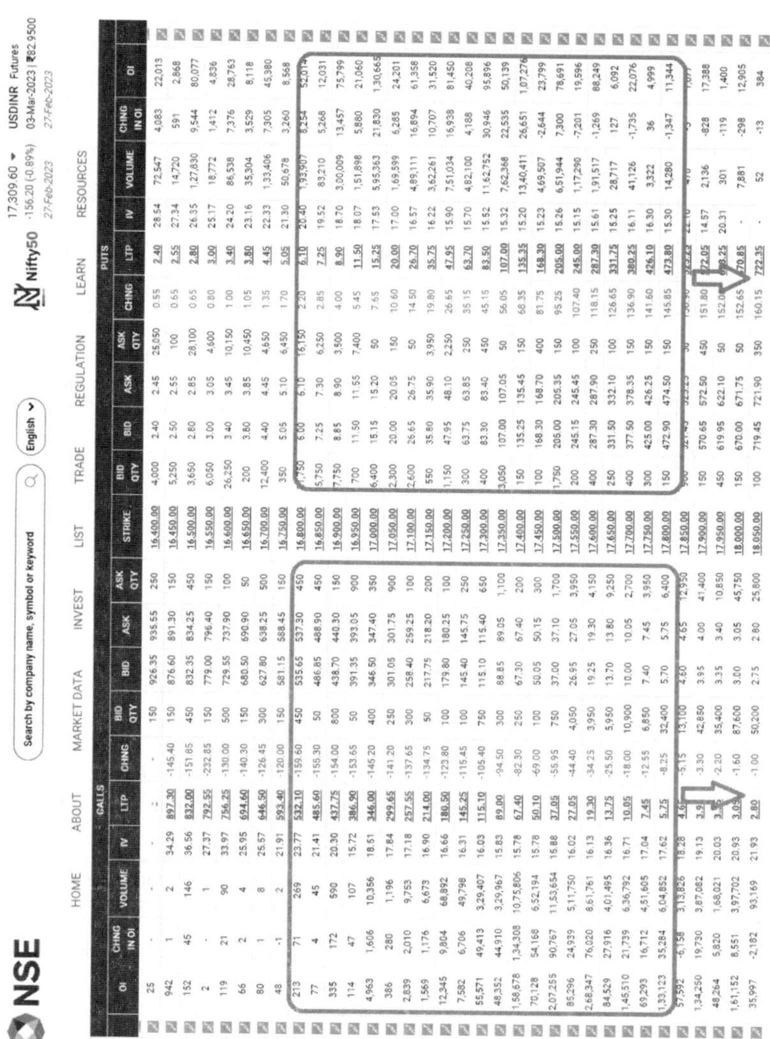


| CALLS | | | | | | | | | | | PUTS | | | | | | | | | |
|---|---|---|---|---|---|---|---|---|---|---|---|---|---|---|---|---|---|---|---|---|
| OI | CHNG IN OI | VOLUME | IV | LTP | CHNG | BID QTY | BID | ASK | ASK QTY | STRIKE | BID QTY | BID | ASK | ASK QTY | CHNG | LTP | IV | VOLUME | CHNG IN OI | OI |
| 25 | - | - | - | - | - | 150 | 926.35 | 935.55 | 250 | 16,400.00 | 4,000 | 2.40 | 2.45 | 25,050 | 0.55 | 2.40 | 28.54 | 72,547 | 4,083 | 22,013 |
| 942 | 1 | 2 | 34.29 | 897.30 | -145.40 | 150 | 876.60 | 891.30 | 150 | 16,450.00 | 5,250 | 2.50 | 2.55 | 100 | 0.65 | 2.55 | 27.34 | 14,720 | 591 | 2,868 |
| 152 | 45 | 146 | 36.56 | 832.00 | -151.85 | 450 | 832.35 | 834.25 | 450 | 16,500.00 | 3,650 | 2.80 | 2.85 | 28,100 | 0.65 | 2.80 | 26.35 | 1,27,830 | 9,544 | 80,077 |
| 2 | - | 1 | 27.37 | 792.55 | -232.85 | 150 | 779.00 | 796.40 | 150 | 16,550.00 | 6,050 | 3.00 | 3.05 | 4,600 | 0.80 | 3.00 | 25.17 | 18,772 | 1,412 | 4,836 |
| 119 | 21 | 90 | 33.97 | 756.25 | -130.00 | 500 | 729.55 | 737.90 | 100 | 16,600.00 | 26,250 | 3.40 | 3.45 | 10,150 | 1.00 | 3.40 | 24.20 | 86,538 | 7,376 | 28,763 |
| 66 | 2 | 4 | 25.95 | 694.60 | -140.30 | 150 | 680.50 | 690.90 | 50 | 16,650.00 | 200 | 3.80 | 3.85 | 10,450 | 1.05 | 3.80 | 23.16 | 35,304 | 3,529 | 8,118 |
| 80 | 1 | 8 | 25.57 | 646.50 | -126.45 | 300 | 627.80 | 638.25 | 500 | 16,700.00 | 12,400 | 4.40 | 4.45 | 4,650 | 1.35 | 4.45 | 22.33 | 1,33,406 | 7,305 | 45,380 |
| 48 | -1 | 2 | 21.91 | 593.40 | -120.00 | 150 | 581.15 | 588.45 | 150 | 16,750.00 | 350 | 5.05 | 5.10 | 6,450 | 1.70 | 5.05 | 21.30 | 50,678 | 3,260 | 8,568 |
| 213 | 71 | 269 | 23.77 | 532.10 | -159.60 | 450 | 535.65 | 537.30 | 450 | 16,800.00 | 1,750 | 6.00 | 6.10 | 16,150 | 2.20 | 6.10 | 20.40 | 1,93,907 | 8,254 | 52,014 |
| 77 | 4 | 45 | 21.41 | 485.60 | -155.30 | 50 | 486.85 | 488.90 | 450 | 16,850.00 | 5,750 | 7.25 | 7.30 | 6,250 | 2.85 | 7.25 | 19.52 | 83,210 | 5,268 | 12,031 |
| 335 | 172 | 590 | 20.30 | 437.75 | -154.00 | 800 | 438.70 | 440.30 | 150 | 16,900.00 | 7,750 | 8.85 | 8.90 | 3,500 | 4.00 | 8.90 | 18.70 | 3,00,009 | 13,457 | 75,799 |
| 114 | 47 | 107 | 15.72 | 386.90 | -153.65 | 50 | 391.35 | 393.05 | 900 | 16,950.00 | 700 | 11.50 | 11.55 | 7,400 | 5.45 | 11.50 | 18.07 | 1,51,898 | 5,880 | 21,060 |
| 4,963 | 1,606 | 10,356 | 18.51 | 346.00 | -145.20 | 400 | 346.50 | 347.40 | 350 | 17,000.00 | 6,400 | 15.15 | 15.20 | 50 | 7.65 | 15.25 | 17.53 | 5,95,363 | 21,830 | 1,30,665 |
| 386 | 280 | 1,196 | 17.84 | 299.65 | -141.20 | 250 | 301.05 | 301.75 | 900 | 17,050.00 | 2,300 | 20.00 | 20.05 | 150 | 10.60 | 20.00 | 17.00 | 1,69,599 | 6,285 | 24,201 |
| 2,839 | 2,010 | 9,753 | 17.18 | 257.55 | -137.65 | 300 | 258.40 | 259.25 | 100 | 17,100.00 | 2,600 | 26.65 | 26.75 | 50 | 14.50 | 26.70 | 16.57 | 4,89,111 | 16,894 | 61,358 |
| 1,569 | 1,176 | 6,673 | 16.90 | 214.00 | -134.75 | 50 | 217.75 | 218.20 | 200 | 17,150.00 | 550 | 35.80 | 35.90 | 3,950 | 19.80 | 35.75 | 16.22 | 3,62,261 | 10,707 | 31,520 |
| 12,345 | 9,804 | 68,892 | 16.66 | 180.50 | -123.80 | 100 | 179.80 | 180.25 | 100 | 17,200.00 | 1,150 | 47.95 | 48.10 | 2,250 | 26.65 | 47.95 | 15.90 | 7,51,034 | 16,938 | 81,450 |
| 7,582 | 6,706 | 49,798 | 16.31 | 145.25 | -115.45 | 100 | 145.40 | 145.75 | 250 | 17,250.00 | 300 | 63.75 | 63.85 | 250 | 35.15 | 63.70 | 15.70 | 4,82,100 | 4,188 | 40,208 |
| 55,571 | 49,413 | 3,29,407 | 16.03 | 115.10 | -105.40 | 750 | 115.10 | 115.40 | 650 | 17,300.00 | 400 | 83.30 | 83.40 | 450 | 45.15 | 83.50 | 15.52 | 11,62,752 | 30,946 | 95,896 |
| 48,352 | 44,910 | 3,29,967 | 15.83 | 89.00 | -94.50 | 300 | 88.85 | 89.05 | 1,100 | 17,350.00 | 3,050 | 107.00 | 107.05 | 50 | 56.05 | 107.00 | 15.32 | 7,62,368 | 22,535 | 50,139 |
| 1,58,678 | 1,34,308 | 10,75,806 | 15.78 | 67.40 | -82.30 | 250 | 67.30 | 67.40 | 200 | 17,400.00 | 150 | 135.25 | 135.45 | 150 | 68.35 | 135.35 | 15.20 | 13,40,411 | 26,651 | 1,07,276 |
| 70,128 | 54,168 | 6,52,194 | 15.78 | 50.10 | -69.00 | 100 | 50.05 | 50.15 | 300 | 17,450.00 | 100 | 168.30 | 168.70 | 400 | 81.75 | 168.30 | 15.23 | 4,69,507 | -2,644 | 23,799 |
| 2,07,255 | 90,767 | 11,53,654 | 15.88 | 37.05 | -55.95 | 750 | 37.00 | 37.10 | 1,700 | 17,500.00 | 1,750 | 205.00 | 205.35 | 150 | 95.25 | 205.00 | 15.26 | 6,51,944 | 7,300 | 78,691 |
| 85,296 | 24,939 | 5,11,750 | 16.02 | 27.05 | -44.40 | 4,050 | 26.95 | 27.05 | 3,950 | 17,550.00 | 200 | 245.15 | 245.45 | 100 | 107.40 | 245.00 | 15.15 | 1,17,290 | -7,201 | 19,596 |
| 2,68,347 | 76,020 | 8,61,761 | 16.13 | 19.30 | -34.25 | 3,950 | 19.25 | 19.30 | 4,150 | 17,600.00 | 400 | 287.30 | 287.90 | 250 | 118.15 | 287.30 | 15.61 | 1,91,517 | -1,269 | 88,249 |
| 84,529 | 27,916 | 4,01,495 | 16.36 | 13.75 | -25.50 | 5,950 | 13.70 | 13.80 | 9,250 | 17,650.00 | 250 | 331.50 | 332.10 | 100 | 126.65 | 331.75 | 15.25 | 28,717 | 127 | 6,092 |
| 1,45,510 | 21,739 | 6,36,792 | 16.71 | 10.05 | -18.00 | 10,900 | 10.00 | 10.05 | 2,700 | 17,700.00 | 400 | 377.50 | 378.35 | 150 | 136.90 | 380.25 | 16.11 | 41,126 | -1,735 | 22,076 |
| 69,293 | 16,712 | 4,51,605 | 17.04 | 7.45 | -12.55 | 6,850 | 7.40 | 7.45 | 3,950 | 17,750.00 | 300 | 425.00 | 426.25 | 150 | 141.60 | 426.10 | 16.30 | 3,322 | 36 | 4,999 |
| 1,33,123 | 35,284 | 6,04,852 | 17.62 | 5.75 | -8.25 | 32,400 | 5.70 | 5.75 | 6,400 | 17,800.00 | 150 | 472.90 | 474.50 | 150 | 145.85 | 473.80 | 15.30 | 14,280 | -1,347 | 11,344 |
| 57,592 | -6,158 | 3,13,826 | 18.28 | [illegible] | -5.15 | 13,100 | 4.60 | 4.65 | 12,950 | 17,850.00 | [illegible] | [illegible] | [illegible] | [illegible] | [illegible] | [illegible] | [illegible] | [illegible] | [illegible] | [illegible] |
| 1,34,250 | 19,730 | 3,87,082 | 19.13 | [illegible] | -3.30 | 42,850 | 3.95 | 4.00 | 41,400 | 17,900.00 | 150 | 570.65 | 572.50 | 450 | 151.80 | [illegible] | 14.57 | 2,136 | -828 | 17,388 |
| 48,264 | 5,820 | 1,68,021 | 20.03 | [illegible] | -2.20 | 35,400 | 3.35 | 3.40 | 10,850 | 17,950.00 | 450 | 619.95 | 622.10 | 50 | [illegible] | [illegible] | 20.31 | 301 | -119 | 1,400 |
| 1,61,152 | 8,551 | 3,97,702 | 20.93 | [illegible] | -1.60 | 87,600 | 3.00 | 3.05 | 45,750 | 18,000.00 | 150 | 670.00 | 671.75 | 50 | 152.65 | [illegible] | - | 7,881 | -298 | 12,905 |
| 35,997 | -2,182 | 93,169 | 21.93 | 2.80 | -1.00 | 50,200 | 2.75 | 2.80 | 25,800 | 18,050.00 | 100 | 719.45 | 721.90 | 350 | 160.15 | 722.35 | - | 52 | -13 | 384 |

## The call open interest

The call OI shows a significant drop in call premium and an increase in open interest. According to OI interpretation principles, call option short build-ups have occurred, which indicates a ***bearish sentiment***.

| | | | | | | | | | | | |
|---|---|---|---|---|---|---|---|---|---|---|---|
| 213 | 71 | 269 | 23.77 | 532.10 | -159.60 | 450 | 535.65 | 537.30 | 450 | 16,800.00 |
| 77 | 4 | 45 | 21.41 | 485.60 | -155.30 | 50 | 486.85 | 488.90 | 450 | 16,850.00 |
| 335 | 172 | 590 | 20.30 | 437.75 | -154.00 | 800 | 438.70 | 440.30 | 150 | 16,900.00 |
| 114 | 47 | 107 | 15.72 | 386.90 | -153.65 | 50 | 391.35 | 393.05 | 900 | 16,950.00 |
| 4,963 | 1,606 | 10,356 | 18.51 | 346.00 | -145.20 | 400 | 346.50 | 347.40 | 350 | 17,000.00 |
| 386 | 280 | 1,196 | 17.84 | 299.65 | -141.20 | 250 | 301.05 | 301.75 | 900 | 17,050.00 |
| 2,839 | 2,010 | 9,753 | 17.18 | 257.55 | -137.65 | 300 | 258.40 | 259.25 | 100 | 17,100.00 |
| 1,569 | 1,176 | 6,673 | 16.90 | 214.00 | -134.75 | 50 | 217.75 | 218.20 | 200 | 17,150.00 |
| 12,345 | 9,804 | 68,892 | 16.66 | 180.50 | -123.80 | 100 | 179.80 | 180.25 | 100 | 17,200.00 |
| 7,582 | 6,706 | 49,798 | 16.31 | 145.25 | -115.45 | 100 | 145.40 | 145.75 | 250 | 17,250.00 |
| 55,571 | 49,413 | 3,29,407 | 16.03 | 115.10 | -105.40 | 750 | 115.10 | 115.40 | 650 | 17,300.00 |
| 48,352 | 44,910 | [illegible] | [illegible] | 89.00 | -94.50 | 300 | 88.85 | 89.05 | 1,100 | 17,350.00 |
| 1,58,673 | 1,34,308 | [illegible] | [illegible] | 67.40 | -82.30 | 250 | 67.30 | 67.40 | 200 | 17,400.00 |
| 70,128 | 54,168 | 6,52,194 | 15.78 | 50.10 | -69.00 | 100 | 50.05 | 50.15 | 300 | 17,450.00 |
| 2,07,255 | 90,767 | 11,53,654 | 15.88 | 37.05 | -55.95 | 750 | 37.00 | 37.10 | 1,700 | 17,500.00 |
| 85,296 | 24,939 | 5,11,750 | 16.02 | 27.05 | -44.40 | 4,050 | 26.95 | 27.05 | 3,950 | 17,550.00 |
| 2,68,347 | 76,020 | 8,61,761 | 16.13 | 19.30 | -34.25 | 3,950 | 19.25 | 19.30 | 4,150 | 17,600.00 |
| 84,529 | 27,916 | 4,01,495 | 16.36 | 13.75 | -25.50 | 5,950 | 13.70 | 13.80 | 9,250 | 17,650.00 |
| 1,45,510 | 21,739 | 6,36,792 | 16.71 | 10.05 | -18.00 | 10,900 | 10.00 | 10.05 | 2,700 | 17,700.00 |
| 69,293 | 16,712 | 4,51,605 | 17.04 | 7.45 | -12.55 | 6,850 | 7.40 | 7.45 | 3,950 | 17,750.00 |
| 1,33,123 | 35,284 | 6,04,852 | 17.62 | 5.75 | -8.25 | 32,400 | 5.70 | 5.75 | 6,400 | 17,800.00 |

Call Short

## The put open interest

On the other hand, open interests were simultaneously added to OTM put options and put premium increases. Trading seems to have resulted in long positions via put options. The ITM (in-the-money) put options also exhibit outstanding short coverage. Put long and short covering both point to a negative market outlook. Hence, by combining call and put options, it can be predicted that the index will decline soon, indicating that the market may continue to be quite bearish.

| | | | | | | | | | | |
|---|---|---|---|---|---|---|---|---|---|---|
| 16,800.00 | [illegible] | 6.00 | 6.10 | 16,150 | 2.20 | 6.10 | 20.40 | 1,93,907 | 8,254 | 52,014 |
| 16,850.00 | 5,750 | 7.25 | 7.30 | 6,250 | 2.85 | 7.25 | 19.52 | 83,210 | 5,268 | 12,031 |
| 16,900.00 | 7,750 | 8.85 | 8.90 | 3,500 | 4.00 | 8.90 | 18.70 | 3,00,009 | 13,457 | 75,799 |
| 16,950.00 | 700 | 11.50 | 11.55 | 7,400 | [illegible] | 11.50 | 18.07 | 1,51,898 | 5,880 | 21,060 |
| 17,000.00 | 6,400 | 15.15 | 15.20 | 50 | 7.65 | 15.25 | 17.53 | 5,95,363 | 21,830 | 1,30,665 |
| 17,050.00 | 2,300 | 20.00 | 20.05 | 150 | 10.60 | 20.00 | 17.00 | 1,69,599 | 6,285 | 24,201 |
| 17,100.00 | 2,600 | 26.65 | 26.75 | 50 | 14.50 | 26.70 | 16.57 | 4,89,111 | 16,894 | 61,358 |
| 17,150.00 | 550 | 35.80 | 35.90 | 3,950 | 19.80 | [illegible] | [illegible] | [illegible] | 10,707 | 31,520 |
| 17,200.00 | 1,150 | 47.95 | 48.10 | 2,250 | 26.65 | [illegible] | [illegible] | 7,51,034 | 16,938 | 81,450 |
| 17,250.00 | 300 | 63.75 | 63.85 | 250 | 35.15 | 63.70 | 15.70 | 4,82,100 | 4,188 | 40,208 |
| 17,300.00 | 400 | 83.30 | 83.40 | 450 | 45.15 | 83.50 | 15.52 | 11,62,752 | 30,946 | 95,896 |
| 17,350.00 | 3,050 | 107.00 | 107.05 | 50 | 56.05 | 107.00 | 15.32 | 7,62,368 | 22,535 | 50,139 |
| 17,400.00 | 150 | 135.25 | 135.45 | 150 | [illegible] | 135.35 | 15.20 | 13,40,411 | [illegible] | 1,07,276 |
| 17,450.00 | 100 | 168.30 | 168.70 | 400 | [illegible] | 168.30 | 15.23 | 4,69,507 | [illegible] | 23,799 |
| 17,500.00 | 1,750 | 205.00 | 205.35 | 150 | 95.25 | 205.00 | 15.26 | 6,51,944 | 7,300 | 78,691 |
| 17,550.00 | 200 | 245.15 | 245.45 | 100 | 107.40 | [illegible] | [illegible] | [illegible] | -7,201 | 19,596 |
| 17,600.00 | 400 | 287.30 | 287.90 | 250 | 118.15 | [illegible] | [illegible] | [illegible] | -1,269 | 88,249 |
| 17,650.00 | 250 | 331.50 | 332.10 | 100 | 126.65 | [illegible] | [illegible] | [illegible] | 127 | 6,092 |
| 17,700.00 | 400 | 377.50 | 378.35 | 150 | 136.90 | 380.25 | 16.11 | 41,126 | -1,735 | 22,076 |
| 17,750.00 | 300 | 425.00 | 426.25 | 150 | 141.60 | 426.10 | 16.30 | 3,322 | 36 | 4,999 |
| 17,800.00 | 150 | 472.90 | 474.50 | 150 | [illegible] | 473.80 | 15.30 | 14,280 | -1,347 | 11,344 |
| 17,850.00 | [illegible] | [illegible] | [illegible] | [illegible] | [illegible] | [illegible] | [illegible] | [illegible] | [illegible] | [illegible] |

Put Long

Put Short Covering

## *Example 2*

The Nifty option chain shown below was also in effect on 29 September 2020, when it was trading at 11,228 (rounded off). The information relates to OI building for the index's 1 October expiration.

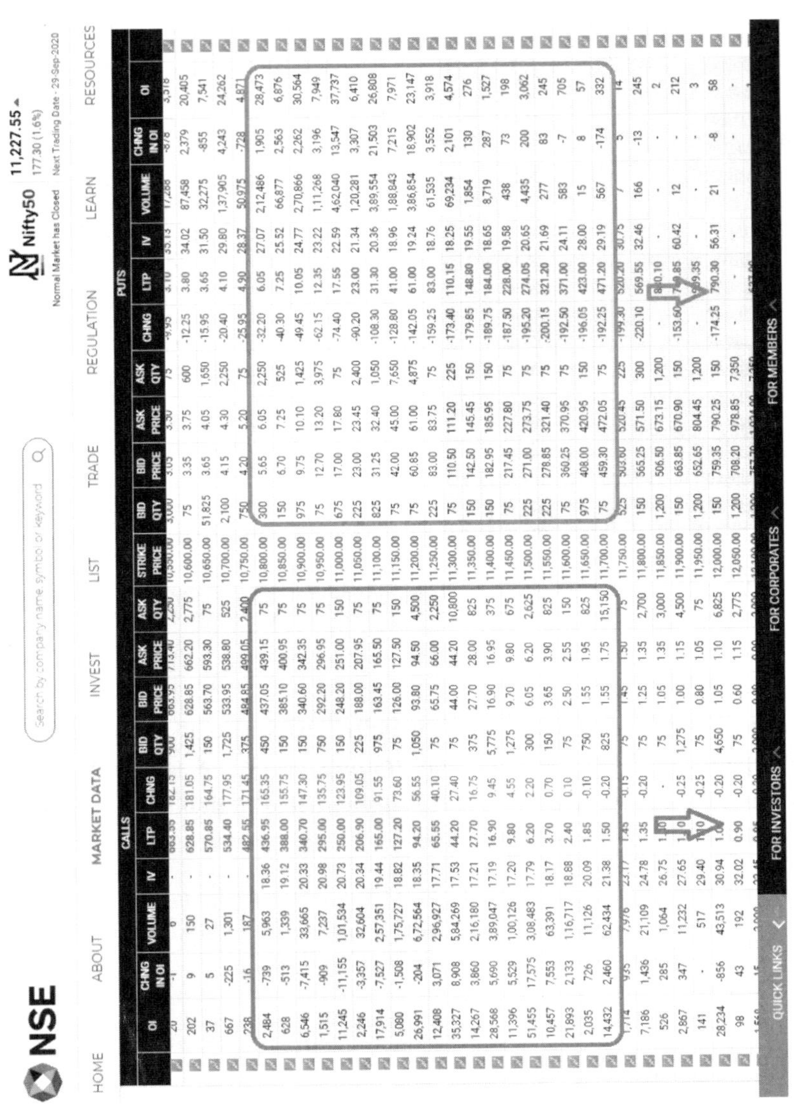

NSE

HOME | ABOUT | MARKET DATA | INVEST | LIST | TRADE | REGULATION | LEARN | RESOURCES

Nifty50 11,227.55 ▲ 177.30 (1.6%)
Normal Market has Closed  Next Trading Date - 29-Sep-2020

| CALLS | | | | | | | | | | | PUTS | | | | | | | | | |
|---|---|---|---|---|---|---|---|---|---|---|---|---|---|---|---|---|---|---|---|---|
| OI | CHNG IN OI | VOLUME | IV | LTP | CHNG | BID QTY | BID PRICE | ASK PRICE | ASK QTY | STRIKE PRICE | BID QTY | BID PRICE | ASK PRICE | ASK QTY | CHNG | LTP | IV | VOLUME | CHNG IN OI | OI |
| 20 | -1 | 6 | - | 683.35 | 182.15 | 900 | 663.95 | 713.40 | 2,250 | 10,550.00 | 3,000 | 3.05 | 3.50 | 75 | -9.95 | 3.10 | 35.13 | 17,288 | -878 | 3,518 |
| 202 | 9 | 150 | - | 628.85 | 181.05 | 1,425 | 628.85 | 662.20 | 2,775 | 10,600.00 | 75 | 3.35 | 3.75 | 600 | -12.25 | 3.80 | 34.02 | 87,458 | 2,379 | 20,405 |
| 37 | 5 | 27 | - | 570.85 | 164.75 | 150 | 563.70 | 593.30 | 75 | 10,650.00 | 51,825 | 3.65 | 4.05 | 1,650 | -15.95 | 3.65 | 31.50 | 32,275 | -855 | 7,541 |
| 667 | -225 | 1,301 | - | 534.40 | 177.95 | 1,725 | 533.95 | 538.80 | 525 | 10,700.00 | 2,100 | 4.15 | 4.30 | 2,250 | -20.40 | 4.10 | 29.80 | 1,37,905 | 4,243 | 24,262 |
| 238 | -16 | 187 | - | 482.55 | 171.45 | 375 | 484.85 | 499.05 | 2,400 | 10,750.00 | 750 | 4.20 | 5.20 | 75 | -25.95 | 4.90 | 28.37 | 50,975 | -728 | 4,871 |
| 2,484 | -739 | 5,963 | 18.36 | 436.95 | 165.35 | 450 | 437.05 | 439.15 | 75 | 10,800.00 | 300 | 5.65 | 6.05 | 2,250 | -32.20 | 6.05 | 27.07 | 2,12,486 | 1,905 | 28,473 |
| 628 | -513 | 1,339 | 19.12 | 388.00 | 155.75 | 150 | 385.10 | 400.95 | 75 | 10,850.00 | 150 | 6.70 | 7.25 | 525 | -40.30 | 7.25 | 25.52 | 66,877 | 2,563 | 6,876 |
| 6,546 | -7,415 | 33,665 | 20.33 | 340.70 | 147.30 | 150 | 340.60 | 342.35 | 75 | 10,900.00 | 975 | 9.75 | 10.10 | 1,425 | -49.45 | 10.05 | 24.77 | 2,70,866 | 2,262 | 30,564 |
| 1,515 | -909 | 7,237 | 20.98 | 295.00 | 135.75 | 750 | 292.20 | 296.95 | 75 | 10,950.00 | 75 | 12.70 | 13.20 | 3,975 | -62.15 | 12.35 | 23.22 | 1,11,268 | 3,196 | 7,949 |
| 11,245 | -11,155 | 1,01,534 | 20.73 | 250.00 | 123.95 | 150 | 248.20 | 251.00 | 150 | 11,000.00 | 675 | 17.00 | 17.80 | 75 | -74.40 | 17.55 | 22.59 | 4,62,040 | 13,547 | 37,737 |
| 2,246 | -3,357 | 32,604 | 20.34 | 206.90 | 109.05 | 225 | 188.00 | 207.95 | 75 | 11,050.00 | 225 | 23.00 | 23.45 | 2,400 | -90.20 | 23.00 | 21.34 | 1,20,281 | 3,307 | 6,410 |
| 17,914 | -7,527 | 2,57,351 | 19.44 | 165.00 | 91.55 | 975 | 163.45 | 165.50 | 75 | 11,100.00 | 825 | 31.25 | 32.40 | 1,050 | -108.30 | 31.30 | 20.36 | 3,89,554 | 21,503 | 26,808 |
| 5,080 | -1,508 | 1,75,727 | 18.82 | 127.20 | 73.60 | 75 | 126.00 | 127.50 | 150 | 11,150.00 | 75 | 42.00 | 45.00 | 7,650 | -128.80 | 41.00 | 18.96 | 1,88,843 | 7,215 | 7,971 |
| 26,991 | -204 | 6,72,564 | 18.35 | 94.20 | 56.55 | 1,050 | 93.80 | 94.50 | 4,500 | 11,200.00 | 75 | 60.85 | 61.00 | 4,875 | -142.05 | 61.00 | 19.24 | 3,86,854 | 18,902 | 23,147 |
| 12,408 | 3,071 | 2,96,927 | 17.71 | 65.55 | 40.10 | 75 | 65.75 | 66.00 | 2,250 | 11,250.00 | 225 | 83.00 | 83.75 | 75 | -159.25 | 83.00 | 18.76 | 61,535 | 3,552 | 3,918 |
| 35,327 | 8,908 | 5,84,269 | 17.53 | 44.20 | 27.40 | 75 | 44.00 | 44.20 | 10,800 | 11,300.00 | 75 | 110.50 | 111.20 | 225 | -173.40 | 110.15 | 18.25 | 69,234 | 2,101 | 4,574 |
| 14,267 | 3,860 | 2,16,180 | 17.21 | 27.70 | 16.75 | 375 | 27.70 | 28.00 | 825 | 11,350.00 | 150 | 142.50 | 145.45 | 150 | -179.85 | 148.80 | 19.55 | 1,854 | 130 | 276 |
| 28,568 | 5,690 | 3,89,047 | 17.19 | 16.90 | 9.45 | 5,775 | 16.90 | 16.95 | 375 | 11,400.00 | 150 | 182.95 | 185.95 | 150 | -189.75 | 184.00 | 18.65 | 8,719 | 287 | 1,527 |
| 11,396 | 5,529 | 1,00,126 | 17.20 | 9.80 | 4.55 | 1,275 | 9.70 | 9.80 | 675 | 11,450.00 | 75 | 217.45 | 227.80 | 75 | -187.50 | 228.00 | 19.58 | 438 | 73 | 198 |
| 51,455 | 17,575 | 3,08,483 | 17.79 | 6.20 | 2.20 | 300 | 6.05 | 6.20 | 2,625 | 11,500.00 | 225 | 271.00 | 273.75 | 75 | -195.20 | 274.05 | 20.65 | 4,435 | 200 | 3,062 |
| 10,457 | 7,553 | 63,391 | 18.17 | 3.70 | 0.70 | 150 | 3.65 | 3.90 | 825 | 11,550.00 | 225 | 278.85 | 321.40 | 75 | -200.15 | 321.20 | 21.69 | 277 | 83 | 245 |
| 21,893 | 2,133 | 1,16,717 | 18.88 | 2.40 | 0.10 | 75 | 2.50 | 2.55 | 150 | 11,600.00 | 75 | 360.25 | 370.95 | 75 | -192.50 | 371.00 | 24.11 | 583 | -7 | 705 |
| 2,035 | 726 | 11,126 | 20.09 | 1.85 | -0.10 | 750 | 1.55 | 1.95 | 825 | 11,650.00 | 975 | 408.00 | 420.95 | 150 | -196.05 | 423.00 | 28.00 | 15 | 8 | 57 |
| 14,432 | 2,460 | 62,434 | 21.38 | 1.50 | -0.20 | 825 | 1.55 | 1.75 | 15,150 | 11,700.00 | 75 | 459.30 | 472.05 | 75 | -192.25 | 471.20 | 29.19 | 567 | -174 | 332 |
| 1,714 | 935 | 7,976 | 23.17 | 1.45 | -0.15 | 75 | 1.45 | 1.50 | 75 | 11,750.00 | 525 | 503.60 | 520.45 | 225 | -199.30 | 520.20 | 30.75 | 7 | 5 | 14 |
| 7,186 | 1,436 | 21,109 | 24.78 | 1.35 | -0.20 | 75 | 1.25 | 1.35 | 2,700 | 11,800.00 | 150 | 565.25 | 571.50 | 300 | -220.10 | 569.55 | 32.46 | 166 | -13 | 245 |
| 526 | 285 | 1,064 | 26.75 | [illegible] | - | 75 | 1.05 | 1.35 | 3,000 | 11,850.00 | 1,200 | 506.50 | 673.15 | 1,200 | - | [illegible] | - | - | - | 2 |
| 2,867 | 347 | 11,232 | 27.65 | [illegible] | -0.25 | 1,275 | 1.00 | 1.15 | 4,500 | 11,900.00 | 150 | 663.85 | 670.90 | 150 | -153.60 | [illegible] | 60.42 | 12 | - | 212 |
| 141 | - | 517 | 29.40 | [illegible] | -0.25 | 75 | 0.80 | 1.05 | 75 | 11,950.00 | 1,200 | 652.65 | 804.45 | 1,200 | - | [illegible] | - | - | - | 3 |
| 28,234 | -856 | 43,513 | 30.94 | [illegible] | -0.20 | 4,650 | 1.05 | 1.10 | 6,825 | 12,000.00 | 150 | 759.35 | 790.25 | 150 | -174.25 | 790.30 | 56.31 | 21 | -8 | 58 |
| 98 | 43 | 192 | 32.02 | 0.90 | -0.20 | 75 | 0.60 | 1.15 | 2,775 | 12,050.00 | 1,200 | 708.20 | 978.85 | 7,350 | - | - | - | - | - | - |

QUICK LINKS | FOR INVESTORS | FOR CORPORATES | FOR MEMBERS

## The call open interest

Examine the call option side initially. Both the open interest and call option prices have significantly increased. Nothing but extraordinary buying in the call option is being done here. The volume indicates that option traders are diligently purchasing options. If call options are being purchased, this indicates a bullish perspective.

| | | | | | | | | | | |
|---|---|---|---|---|---|---|---|---|---|---|
| [illegible] | [illegible] | [illegible] | [illegible] | [illegible] | [illegible] | [illegible] | [illegible] | [illegible] | [illegible] | 10,750.00 |
| 2,484 | -739 | 5,963 | 18.36 | 436.95 | 165.35 | 450 | 437.05 | 439.15 | 75 | 10,800.00 |
| 628 | -513 | 1,339 | 19.12 | 388.00 | 155.75 | 150 | 385.10 | 400.95 | 75 | 10,850.00 |
| 6,546 | -7,415 | 33,665 | 20.33 | 340.70 | 147.30 | 150 | 340.60 | 342.35 | 75 | 10,900.00 |
| 1,515 | -909 | 7,237 | 20.98 | 295.00 | 135.75 | 750 | 292.20 | 296.95 | 75 | 10,950.00 |
| 11,245 | -11,155 | 1,01,534 | 20.73 | 250.00 | 123.95 | 150 | 248.20 | 251.00 | 150 | 11,000.00 |
| 2,246 | -3,357 | 32,6 | Call Short | 206.90 | 109.05 | 225 | 188.00 | 207.95 | 75 | 11,050.00 |
| 17,914 | -7,527 | 2,57, | Covering | 165.00 | 91.55 | 975 | 163.45 | 165.50 | 75 | 11,100.00 |
| 5,080 | -1,508 | 1,75,727 | 18.82 | 127.20 | 73.60 | 75 | 126.00 | 127.50 | 150 | 11,150.00 |
| 26,991 | -204 | 6,72,564 | 18.35 | 94.20 | 56.55 | 1,050 | 93.80 | 94.50 | 4,500 | 11,200.00 |
| 12,408 | 3,071 | 2,96,927 | 17.71 | 65.55 | 40.10 | 75 | 65.75 | 66.00 | 2,250 | 11,250.00 |
| 35,327 | 8,908 | 5,84,269 | 17.53 | 44.20 | 27.40 | 75 | 44.00 | 44.20 | 10,800 | 11,300.00 |
| 14,267 | 3,860 | 2,16,180 | 17.21 | 27.70 | 16.75 | 375 | 27.70 | 28.00 | 825 | 11,350.00 |
| 28,568 | 5,690 | 3,89,( | Call Long | 16.90 | 9.45 | 5,775 | 16.90 | 16.95 | 375 | 11,400.00 |
| 11,396 | 5,529 | 1,00,1 | Build-up | 9.80 | 4.55 | 1,275 | 9.70 | 9.80 | 675 | 11,450.00 |
| 51,455 | 17,575 | 3,08,483 | 17.79 | 6.20 | 2.20 | 300 | 6.05 | 6.20 | 2,625 | 11,500.00 |
| 10,457 | 7,553 | 63,391 | 18.17 | 3.70 | 0.70 | 150 | 3.65 | 3.90 | 825 | 11,550.00 |
| 21,893 | 2,133 | 1,16,717 | 18.88 | 2.40 | 0.10 | 75 | 2.50 | 2.55 | 150 | 11,600.00 |
| 2,035 | 726 | 11,126 | 20.09 | 1.85 | -0.10 | 750 | 1.55 | 1.95 | 825 | 11,650.00 |
| 14,432 | 2,460 | 62,434 | 21.38 | 1.50 | -0.20 | 825 | 1.55 | 1.75 | 15,150 | 11,700.00 |
| [illegible] | [illegible] | [illegible] | [illegible] | [illegible] | [illegible] | [illegible] | [illegible] | [illegible] | [illegible] | 11,750.00 |

## The put open interest

Keep an eye on the put side right now as there are more open interests and a declining option price. It looks like the put option traders have taken a short position in the index. The huge volume in this instance also suggests that the writers of the put are very active. As a result, traders of call and put options want the price of the Nifty to increase. Massive short coverage in at-the-money and in-the-money call options have also occurred, pushing the index higher. If no overnight breaking news materialises, the index may therefore continue to trend strongly upward.

| | | | | | | | | | | |
|---|---|---|---|---|---|---|---|---|---|---|
| 10,750.00 | 750 | 4.20 | 5.20 | 75 | -25.95 | 4.90 | 28.37 | 50,975 | -728 | 4,871 |
| 10,800.00 | 300 | 5.65 | 6.05 | 2,250 | -32.20 | 6.05 | 27.07 | 2,12,486 | 1,905 | 28,473 |
| 10,850.00 | 150 | 6.70 | 7.25 | 525 | -40.30 | 7.25 | 25.52 | 66,877 | 2,563 | 6,876 |
| 10,900.00 | 975 | 9.75 | 10.10 | 1,425 | -49.45 | 10.05 | 24.77 | 2,70,866 | 2,262 | 30,564 |
| 10,950.00 | 75 | 12.70 | 13.20 | 3,975 | -62.15 | 12.35 | 23.22 | 1,11,268 | 3,196 | 7,949 |
| 11,000.00 | 675 | 17.00 | 17.80 | 75 | -74.40 | 17.55 | 22.59 | 4,62,040 | 13,547 | 37,737 |
| 11,050.00 | 225 | 23.00 | 23.45 | 2,400 | -90.20 | 23.00 | 21.34 | 1,20,281 | 3,307 | 6,410 |
| 11,100.00 | 825 | 31.25 | 32.40 | 1,050 | -108.30 | 31.30 | 20.36 | 3,89,554 | 21,503 | 26,808 |
| 11,150.00 | 75 | 42.00 | 45.00 | 7,650 | -128.80 | 41.00 | 18.96 | 1,88,843 | 7,215 | 7,971 |
| 11,200.00 | 75 | 60.85 | 61.00 | 4,875 | -142.05 | 61.00 | 19.24 | 3,86,854 | 18,902 | 23,147 |
| 11,250.00 | 225 | 83.00 | 83.75 | 75 | -159.25 | 83.00 | Put Short | 1,535 | 3,552 | 3,918 |
| 11,300.00 | 75 | 110.50 | 111.20 | 225 | -173.40 | 110.1[illegible] | Build-up | 9,234 | 2,101 | 4,574 |
| 11,350.00 | 150 | 142.50 | 145.45 | 150 | -179.85 | 148.80 | 19.55 | 1,854 | 130 | 276 |
| 11,400.00 | 150 | 182.95 | 185.95 | 150 | -189.75 | 184.00 | 18.65 | 8,719 | 287 | 1,527 |
| 11,450.00 | 75 | 217.45 | 227.80 | 75 | -187.50 | 228.00 | 19.58 | 438 | 73 | 198 |
| 11,500.00 | 225 | 271.00 | 273.75 | 75 | -195.20 | 274.05 | 20.65 | 4,435 | 200 | 3,062 |
| 11,550.00 | 225 | 278.85 | 321.40 | 75 | 200.15 | 321.20 | 21.69 | 277 | 83 | 245 |
| 11,600.00 | 75 | 360.25 | 370.95 | 75 | -192.50 | 371.00 | 24.11 | 583 | 7 | 705 |
| 11,650.00 | 975 | 408.00 | 420.95 | 150 | -196.05 | 423.00 | 28.00 | 15 | 8 | 57 |
| 11,700.00 | 75 | 459.30 | 472.05 | 75 | -192.25 | 471.20 | 29.19 | 567 | -174 | 332 |
| 11,750.00 | 525 | 503.60 | 520.45 | 225 | -199.30 | 520.20 | 30.75 | 7 | 5 | 14 |

## *Example 3:*

You have seen the option chain for markets that are moving, or when market sentiment is strongly bullish or bearish. The two option chains described in the previous two examples belonged to the Nifty index. Now, let's look at a stock option example. See the option chain data for ASHOKLEY below. Data was collected on 3 March 2023, and it will expire on 29 March 2023. Even though there isn't a lot of open interest build-up, attempt to comprehend the potential interpretations. Before 2021, the NSE option chain showed an open interest in the number of shares of that specific security. Open interest is now displayed as a number of contracts. If you want to view the open interest in quantity, you simply multiply it by the lot size, which is 5,000 for ASHOKLEY. This explains why the option chain for ASHOKLEY appears to have sparse open interest building.

**Option Chain (Equity Derivatives)**

Futures contracts

View Options Contracts for: Select ∨ OR

Select Symbol: ASHOKLEY ∨

Expiry Date: 29-Mar-2023 ∨ OR

Strike Price: Select ∨

Underlying Index: **ASHOKLEY 145.00** As on 03-Mar-2023 15:30:00 IST

Terms of Use | Best View | Download (.csv)

| CALLS | | | | | | | | | | | PUTS | | | | | | | | | |
|---|---|---|---|---|---|---|---|---|---|---|---|---|---|---|---|---|---|---|---|---|
| OI | CHNG IN OI | VOLUME | IV | LTP | CHNG | BID QTY | BID | ASK | ASK QTY | STRIKE | BID QTY | BID | ASK | ASK QTY | CHNG | LTP | IV | VOLUME | CHNG IN OI | OI |
| - | - | - | - | - | - | 15,000 | 26.10 | 30.45 | 15,000 | 117.50 | - | - | 0.25 | 5,000 | - | - | - | - | - | - |
| 1 | - | - | - | - | - | 15,000 | 23.65 | 27.75 | 25,000 | 120.00 | - | - | 0.10 | 70,000 | - | 0.05 | 32.83 | 18 | -4 | 122 |
| 6 | - | - | - | - | - | 5,000 | 22.75 | 25.55 | 15,000 | 122.50 | 5,000 | 0.10 | 0.35 | 10,000 | 0.25 | 0.35 | 41.44 | 1 | - | 7 |
| 1 | - | - | - | - | - | 5,000 | 20.35 | 21.05 | 5,000 | 125.00 | 3,35,000 | 0.10 | 0.20 | 40,000 | - | 0.15 | 31.82 | 4 | -2 | 84 |
| - | - | - | - | - | - | 5,000 | 17.75 | 18.55 | 5,000 | 127.50 | 1,70,000 | 0.10 | 0.25 | 5,000 | - | 0.20 | 29.98 | 1 | - | 33 |
| 47 | - | - | - | - | - | 5,000 | 15.45 | 16.00 | 5,000 | 130.00 | 5,55,000 | 0.20 | 0.25 | 45,000 | - | 0.25 | 27.70 | 65 | -37 | 391 |
| 1 | - | - | - | - | - | 5,000 | 13.10 | 13.60 | 10,000 | 132.50 | 45,000 | 0.30 | 0.40 | 10,000 | -0.15 | 0.30 | 26.00 | 37 | 1 | 92 |
| 35 | - | - | - | - | - | 5,000 | 10.85 | 11.20 | 5,000 | 135.00 | 65,000 | 0.45 | 0.55 | 1,10,000 | -0.15 | 0.50 | 24.37 | 269 | 4 | 585 |
| 11 | - | 2 | 24.35 | 9.35 | 0.15 | 5,000 | 8.70 | 9.20 | 5,000 | 137.50 | 10,000 | 0.75 | 0.90 | 25,000 | -0.15 | 0.85 | 24.11 | 44 | 11 | 184 |
| 274 | -9 | 46 | 20.72 | 7.00 | -0.25 | 5,000 | 7.00 | 7.05 | 5,000 | 140.00 | 10,000 | 1.35 | 1.45 | 10,000 | -0.15 | 1.40 | 24.48 | 353 | -2 | 712 |
| 112 | 2 | 23 | 20.57 | 5.20 | -0.35 | 10,000 | 5.15 | 5.40 | 10,000 | 142.50 | 15,000 | 2.05 | 2.15 | 5,000 | -0.05 | 2.20 | 23.87 | 71 | 16 | 153 |
| 647 | 4 | 565 | 21.52 | 3.85 | -0.20 | 20,000 | 3.80 | 3.90 | 10,000 | 145.00 | 5,000 | 3.15 | 3.25 | 15,000 | -0.10 | 3.20 | 23.67 | 438 | 8 | 511 |
| 244 | 3 | 196 | 22.09 | 2.80 | -0.05 | 5,000 | 2.75 | 2.85 | 10,000 | 147.50 | 5,000 | 4.40 | 4.75 | 15,000 | -0.30 | 4.35 | 23.05 | 5 | 2 | 34 |
| 1,270 | 23 | 537 | 22.87 | 1.95 | -0.05 | 1,15,000 | 1.90 | 1.95 | 20,000 | 150.00 | 5,000 | 6.10 | 6.35 | 5,000 | -0.15 | 6.15 | 24.72 | 26 | 3 | 325 |
| 143 | 11 | 79 | 23.51 | 1.35 | -0.05 | 10,000 | 1.25 | 1.35 | 15,000 | 152.50 | 5,000 | 7.85 | 8.45 | 5,000 | - | - | - | - | - | 6 |
| 591 | -15 | 386 | 23.42 | 0.90 | - | 20,000 | 0.85 | 0.90 | 10,000 | 155.00 | 10,000 | 10.00 | 10.35 | 15,000 | -0.20 | 9.90 | 24.87 | 7 | - | 39 |
| 80 | 5 | 34 | 24.45 | 0.55 | -0.05 | 25,000 | 0.50 | 0.95 | 5,000 | 157.50 | 5,000 | 12.05 | 12.95 | 10,000 | - | - | - | - | - | - |
| 684 | -20 | 399 | 25.80 | [illegible] | - | 1,05,000 | 0.40 | 0.45 | 1,20,000 | 160.00 | 5,000 | 14.55 | 14.80 | 10,000 | -0.05 | [illegible] | 30.78 | 2 | -1 | 39 |
| 38 | -2 | 15 | 25.29 | [illegible] | - | 60,000 | 0.20 | 1.30 | 5,000 | 162.50 | 5,000 | 16.75 | 18.70 | 5,000 | - | - | - | - | - | - |
| 138 | 1 | 11 | 28.07 | [illegible] | - | 1,20,000 | 0.20 | 0.25 | 4,40,000 | 165.00 | 5,000 | 19.15 | 19.80 | 5,000 | - | - | - | - | - | - |
| 23 | - | 1 | 27.95 | 0.15 | - | 20,000 | 0.10 | 0.20 | 10,000 | 167.50 | 5,000 | 21.50 | 22.20 | 5,000 | - | - | - | - | - | - |
| 121 | - | 8 | 30.38 | 0.15 | - | 6,20,000 | 0.10 | 0.15 | 1,30,000 | 170.00 | 5,000 | 24.00 | 24.70 | 5,000 | - | - | - | - | - | 1 |
| - | - | - | - | - | - | - | - | 0.45 | 10,000 | 172.50 | 15,000 | 24.85 | 29.35 | 15,000 | - | - | - | - | - | - |
| 54 | - | 2 | 32.88 | 0.10 | - | 3,25,000 | 0.05 | 0.10 | 25,000 | 175.00 | 15,000 | 28.25 | 31.45 | 15,000 | - | - | - | - | - | 1 |
| 1 | - | - | - | - | - | - | - | 0.25 | 20,000 | 177.50 | 15,000 | 29.80 | 34.15 | 15,000 | - | - | - | - | - | - |
| Tot 4,522 | | 2,304 | | | | | | | | | | | | | | | | 1,341 | | 3,319 |

| | | | | | | | | | | |
|---|---|---|---|---|---|---|---|---|---|---|
| 11 | - | 2 | 24.35 | 9.35 | 0.15 | 5,000 | 8.70 | 9.20 | 5,000 | 137.50 |
| 274 | -9 | 46 | 20.72 | 7.00 | -0.25 | 5,000 | 7.00 | 7.05 | 5,000 | 140.00 |
| 112 | 2 | 23 | 20.57 | 5.20 | -0.35 | 10,000 | 5.15 | 5.40 | 10,000 | 142.50 |
| 647 | 4 | 565 | 21.52 | 3.85 | -0.20 | 20,000 | 3.80 | 3.90 | 10,000 | 145.00 |
| 244 | 3 | 190 | [illegible] | 2.80 | -0.05 | 5,000 | 2.75 | 2.85 | 10,000 | 147.50 |
| 1,270 | 23 | 537 | 22.87 | 1.95 | -0.05 | 1,15,000 | 1.90 | 1.95 | 20,000 | 150.00 |
| 143 | 11 | 79 | 23.51 | 1.35 | -0.05 | 10,000 | 1.25 | 1.35 | 15,000 | 152.50 |
| 591 | -15 | 386 | 23.42 | 0.90 | | 20,000 | 0.85 | 0.90 | 10,000 | 155.00 |
| 80 | 5 | 34 | 24.45 | 0.55 | -0.05 | 25,000 | 0.50 | 0.95 | 5,000 | 157.50 |

Short Build-up

| | | | | | | | | | | |
|---|---|---|---|---|---|---|---|---|---|---|
| 137.50 | 10,000 | 0.75 | 0.90 | 25,000 | -0.15 | 0.85 | 24.11 | 44 | 11 | 184 |
| 140.00 | 10,000 | 1.35 | 1.45 | 10,000 | -0.15 | 1.40 | 24.48 | 353 | -2 | 712 |
| 142.50 | 15,000 | 2.05 | 2.15 | 5,000 | -0.05 | 2.20 | 23.87 | 71 | 16 | 153 |
| 145.00 | 5,000 | 3.15 | 3.25 | 15,000 | -0.10 | 3.20 | 23.67 | 438 | 8 | 511 |
| 147.50 | 5,000 | 4.40 | 4.75 | 15,000 | -0.30 | 4.35 | 23.05 | 5 | 2 | 34 |
| 150.00 | 5,000 | 6.10 | 6.35 | 5,000 | -0.15 | 6.15 | 24.72 | 26 | 3 | 325 |
| 152.50 | 5,000 | 7.85 | 8.45 | 5,000 | - | - | - | - | - | 6 |
| 155.00 | 10,000 | 10.00 | 10.35 | 15,000 | -0.20 | 9.90 | 24.87 | 7 | - | 39 |

Short Build-up

The call open interest indicates that writing occurred, and the put open interest also indicates that put writers were active. Call writers will prevent price increases and put sellers will prevent ASHOKLEY price declines. The stock is, therefore, anticipated to move in a range-bound scenario for the upcoming trading sessions.

## HOW TO IDENTIFY SHORT-TERM MARKET TREND?

Before going any further, allow me to mention a few market participants in the Indian market who are crucial in influencing market price, *viz.*, FIIs DIIs and Pro traders. Here is a quick description of each:

***Foreign institutional investors (FII):*** Institutional investors based outside India and who invest in the Indian stock market are known as FIIs. These investors include mutual funds, pension funds, and hedge funds. FIIs can significantly affect Indian markets by bringing in foreign cash. Regarding the sum of money, they are permitted to invest in Indian debt and equity markets. However, there are a number of rules and limitations.

***Domestic institutional investors (DII):*** Institutional investors with a presence in India, like mutual funds, insurance companies, and banks, participate in the Indian stock market as DIIs. They are prominent market participants in India and have a big say in how the market behaves. Additionally, some rules and limitations apply to DIIs.

***Professional Traders (Pro traders):*** Pro traders are people or businesses who conduct trading operations on the Indian stock market on a full-time basis. To make trading judgements, they may employ a range of trading methodologies, including technical analysis, fundamental analysis, and quantitative analysis. Proprietary trading companies, high-frequency traders, and algorithmic traders are a few examples of professional traders.

It is worth mentioning that the FII, DII and Pro traders are the most sophisticated market participants in India. They are competent and experienced, have strong research teams, and have plenty of trading capital. In essence, they make informed decisions when trading. As a result, they frequently make money from the market. The good news is that their data is publicly available and is closely monitored by market participants as it can provide insights into investor sentiment and market trends. It is generally believed that markets move in the direction that they perceive. The market will remain bullish if they establish long holdings and become bearish if they build short positions. Doesn't that sound great? What if you are aware of the positions they are developing in the marketplace? It won't be simple for you to guess the market's direction, though. Yes! You can determine the short-term trend by just following them because they hold their positions for a limited number of trading sessions much of the time. How we find out about the positions they have taken is the following question. Exactly this is what we'll be talking about in this section.

# FII, DII & PRO TRADERS POSITION IN DERIVATIVE MARKET

You need to do some research in order to understand what the major players in the market are doing. Frequent monitoring of their positions is required. Nothing is simple. Thankfully, the data is made available to us each day as the market closes, by the NSE (National Stock Exchange of India). On their website, after-hours data is frequently updated. The data must be downloaded and processed in a way that you can understand. Break the information down in a way that you can grasp.

First, download the data from the NSE website. The procedures are listed below.

1. Go to www.nseindia.com and select **Daily Market Reports** under **RESOURCES** tab as shown in the image below.

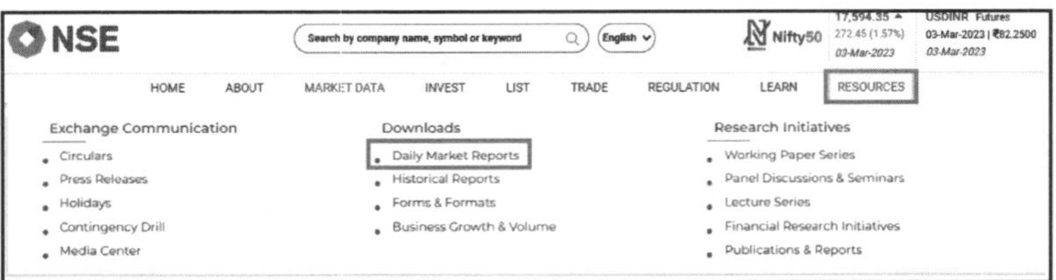


2. Next, select the **Daily Reports** category in the **DERIVATIVES** area and download the **Participant wise Open Interest (csv)** file.

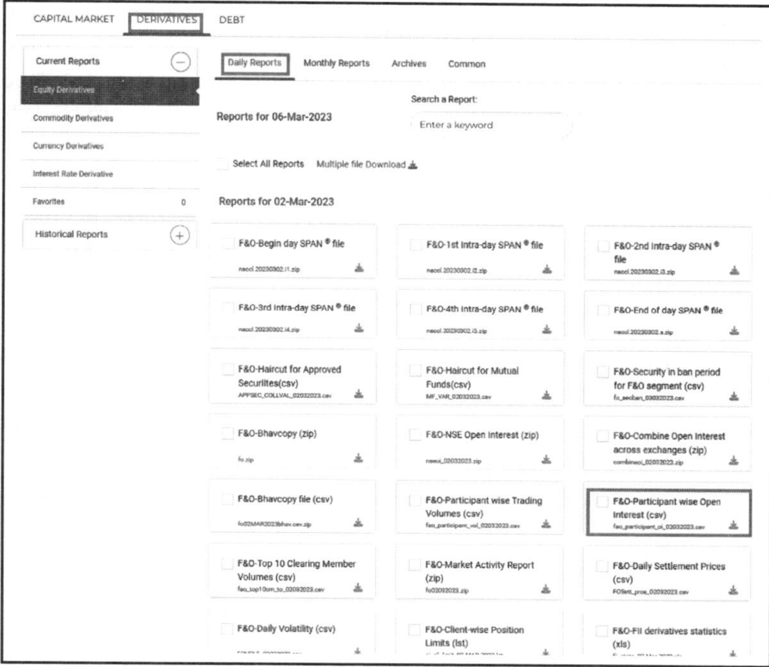


This csv file contains end-of-day (EOD) transaction data for the derivatives market. These are cumulative positions taken on stock futures and options as well as index futures and options by various market participants, including FII, DII, Pro and Client. The positions in index futures and options that are listed in the sheet refer to NIFTY and BANKNIFTY positions with weekly and monthly expirations. You can now extract the data as needed. First, have a glance at the sheet.

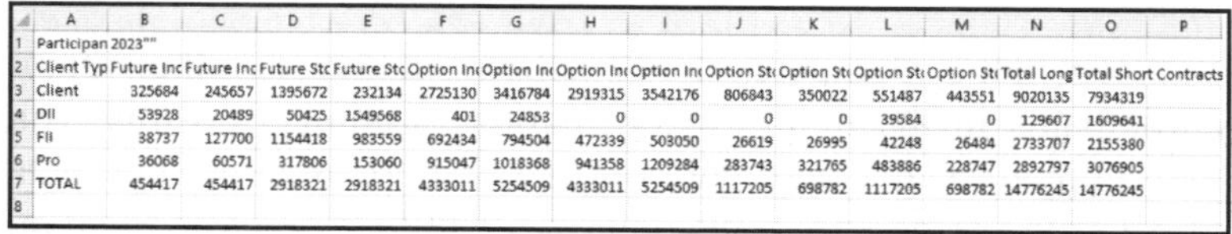

| | A | B | C | D | E | F | G | H | I | J | K | L | M | N | O | P |
|---|---|---|---|---|---|---|---|---|---|---|---|---|---|---|---|---|
| 1 | Participan 2023"" | | | | | | | | | | | | | | | |
| 2 | Client Typ | Future Inc | Future Inc | Future Stc | Future Stc | Option In | Option In | Option In | Option In | Option St | Option St | Option St | Option St | Total Long | Total Short | Contracts |
| 3 | Client | 325684 | 245657 | 1395672 | 232134 | 2725130 | 3416784 | 2919315 | 3542176 | 806843 | 350022 | 551487 | 443551 | 9020135 | 7934319 | |
| 4 | DII | 53928 | 20489 | 50425 | 1549568 | 401 | 24853 | 0 | 0 | 0 | 0 | 39584 | 0 | 129607 | 1609641 | |
| 5 | FII | 38737 | 127700 | 1154418 | 983559 | 692434 | 794504 | 472339 | 503050 | 26619 | 26995 | 42248 | 26484 | 2733707 | 2155380 | |
| 6 | Pro | 36068 | 60571 | 317806 | 153060 | 915047 | 1018368 | 941358 | 1209284 | 283743 | 321765 | 483886 | 228747 | 2892797 | 3076905 | |
| 7 | TOTAL | 454417 | 454417 | 2918321 | 2918321 | 4333011 | 5254509 | 4333011 | 5254509 | 1117205 | 698782 | 1117205 | 698782 | 14776245 | 14776245 | |
| 8 | | | | | | | | | | | | | | | | |

The sheet is complex and contains a lot of information. I'll explain it so that you may comprehend it better. You can ignore the stock futures and options data since you just want to determine the direction of the NIFTY & BANKNIFTY. If you examine closely, DII has relatively little exposure to index options, hence the value of their data is small. In addition, since clients are traders in addition to FII, DII and Pro traders, you can disregard their statistics. The majority of them are retail traders and they are pitiful at market analysis. But the prediction will be more accurate if you consider more facts. In any case, you'll be able to create a simpler sheet immediately.

Copy the Future Index Long and Future Index Short values for DII, FII, and Pro from the downloaded sheet, then paste them into the calculation sheet as indicated in the figure below to finish preparing the page. To maintain the sheet, the calculation sheet must first be constructed.

| | A | B | C | D | E |
|---|---|---|---|---|---|
| 3 | | | | | |
| 4 | | INDEX FUTURES | | | |
| 5 | | **Future Index Long** | **Future Index Short** | **Net** | |
| 6 | **DII** | 53928 | 20489 | **33439** | |
| 7 | **FII** | 38737 | 127700 | **-88963** | |
| 8 | **PRO** | 36068 | 60571 | **-24503** | |
| 9 | | | | | |

The 'Net' column lists the traders' net positions (DII, FII, & PRO). It is determined by deducting the Future Index Short column from the Future Index Long column. Positive net positions signify a long build-up by them, while negative net positions suggest a short build-up. Positions in index futures are determined in this manner.

Now let's compute the positions taken by the major participants in the index option market. Again, to do this, you must copy the Call Long, Put Long, Call Short, and Put Short data of FII & Pro traders from the downloaded file, then paste them on the calculation sheet.

| | Call Long | Put Long | Call Short | Put Short | Net Call | Net Put | Net OI |
|---|---|---|---|---|---|---|---|
| | | | INDEX OPTIONS | | | | |
| FII | 692434 | 794504 | 472339 | 503050 | 220095 | 291454 | **-71359** |
| PRO | 915047 | 1018368 | 941358 | 1209284 | -26311 | -190916 | **164605** |

On the preceding sheet, the Net Call is (Call Long – Call Short) and the Net Put is (Put Long – Put Short), while the Net OI is just the total amount invested (Net Call – Net Put). Once more, positive net positions suggest building up long bets, while negative positions indicate building up short positions by FII and professional traders. It is important to note right now that we cannot determine the market trend by focusing solely on one-day positions. We must monitor the build-up of positions for at least a few days. This means that you must regularly update and maintain a data sheet. Look at the next couple of steps to maintain the sheet now.

Check out the information on the master sheet first. It comprises NIFTY & BANKNIFTY closing prices as well as cumulative, expiry, 10-day, and daily positions created by various market participants on index futures and options. The various components of the sheet will be covered later. Let's first update the spreadsheet. In order to add a new row to the master sheet, copy the index futures and options data from the computation sheet and paste them one at a time. Because the data in the calculation sheet also contains a formula, remember to paste the data as 'value' (paste special as value). To obtain the combined positions, simply add the values of DII, FII, and/or Pro traders to the index futures and index options columns.

| | A | B | C | D | E | F | G | H | I | J | K | L |
|---|---|---|---|---|---|---|---|---|---|---|---|---|
| 1 | | | | | | | | | | | | |
| 2 | Date | INDEX FUTURES | | | | INDEX OPTIONS | | | INDEX FUTURES | INDEX OPTIONS | NIFTY | BANKNIFTY |
| 3 | | DII | FII | PRO | Combine | FII | PRO | Combine | | | | |
| 4 | Expiry Position | 16509 | 15888 | -25818 | 6579 | 214833 | 335084 | 549917 | | | | |
| 5 | 10 Day' net position | 25123 | -406 | -32204 | -7487 | 244212 | 668166 | 912378 | | | | |
| 6 | 03-Mar-23 | 33439 | -88963 | -24503 | -80027 | -71359 | 164605 | 93246 | 37163 | 493562 | 17594 | 41251 |
| 7 | 02-Mar-23 | 31685 | -131240 | -17635 | -117190 | -260624 | -139692 | -400316 | -10912 | -343805 | 17322 | 40390 |
| 8 | 01-Mar-23 | 29617 | -125604 | -10291 | -106278 | -192361 | 135850 | -56511 | -9470 | 411607 | 17451 | 40698 |
| 9 | 28-Feb-23 | 32353 | -131767 | 2606 | -96808 | -227463 | -240655 | -468118 | -821 | -163503 | 17304 | 40269 |
| 10 | 27-Feb-23 | 23118 | -116233 | -2872 | -95987 | -212875 | -91740 | -304615 | -8719 | 283839 | 17393 | 40307 |
| 11 | 24-Feb-23 | 16941 | -107761 | 3552 | -87268 | -284227 | -304227 | -588454 | -662 | -131783 | 17466 | 39909 |
| 12 | 23-Feb-23 | 16930 | -104851 | 1315 | -86606 | -286192 | -170479 | -456671 | -3152 | 407439 | 17511 | 40001 |
| 13 | 22-Feb-23 | 12243 | -108504 | 12807 | -83454 | -339089 | -525021 | -864110 | -24229 | -294068 | 17554 | 39996 |
| 14 | 21-Feb-23 | 6109 | -78250 | 12916 | -59225 | -267188 | -302854 | -570042 | 13315 | 249090 | 17827 | 40674 |
| 15 | 20-Feb-23 | 8316 | -88557 | 7701 | -72540 | -315571 | -503561 | -819132 | -5141 | -196961 | 17845 | 40702 |
| 16 | 17-Feb-23 | 14381 | -80664 | -1116 | -67399 | -319494 | -302677 | -622171 | -1703 | -327805 | 17944 | 41131 |
| 17 | 16-Feb-23 | 12188 | -69324 | -8560 | -65696 | -179671 | -114695 | -294366 | -8321 | -471100 | 18036 | 41631 |
| 18 | 15-Feb-23 | 12247 | -66257 | -3365 | -57375 | -80332 | 257066 | 176734 | -4325 | 138574 | 18016 | 41731 |
| 19 | 14-Feb-23 | 13373 | -63675 | -2748 | -53050 | -59118 | 97278 | 38160 | 26055 | 597921 | 17930 | 41648 |
| 20 | 13-Feb-23 | 17432 | -104752 | 8215 | -79105 | -237204 | -322557 | -559761 | 7188 | -247933 | 17771 | 41282 |
| 21 | 10-Feb-23 | 24743 | -105540 | -5496 | -86293 | -204636 | -107192 | -311828 | -9603 | -129019 | 17856 | 41559 |
| 22 | 09-Feb-23 | 21883 | -95054 | -3519 | -76690 | -126547 | -56262 | -182809 | 5976 | -105654 | 17893 | 41554 |
| 23 | 08-Feb-23 | 21483 | -96684 | -7465 | -82666 | -139117 | 61962 | -77155 | 5660 | 222524 | 17872 | 41538 |
| 24 | 07-Feb-23 | 29218 | -110680 | -6864 | -88326 | -127755 | -171924 | -299679 | 3714 | 90037 | 17721 | 41491 |
| 25 | 06-Feb-23 | 29616 | -111392 | -10264 | -92040 | -218820 | -170896 | -389716 | -17727 | -323396 | 17765 | 41375 |
| 26 | 03-Feb-23 | 27590 | -87769 | -14134 | -74313 | -91040 | 24720 | -66320 | 27169 | 301370 | 17854 | 41499 |

Let's look at an example to better understand what the various values on the sheet imply. The combined index futures position as of 3 March 2023, is -80,027, which means the major participants (DII, FII, and Pro) have combined a total short position in the index futures of 80,027 contracts. Similarly, as of 3 March 2023, they had long positions totalling 93,246 contracts in index options, including all expiries. The 10-day net position represents their positions over the previous 10 days. It is derived by deducting the position of 10 days ago from the position today. The upper sheet's purple-coloured row indicates the spot that is 10 days earlier. Likewise, like how daily position is determined by subtracting yesterday's position from today's cumulative position, expiry position is determined by subtracting the last expiry day data from today's data.

After a significant amount of more copy, paste, addition, and subtraction activity, we have finally finished creating the master sheet. The master sheet is completed. In order to forecast the general market direction, we will now focus on the analysis of this data. Look at the daily open interest build-up for both index options and futures first. If these pieces of information indicate that long holdings have been amassing over the past few days, the market is likely to turn bullish soon. Conversely, short positions suggest that the market may decline. Yet, it provides the appearance that there is no clear direction among the major players and the indices are predicted to trade in a range-bound zone if the index futures shows a long build-up and the index options shows a short build-up and vice versa.

For illustration, have a look at the open interest range from 3 February to 13 February 2023, on the sheet below. At that time, traders made short bets in index options while simultaneously accumulating long positions in index futures. The market should decline, according to options traders, and the market should rise, according to futures traders. Hence, throughout the course of ten trading sessions, the NIFTY index fluctuates between 17,854 and 17,771 and the BANKNIFTY index between 41,499 and 41,282.

| Date | INDEX FUTURES | | | | INDEX OPTIONS | | | INDEX FUTURES | INDEX OPTIONS | NIFTY | BANKNIFTY |
|---|---|---|---|---|---|---|---|---|---|---|---|
| | DII | FII | PRO | Combine | FII | PRO | Combine | | | | |
| Expiry Position | 16509 | 15888 | -25818 | 6579 | 214833 | 335084 | 549917 | | | | |
| 10 Day' net position | 25123 | -406 | -32204 | -7487 | 244212 | 668166 | 912378 | | | | |
| 15-Feb-23 | 12247 | -66257 | -3365 | -57375 | -80332 | 257066 | 176734 | -4325 | 138574 | 18016 | 41731 |
| 14-Feb-23 | 13373 | -63675 | -2748 | -53050 | -59118 | 97278 | 38160 | 26055 | 597921 | 17930 | 41648 |
| 13-Feb-23 | 17432 | -104752 | 8215 | -79105 | -237204 | -322557 | -559761 | 7188 | -247933 | 17771 | 41282 |
| 10-Feb-23 | 24743 | -105540 | -5496 | -86293 | -204636 | -107192 | -311828 | -9603 | -129019 | 17856 | 41559 |
| 09-Feb-23 | 21883 | -95054 | -3519 | -76690 | -126547 | -56262 | -182809 | 5976 | -105654 | 17893 | 41554 |
| 08-Feb-23 | 21483 | -96684 | -7465 | -82666 | -139117 | 61962 | -77155 | 5660 | 222524 | 17872 | 41538 |
| 07-Feb-23 | 29218 | -110680 | -6864 | -88326 | -127755 | -171924 | -299679 | 3714 | 90037 | 17721 | 41491 |
| 06-Feb-23 | 29616 | -111392 | -10264 | -92040 | -218820 | -170896 | -389716 | -17727 | -323396 | 17765 | 41375 |
| 03-Feb-23 | 27590 | -87769 | -14134 | -74313 | -91040 | 24720 | -66320 | 27169 | 301370 | 17854 | 41499 |
| 02-Feb-23 | 29660 | -112699 | -18443 | -101482 | -209277 | -158413 | -367690 | -20883 | 152394 | 17610 | 40669 |
| 01-Feb-23 | 24714 | -85804 | -19509 | -80599 | -198891 | -321193 | -520084 | 23130 | -206951 | 17616 | 40513 |
| 31-Jan-23 | 22419 | -93630 | -32518 | -103729 | -150207 | -162926 | -313133 | -3594 | 122570 | 17662 | 40655 |
| 30-Jan-23 | 3339 | -75637 | -27837 | -100135 | -197768 | -237935 | -435703 | -3622 | 101996 | 17649 | 40420 |
| 27-Jan-23 | -18403 | -58622 | -19488 | -96513 | -227427 | -310272 | -537699 | -23725 | -182283 | 17604 | 40345 |

Now consider a different illustration. According to the graphic below, from 21 October through 1 November 2022, large long holdings on index futures as well as index options were created by FII, DII, and professional traders. As a result, the NIFTY index rose from 17,576 to 18,145 and the BANKNIFTY index rose from 40,584 to 41,290 within just six trading sessions. That is the aura of examining open interest. It gives us a more accurate picture of the market than any other tool available. Moreover, remember to have a look at the expiry and 10-day net position for the index futures and options. You will have even more clarity regarding the upcoming market trend as a result.

| Date | INDEX FUTURES | | | | INDEX OPTIONS | | | INDEX FUTURES | INDEX OPTIONS | NIFTY | BANKNIFTY |
|---|---|---|---|---|---|---|---|---|---|---|---|
| | DII | FII | PRO | Combine | FII | PRO | Combine | | | | |
| Expiry Position | 16509 | 15888 | -25818 | 6579 | 214833 | 335084 | 549917 | | | | |
| 10 Day' net position | 25123 | -406 | -32204 | -7487 | 244212 | 668166 | 912378 | | | | |
| 09-Nov-22 | -70963 | 27425 | -17616 | -61154 | -287471 | 452941 | 165470 | 3033 | -47169 | 18157 | 41783 |
| 07-Nov-22 | -70945 | 23213 | -16455 | -64187 | -224579 | 437218 | 212639 | -121 | 17059 | 18203 | 41686 |
| 04-Nov-22 | -70802 | 24810 | -18074 | -64066 | -226789 | 422369 | 195580 | -12639 | -34828 | 18117 | 41258 |
| 03-Nov-22 | -70229 | 26774 | -7972 | -51427 | -186986 | 417394 | 230408 | -7109 | 31304 | 18053 | 41298 |
| 02-Nov-22 | -69812 | 38132 | -12638 | -44318 | -252712 | 451816 | 199104 | -1953 | -112018 | 18083 | 41147 |
| 01-Nov-22 | -67273 | 45181 | -20273 | -42365 | -214984 | 526106 | 311122 | 14808 | 11771 | 18145 | 41290 |
| 31-Oct-22 | -68088 | 33804 | -22889 | -57173 | -164308 | 463659 | 299351 | 425 | 166286 | 18012 | 41308 |
| 28-Oct-22 | -68874 | 17394 | -6118 | -57598 | -185973 | 319038 | 133065 | 806 | -65706 | 17786 | 40990 |
| 27-Oct-22 | -66979 | 23285 | -14710 | -58404 | -156997 | 355768 | 198771 | 46803 | 103138 | 17737 | 41299 |
| 25-Oct-22 | -66597 | -57598 | 18988 | -105207 | -323492 | 419125 | 95633 | 19142 | 297724 | 17656 | 41123 |
| 21-Oct-22 | -62051 | -76850 | 14552 | -124349 | -188406 | -13685 | -202091 | 16349 | 9464 | 17576 | 40584 |
| 20-Oct-22 | -59084 | -81893 | 279 | -140698 | -185406 | -26149 | -211555 | -19458 | -169677 | 17564 | 40100 |
| 19-Oct-22 | -57509 | -62756 | -975 | -121240 | -153466 | 111588 | -41878 | 219 | -116390 | 17512 | 40373 |
| 18-Oct-22 | -52603 | -60403 | -8453 | -121459 | -69742 | 144254 | 74512 | 27563 | 48554 | 17487 | 40318 |
| 17-Oct-22 | -55557 | -87799 | -5666 | -149022 | -114599 | 140557 | 25958 | 4579 | 316233 | 17312 | 39920 |
| 14-Oct-22 | -57607 | -91582 | -4412 | -153601 | -180680 | -109595 | -290275 | 6260 | 21754 | 17185 | 39306 |

## FII, FPI & DII POSITION IN CASH MARKET

As we have discussed in the earlier section, foreign institutional investors (FIIs) are entities that pool money from various sources and invest it in the financial markets of another country. For example, when American hedge funds invest in the Indian stock market, they are considered FIIs. However, they have some restrictions to invest in equity of Indian companies. For example:

(i) FII are permitted to invest up to 10% of a single company's equity.

(ii) The maximum investment limit in Indian companies is 24% of paid-up capital. If individual companies obtain shareholder approval, the maximum limit can be raised to 30%.

(iii) The maximum investment limit in public sector banks is 20% of paid-up capital.

Foreign Portfolio Investment (FPI) is the purchase of foreign financial assets by an investor. It consists of a variety of financial assets such as fixed deposits, stocks and mutual funds. The investors hold all of the investments in a passive manner. Foreign portfolio investors are investors who invest in foreign portfolios.

Foreign portfolios raise volatility. As a result, the risk is increased. The goal of investing in foreign markets is to diversify the portfolio while also earning a good return on investment. Because of the risk they are willing to take, investors expect high returns.

Foreign Portfolio Investment is a popular investment option these days. Individuals, corporations, and even governments invest in foreign portfolios.

DII is an abbreviation for 'domestic institutional investors'. DIIs are a type of investor who undertakes to invest in financial assets and securities of the country in which they currently reside. DII investment decisions are influenced by both political and economic trends. Domestic institutional investors (DIIs), like foreign institutional investors (FIIs), can have an impact on the economy's net investment flows. There are four types of domestic institutional investors. They are: Mutual Funds, Insurance Companies, Local Pension Funds and Banking & Financial Institutions.

Let us first observe how the FII and DII cash market data appear on the NSE website. Then we'll look at data processing and interpretation.

Home > FII/FPI & DII trading activity on NSE, BSE and MSEI

FII/FPI & DII trading activity on NSE, BSE and MSEI

Download (.csv)

| CATEGORY | DATE | BUY VALUE (₹ Crores) | SELL VALUE (₹ Crores) | NET VALUE (₹ Crores) |
|---|---|---|---|---|
| DII ** | 15-Nov-2023 | 8,165.17 | 7,555.35 | 609.82 |
| FII/FPI * | 15-Nov-2023 | 15,620.95 | 15,070.76 | 550.19 |

The above screen displays the trading activity of the major players for one day only, and we cannot gauge market sentiment based solely on one-day data. In order to assess the market trend, we must observe the position build-ups for at least a few days. Therefore, we will maintain a sheet of their daily position once the data is available on the NSE website.

| | A | B | C | D | E | F | G | H | I |
|---|---|---|---|---|---|---|---|---|---|
| 1 | | | | | | | | | |
| 2 | | Cash Market | | | | | | | NET |
| 3 | | FII/FPI | | | | DII | | | |
| 4 | Date | Buy Value | Sell Value | Net Value | | Buy Value | Sell Value | Net Value | |
| 148 | 17-Aug-22 | 8,665.90 | 6,318.70 | 2347.2 | | 5,729.80 | 6,240.10 | -510.3 | 1836.9 |
| 149 | 16-Aug-22 | 19,799.10 | 18,422.26 | 1376.84 | | 5,260.39 | 5,396.63 | -136.24 | 1240.6 |
| 150 | 12-Aug-22 | 8,260.13 | 5,219.67 | 3040.46 | | 5,752.42 | 6,591.87 | -839.45 | 2201.01 |
| 151 | 11-Aug-22 | 9,030.90 | 6,732.82 | 2298.08 | | 5,758.11 | 6,487.67 | -729.56 | 1568.52 |
| 152 | 10-Aug-22 | 9,357.94 | 8,296.06 | 1061.88 | | 5,466.36 | 6,234.81 | -768.45 | 293.43 |
| 153 | 8-Aug-22 | 15,834.69 | 14,384.99 | 1449.7 | | 5,126.30 | 5,267.03 | -140.73 | 1308.97 |
| 154 | 5-Aug-22 | 8,348.69 | 6,742.88 | 1605.81 | | 7,260.62 | 7,756.56 | -495.94 | 1109.87 |
| 155 | 4-Aug-22 | 8,705.19 | 7,230.42 | 1474.77 | | 5,255.26 | 5,302.05 | -46.79 | 1427.98 |
| 156 | 3-Aug-22 | 10,148.58 | 9,383.41 | 765.17 | | 5,865.37 | 6,383.79 | -518.42 | 246.75 |
| 157 | 2-Aug-22 | 7,526.33 | 6,701.15 | 825.18 | | 6,208.86 | 6,091.07 | 117.79 | 942.97 |
| 158 | 1-Aug-22 | 16,377.49 | 14,056.88 | 2320.61 | | 5,331.92 | 6,154.15 | -822.23 | 1498.38 |
| 159 | 29-Jul-22 | 8,531.17 | 7,484.85 | 1046.32 | | 6,720.39 | 6,721.30 | -0.91 | 1045.41 |
| 160 | 28-Jul-22 | 7,300.21 | 5,662.52 | 1637.69 | | 6,941.15 | 6,340.86 | 600.29 | 2237.98 |
| 161 | 27-Jul-22 | 4,940.81 | 5,377.62 | -436.81 | | 5,448.69 | 4,736.66 | 712.03 | 275.22 |
| 162 | 26-Jul-22 | 4,031.75 | 5,580.04 | -1548.29 | | 6,428.26 | 5,428.90 | 999.36 | -548.93 |
| 163 | 25-Jul-22 | 13,602.03 | 14,446.81 | -844.78 | | 5,270.58 | 5,342.84 | -72.26 | -917.04 |
| 164 | 22-Jul-22 | 5,335.17 | 6,010.62 | -675.45 | | 5,072.01 | 4,332.63 | 739.38 | 63.93 |
| 165 | 21-Jul-22 | 8,279.42 | 6,480.10 | 1799.32 | | 5,071.58 | 5,383.87 | -312.29 | 1487.03 |
| 166 | 20-Jul-22 | 7,606.04 | 5,825.10 | 1780.94 | | 6,032.73 | 6,262.95 | -230.22 | 1550.72 |
| 167 | 19-Jul-22 | 6,177.59 | 5,201.19 | 976.4 | | 5,085.73 | 5,186.46 | -100.73 | 875.67 |
| 168 | 18-Jul-22 | 15,055.01 | 14,898.93 | 156.08 | | 6,273.77 | 5,429.44 | 844.33 | 1000.41 |
| 169 | 15-Jul-22 | 5,300.67 | 6,950.03 | -1649.36 | | 5,278.66 | 4,219.20 | 1059.46 | -589.9 |
| 170 | 14-Jul-22 | 7,139.02 | 6,829.96 | 309.06 | | 4,224.29 | 4,780.69 | -556.4 | -247.34 |
| 171 | 13-Jul-22 | 5,093.20 | 7,932.72 | -2839.52 | | 6,217.62 | 4,418.40 | 1799.22 | -1040.3 |

Take a look at the positions established by the major players from 18 July to 17 August 2022. FII/FPIs are consistently taking long positions in the equity cash market, while DIIs are trying to take small profits. However, FII/FPI long positions are more aggressive than domestic investors' sell positions, resulting in a positive net position figure. As a result, the Nifty has risen from 16,150 to 17,940 in the time specified. That is the allure of watching the major players consolidate their positions.

Look at the table below to see the positions the major players created from 9 January 2023 to 9 February 2023. The market appeared to be falling because FII and FPIs were selling the companies they had in their portfolios. Nonetheless, DIIs were actively purchasing equities in the belief that excellent stocks were being purchased at fantastic prices, which the market generally favours. Both buying and selling pressure were present concurrently in the equities market. As a result, the index Nifty remained stable between 18,101 and 17,893 during that time. In this manner, you can forecast market trends by only examining the positions taken by the key firms.

| 2 | | Cash Market | | | | | | |
|---|---|---|---|---|---|---|---|---|
| 3 | | FII/FPI | | | DII | | | NET |
| 4 | Date | Buy Value | Sell Value | Net Value | Buy Value | Sell Value | Net Value | |
| 29 | 09-Feb-23 | 7,049.05 | 7,193.78 | -144.73 | 5,589.08 | 5,794.33 | -205.25 | -349.98 |
| 30 | 08-Feb-23 | 7,617.80 | 8,354.62 | -736.82 | 6,154.12 | 5,212.96 | 941.16 | 204.34 |
| 31 | 07-Feb-23 | 7,126.37 | 9,686.33 | -2559.96 | 6,009.70 | 5,369.88 | 639.82 | -1920.14 |
| 32 | 06-Feb-23 | 6,853.35 | 8,071.49 | -1218.14 | 5,771.18 | 4,568.09 | 1203.09 | -15.05 |
| 33 | 03-Feb-23 | 9,482.09 | 10,414.53 | -932.44 | 7,473.98 | 6,209.24 | 1264.74 | 332.3 |
| 34 | 02-Feb-23 | 9,780.82 | 12,846.17 | -3065.35 | 9,470.68 | 7,099.32 | 2371.36 | -693.99 |
| 35 | 01-Feb-23 | 14,366.67 | 12,581.46 | 1785.21 | 10,711.50 | 10,182.03 | 529.47 | 2314.68 |
| 36 | 31-Jan-23 | 14,776.22 | 20,215.86 | -5439.64 | 10,974.09 | 6,467.78 | 4506.31 | -933.33 |
| 37 | 30-Jan-23 | 11,487.01 | 5,974.38 | 5512.63 | 10,904.18 | 17,696.98 | -6792.8 | -1280.17 |
| 38 | 27-Jan-23 | 12,414.78 | 18,392.64 | -5977.86 | 12,373.41 | 8,121.08 | 4252.33 | -1725.53 |
| 39 | 25-Jan-23 | 5,859.15 | 8,253.09 | -2393.94 | 8,111.61 | 6,733.12 | 1378.49 | -1015.45 |
| 40 | 24-Jan-23 | 6,403.88 | 7,164.39 | -760.51 | 6,849.63 | 5,704.88 | 1144.75 | 384.24 |
| 41 | 23-Jan-23 | 5,803.43 | 6,023.30 | -219.87 | 5,925.39 | 5,490.43 | 434.96 | 215.09 |
| 42 | 20-Jan-23 | 8,288.80 | 10,291.05 | -2002.25 | 5,809.29 | 4,299.34 | 1509.95 | -492.3 |
| 43 | 19-Jan-23 | 7,780.87 | 7,380.89 | 399.98 | 4,321.53 | 4,450.49 | -128.96 | 271.02 |
| 44 | 18-Jan-23 | 8,386.64 | 8,705.87 | -319.23 | 6,873.15 | 5,647.19 | 1225.96 | 906.73 |
| 45 | 17-Jan-23 | 8445.26 | 8234.2 | 211.06 | 5239.45 | 5148.64 | 90.81 | 301.87 |
| 46 | 16-Jan-23 | 6260.07 | 7010.66 | -750.59 | 5220.03 | 4534.07 | 685.96 | -64.63 |
| 47 | 13-Jan-23 | 9305.72 | 11728.11 | -2422.39 | 5700.6 | 3747.2 | 1953.4 | -468.99 |
| 48 | 12-Jan-23 | 8,707.37 | 10,370.00 | -1662.63 | 6,087.85 | 3,960.20 | 2127.65 | 465.02 |
| 49 | 11-Jan-23 | 6,859.92 | 4,429.30 | 2430.62 | 6,980.52 | 10,188.67 | -3208.15 | -777.53 |
| 50 | 10-Jan-23 | 6,287.46 | 8,396.80 | -2109.34 | 6,558.15 | 4,751.53 | 1806.62 | -302.72 |
| 51 | 09-Jan-23 | 8,643.63 | 8,846.76 | -203.13 | 6,476.52 | 4,752.73 | 1723.79 | 1520.66 |
| 52 | 06-Jan-23 | 3,855.85 | 6,758.31 | -2902.46 | 6,638.39 | 5,555.22 | 1083.17 | -1819.29 |
| 53 | 05-Jan-23 | 7,275.08 | 8,724.53 | -1449.45 | 6,898.17 | 7,092.26 | -194.09 | -1643.54 |
| 54 | 04-Jan-23 | 4,508.21 | 7,129.10 | -2620.89 | 5,601.36 | 4,827.78 | 773.58 | -1847.31 |
| 55 | 03-Jan-23 | 3,077.09 | 3,705.16 | -628.07 | 5,243.44 | 4,892.87 | 350.57 | -277.5 |
| 56 | 02-Jan-23 | 1,381.14 | 1,593.71 | -212.57 | 4,660.71 | 3,917.36 | 743.35 | 530.78 |

We discussed how to identify market trends using major players' derivative and cash market data in this section of the book. Although we examined the data separately, it is always advisable to assess market sentiment by combining both data sets. Rather than assessing the data individually, combining them provides a more complete picture of the market.

## How to gauge market sentiment using put call ratio (PCR)?

Any F&O trader will immediately identify a widely used terminology as the put call ratio (PCR) if you ask them. As the name would imply, it is the ratio of puts to calls, although we will go into that more specifically later. Understanding put call ratio options and how to find them for a stock are the more important questions. Reading put call ratio charts is particularly crucial since the alterations they show are important predictors of future market movement. The PCR ratio is a popular indication of market direction used by most traders.

## What is put call ratio?

Put call ratio (PCR) is a well-liked derivative indicator that was created expressly to assist traders in determining the general mood (sentiment) of the market. Either the open interest for a given period or the volume of options traded is used to determine the ratio. More puts were traded during the day if the ratio is greater than 1, and more calls were exchanged during the day if the ratio is less than 1. The PCR can be computed for the entire option segment, which includes both specific stocks and indexes.

## How to interpret put call ratio?

The put call ratio is mostly utilised as a contrarian indicator. Fundamentals are less important in the short term than emotions are. Very high or low PCR are indicators of market greed and fear. Contrary to popular belief, PCR is typically going in the wrong direction. Put options are traded more frequently than call options when the PCR is high. But it is true that a seller is also necessary for a bought option. A transaction must involve both the buyer and the seller at the same time. Without a seller, option contracts cannot be bought into and vice versa. The meaning will be quite different from the case of buying options if you think of options as sold rather than bought. Put options are purchased more frequently when the PCR is more than one, hence the market should decline. But in practice, the market usually rises in these situations. Only if you suppose that options are being sold rather than bought can you justify this. When the seller undertakes a significant amount of risk for a small amount of reward and also uses a significant amount of cash, the argument seems to be rather straightforward: option writers are smarter than option holders. Thus, you can conclude put option writers are more active than call option writers if the PCR is greater than one. Hence, the market seems positive, and more put option sellers are anticipated to support the upswing. In contrast, PCR values below one show that more call option writers are active than put option sellers, which could cause the market to decline even more. The market may top out and see a reversal or a correction when PCR is too high, since put option sellers may become fatigued. Similar to this, excessively low PCR signals an oversold market that may experience a sharp pullback or reversal. In conclusion, the PCR can be understood as follows.

| Put/Call Ratio | Interpretation |
|---|---|
| Put call ratio > 1.00 | Bullish sentiment. It indicates that put writers are actively writing during dips in anticipation of the trend strengthening. |
| Put call ratio < 1.00 | Bearish sentiment. It indicates that call option strikes are being aggressively sold by option writers. |
| Put call ratio around 1.50 | Overbought situation. The put writers are exhausted and might book profit. A correction or reversal of the upward trend could happen. |
| Put call ratio around 0.50 | Oversold circumstances. The downtrend may have reached its bottom and a pullback is about to occur. |

Nevertheless, the interpretations are speculative, and the PCR range stated here is not set in stone. The PCR range and interpretations can vary from trader to trader. Just my prior trading experiences were used to inform the aforementioned interpretations. Someone may have the right interpretation if their alternative interpretation yields positive consequences.

## How to estimate trading range with implied volatility (IV)?

It's fascinating to discover that implied volatility (IV) provides many insights, the most valuable of which is the expected levels of movement. I'll talk about how we can use implied volatility to get a better estimate of this range. However, first, let me define implied volatility (IV). The volatility figure implied by the options premium is denoted by IV. A simple calculation yields the IV.

Option premium calculation involves the following

1. Stock price (known and definite information)
2. Strike price (factual input)
3. Volatility (unknown and could have many answers)
4. Time to expiry (known and definite Information)
5. Risk-free interest rate (not a lot impactful)

Given an option premium and inputs 1, 2, 3, and 5, the volatility figure is calculated and it is referred to as implied volatility. The good news about IV is that it does not represent historical volatility, but rather volatility anticipated by option traders. This figure represents the annualised volatility forecasted by options. This means that if this figure is 20% and the stock on which we are trading options is trading at 100, then the stock is expected to trade at 100 +/- 20%, or in the range of 80 to 120.

If you want to estimate the trading range for fewer days, say one month, you can reduce the IV figure proportionally to represent the smaller part of the year. Proportionate reduction means that if the rent for a year is ₹12,000, the rent for a month will be ₹1,000. The difference in proportionate volatility reduction is that time cannot be multiplied directly. Volatility can be scaled (apportioned) by multiplying or dividing by the square root of time.

Assuming there are 252 trading days in a year, you want to find the range for 30 trading days, and your IV is 20%.

30 days of IV reduction = 20%/square root (252) × square root (30)

= 20%/15.9 × 5.5

= 6.9% ~ 7%

So, using this simple calculation, we can estimate that option traders are expecting 7% volatility. This means that for a ₹100 rupee stock, a trading range of 93 to 107 is an expected range indicated by IV for the 30 trading days. This calculation is also applicable to the index. Instead of simply selling options with a range assumption based on historical data, option writers can now sell higher strike call and lower strike put options based on the range indicated by the expectation of future volatility during the option's life.

## MAX PAIN THEORY

Maximum pain is a term used to describe the somewhat controversial Maximum Pain theory, which states that investors who buy and hold option contracts until the expiration date will incur a maximum loss. The occurrence is based primarily on two assumptions.

1. The first assumption is based on price movements, which are the result of traders legitimately buying and selling stock options for hedging purposes. During the last few days, the index has moved closer to the strike prices at which the option buyer suffers the greatest loss.
2. The second assumption is that option sellers, such as large institutions that hedge large positions in their portfolios, will

manipulate the market. Because they are large institutions, they can manipulate index prices, resulting in no obligation to fulfil contracts and thus hedging their payouts to buyers.

Alternatively, as the strategy nears its end, different groups compete based on purchasing power to drive prices towards a more profitable closing price.

When market makers reach a net positive position of call and put options at a strike price where option holders stand to lose the most money, this is known as max pain. Option sellers, on the other hand, may profit the most if they sell more options than they buy, causing them to expire worthless.

The Maximum Pain theory is a bit contentious. The theory's naysayers disagree on whether the maximum pain behaviour of close stock prices is accidental or the result of market manipulation. The latter reason raises more serious concerns about market oversight.

## MAX PAIN CALCULATION

To understand this, consider a simple example. For the sake of this example, I'll assume the market has only three Nifty strikes available. I've taken note of the open interest for both call and put options at each strike.

| Strike | Call Option OI | Put Option OI |
|---|---|---|
| 17900 | 1,41,963 | 1,33,103 |
| 18000 | 1,26,673 | 1,38,707 |
| 18100 | 1,00,174 | 58,663 |

### Case 1: Markets expire at 17,900

Keep in mind that if you write a call option, you will only lose money if the market rises above the strike price. Similarly, if you write a put option, you will only lose money if the market falls below the strike price.

As a result, if the market closes at 17,900, none of the call option writers or sellers will be out of money. This means that call option sellers with strikes of 17900, 18000, and 18100 will keep the premiums received.

Put option sellers, on the other hand, will be in big trouble. Let us begin with the 18100 PE sellers.

18100 PE seller would lose 200 points if Nifty expires at 17,900. Because the OI is 58,663, the loss in rupees is:

= 200 × 58,663 = ₹1,17,32,600/-

18000 PE seller will lose 100 points. In terms of rupees, it would be

= 100 × 1,38,707 = ₹1,38,70,700/-

17900 PE seller won't lose any money.

So, the total amount of money lost by the option seller if the markets expire at 17,900 is:

Total money lost by call option seller + Total money lost by put option seller

= 0 + 1,17,32,600 + 1,38,70,700

= **₹2,56,03,300/-**

Remember that the total amount of money lost by call option sellers equals the sum of the amounts lost by 17900 CE sellers, 18000 CE sellers, and 18100 CE sellers.

Similarly, the total amount lost by put option sellers is equal to the sum of the amounts lost by 17700 PE sellers, 17800 PE sellers, and 17900 PE sellers.

## Case 2: Markets expire at 18,000

At 18,000, the call option sellers listed below would lose money:

17900 CE sellers would lose 100 points, which we can multiply by the open interest to get the rupee value of the loss.

100 × 1,41,963 = ₹1,41,96,300 /-

Both 18000 CE and 18100 CE sellers will not lose money.

The 17900 and 18000 PE sellers wouldn't lose money

The 18100 PE will lose 100 points. Multiplying with the open interest, we get the rupee value of the loss.

100 × 58,663 = ₹58,66,300/-

So, the total loss for option sellers if the market expires at 18,000 is:

= 1,41,96,300 + 58,66,300

= **₹2,00,62,600/-**

## Case 3: Markets expire at 18,100

At 18,100, the call option sellers listed below would lose money:

17900 CE sellers will lose 200 points, with a monetary value of:

200 × 1,41,963 = ₹2,83,92,600/-

18000 CE seller will lose 100 points, with a monetary value of:

100 × 1,26,673 = ₹1,26,67,300/-

18100 CE sellers will keep the premiums received.

Because the market expires at 18,100, all put option sellers will keep the premiums received.

As a result, the total loss of option sellers would be:

= 2,83,92,600 + 1,26,67,300 = **₹4,10,59,900/-**

So far, we've calculated the total rupee value loss for option writers at each possible expiry level. The above calculations can now be summarised in a table format:

| Strike | Call Option OI | Put Option OI | Loss of Calls (`) | Loss of Puts (`) | Total loss (`) |
|---|---|---|---|---|---|
| **17900** | 1,41,963 | 1,33,103 | 0 | 2,56,03,300 | 2,56,03,300 |
| **18000** | 1,26,673 | 1,38,707 | 1,41,96,300 | 58,66,300 | 2,00,62,600 |
| **18100** | 1,00,174 | 58,663 | 4,10,59,900 | 0 | 4,10,59,900 |

Now, we can easily identify the point at which the market is likely to expire. We have identified the combined loss that option writers would experience at various expiry levels. According to the option pain theory, the market will expire at the point where option sellers experience the least amount of pain, i.e., the least amount of loss.

According to the table above, this point is 18,000, where the combined loss is around 2,00,62,600 which is less than the combined loss at 17,900 and 18,100.

That's all there is to the calculation. However, for the sake of simplicity, only three strikes were considered in the example. However, there are numerous strikes for any given underlying, particularly the Nifty. Calculations become cumbersome and confusing, necessitating the use of a tool such as Excel.

As a result, real open interest build-ups of the Nifty option chain were calculated on 23 March 2023 for 29 March expiry. Only ten strike prices and strike prices with 100 multiples are considered for simplicity. Take a look at the image below.

| Strikes | Call OI | Put OI | Call Pain | Put Pain | Total Pain |
|---|---|---|---|---|---|
| 16500 | 4,597 | 92,124 | 0 | 332132500 | 332132500 |
| 16600 | 1,841 | 42,548 | 459700 | 269434000 | 269893700 |
| 16700 | 2,323 | 38,559 | 1103500 | 210990300 | 212093800 |
| 16800 | 6,169 | 66,788 | 1979600 | 156402500 | 158382100 |
| 16900 | 12,150 | 49,623 | 3472600 | 108493500 | 111966100 |
| 17000 | 54,443 | 1,33,103 | 6180600 | 65546800 | 71727400 |
| 17100 | 1,41,963 | 1,38,707 | 14332900 | 35910400 | 50243300 |
| 17200 | 1,26,673 | 58,663 | 36681500 | 20144700 | 56826200 |
| 17300 | 1,00,174 | 34,619 | 71697400 | 10245300 | 81942700 |
| 17400 | 87,945 | 26,297 | 116730700 | 3807800 | 120538500 |
| 17500 | 1,16,270 | 38,078 | 170558500 | 0 | 170558500 |

It assumed that the market would expire at that point for all available strikes and then computed the rupee value of the loss for CE and PE option writers. This number is shown in the final column, titled 'Total Pain'. Once you've calculated the total pain, you can simply identify the point at which the option writer loses the least amount of money. This can be determined by plotting a 'bar graph' of total pain. The bar graph would look something like this:

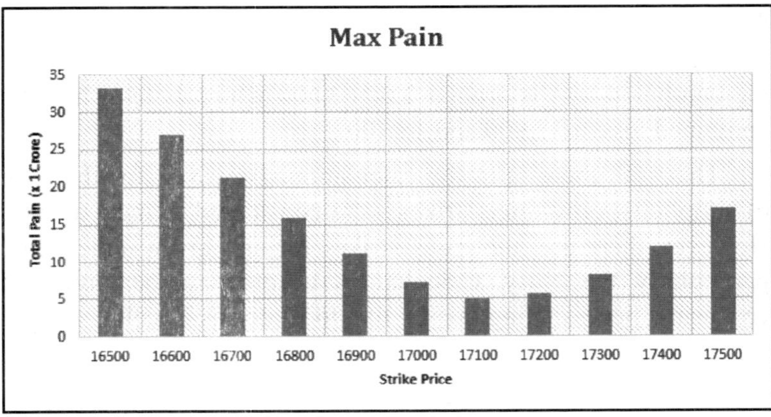


As you can see, the 17100 strike is where option writers would lose the least money, hence in accordance with the theory of option pain, this is the strike where the market for the March series is most likely to expire.

Now, how can you put this knowledge to use now that you've determined the expiry level? Well, there are many applications for this knowledge. The majority of traders identify the strikes they can write using this maximum threshold for pain. As 17,100 is the anticipated expiration level in this scenario, one can choose to write call options above 17,100 or put options below 17,100 and keep all of the premiums.

❑

# Option Trading Strategies

You should have a solid trading plan in place before you begin trading options. There are numerous choice strategies accessible, as was previously described. You need to be aware of your trading or investment goals in order to choose the best strategy. Once you've determined your trading objectives, pick a plan of action that will get you there. Investors who want to safeguard themselves against potential losses on securities they already own will choose a different approach than those who want to benefit from the greater leverage that options might offer.

Option strategies can also be used, depending on the state of the market. Very bullish or bearish, moderately bullish or bearish, and range-bound market behaviour are all possible. At this point, I feel compelled to say that options are a fantastic trading tool that can be used to create a variety of strategies for any market situation. I covered a few strategies for each market emotion in one of my prior books, *Option Chain Analysis: The CT Scan of Derivative Market*. Those were fairly straightforward but effective approaches. Here, I'll go over a few additional tactics with various legs to choose from.

As you can see, selecting the best option strategy is crucial to success in option trading. In this case, let me tell you that managing your holdings when the market doesn't move in your favour is more crucial. As no one can foresee market movement with 100% accuracy, managing deals that aren't in your favour is even more important for long-term success. Option strategy adjustments refer to the management of option positions when the market moves counter to your perception of the direction. It gives option traders the ability to turn a losing deal around and make a profit. The goal of option strategy adjustment is to increase a strategy's potential for profit or recover money from a losing deal.

The two methods for making adjustments are as follows:

1. Adding or removing additional option positions while keeping the strategy's option Greek values, particularly the delta, constant.
2. Realigning the current positions with a new option strategy.

In this book, we will explore option strategy for various market outlooks as well as changes in case the market begins to go in the opposite direction of what you had forecasted. Let's first familiarise ourselves with the many market outlooks that are now in use. They are:

1. Bullish market
2. Bearish market
3. Moderately bullish market
4. Moderately bearish market and
5. Range-bound market

I'll demonstrate a couple of option strategies for each possible market situation. However, before continuing, you should understand what an option trading payoff chart is. Option traders use this tool in order to visualise the risks and rewards of their trades and to decide on their trading strategy with intelligence.

## What is a payoff chart in options trading?

A payoff chart is a blueprint of an option strategy that shows the potential outcomes of the strategy at expiration. A payoff chart, commonly referred to as a profit and loss diagram or risk graph, shows graphically the potential gains and losses connected to an option trading strategy at expiration. Option traders can use this tool to visualise the potential results of their trades before they execute them.

The security price at expiration is plotted on the x-axis of a standard payoff chart, and the profit or loss from the options position on the y-axis. The chart normally has two lines, one for the potential profit or loss of the options' position and the other for the breakeven point. The stock price at which the option position neither gains nor loses money at expiration is known as the breakeven point.

The payoff chart for a long call option position, for example, would show a profit if the stock price at expiration is higher than the strike price of the call option plus the premium paid. Conversely, the chart would show a loss if the stock price at expiration is below the strike price plus the premium paid. The breakeven point for this position would be the strike price plus the premium paid.

To help you understand, I'll give you an example and walk you through the process of creating a payoff chart for a long call option strategy.

Here are the steps to follow:

***Determine the strike price:*** The price at which the option may be exercised is known as the strike price. Pick a strike price that fits in with your trading objectives and strategy.

***Determine the premium***: The premium is the cost incurred when purchasing a call option. It is the price of the option and reflects the biggest possible loss for the trade.

***Identify the expiration date:*** The expiration date is the date on which the option contract expires. It is important to note that the payoff chart assumes that the position is held until expiration.

***Calculate the maximum profit***: The maximum profit for a long call option strategy is unlimited, as the stock price can rise indefinitely. The profit at expiration can be calculated as the difference between the stock price at expiration and the strike price, minus the premium paid.

Maximum profit = (Stock price at expiration – Strike price) – Premium paid

***Calculate the breakeven point***: The breakeven point is the stock price at which the position neither gains nor loses money at expiration. It can be calculated as the strike price plus the premium paid.

Breakeven point = Strike price + Premium paid

***Plot the payoff chart:*** Once you have calculated the maximum profit and breakeven point, you can plot the payoff chart. On the x-axis, plot a range of stock prices at expiration, and on the y-axis, plot the profit or loss of the position. The payoff chart will show a profit if the stock price at expiration is above the breakeven point, and a loss if the stock price is below the breakeven point. The profit potential is unlimited, while the maximum loss is limited to the premium paid.

Given below is an illustration of a payoff chart for a long call option strategy with a 100-strike price, a ₹20/- premium, and a 30-day expiration date:

Here are the calculations and the resulting chart:

Strike price: ₹100/-

Premium: ₹20/-

Expiration date: 30 days from now

Maximum profit = Unlimited

Breakeven point = Strike price + Premium = ₹100/- + ₹20/- = ₹120/-

The table below shows the profit or loss at expiration for different stock prices:

| Stock Price at Expiration | Profit or Loss |
|---|---|
| ₹70 or below | -₹20/- |
| ₹80 or below | -₹20/- |
| ₹90 | -₹20/- |
| ₹100 | -₹20/- |
| ₹110 | -₹10/- |
| ₹120 (Breakeven Point) | ₹0/- |
| ₹130 | ₹10/- |
| ₹140 | ₹20/- |
| ₹150 | ₹30/- |
| ₹160 or higher | ₹40/- or higher |

The chart below represents the same data graphically:

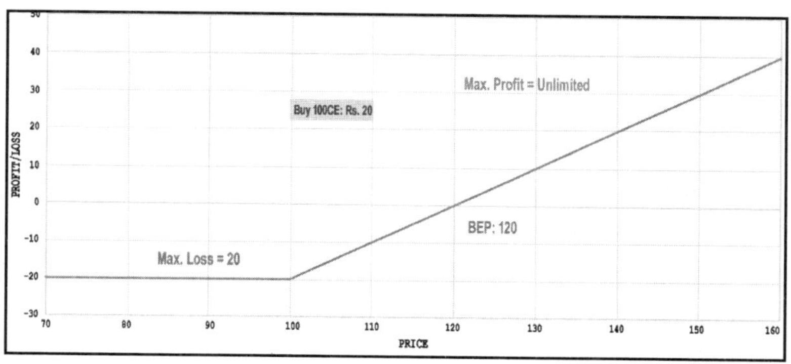

The figure shows that while the potential for profit is limitless, the maximum loss is restricted to the premium paid. The sum of the strike price and the premium paid, or the breakeven point, is ₹120/-. The trade will start to make money if the stock price rises above the breakeven level.

## OPTION STRATEGY ADJUSTMENT

The act of modifying an existing option position in reaction to market or underlying stock price movements is referred to as option strategy adjustment. In order to control risk, secure earnings, or grab fresh trading opportunities, option traders may modify their strategy. The adjustment aims to enhance the position's overall risk-reward profile.

There are various reasons why an option trader may need to adjust their position, including:

1. Changes in the price of the underlying stock: If the stock price swings against the option position, adjustments may be required to minimise losses or capture fresh chances.
2. Changes in implied volatility: Traders may need to make adjustments to their positions in order to profit from changes in implied volatility, which can have an impact on the value of options.
3. Expiration approaching: As options approach expiration, traders may need to adjust their positions to avoid or mitigate potential losses.
4. Change in the underlying stock's outlook or fundamentals: If the underlying stock's outlook or fundamentals change, the option position could need to be modified.

Here are a few typical methods for adjusting option positions:

*1.* ***Rolling***: In this process, a current option position is closed out and a new one is started with a different strike price or expiration date. For instance, if the underlying stock has increased and is now close to the option's strike price, a trader can roll a short call option to a higher strike price.

2. ***Hedging***: This involves opening a new position that is designed to offset the risk of an existing position. For example, a trader may buy a put option to hedge against a long call option position if they are concerned about a potential decline in the underlying stock price.
3. ***Scaling***: This entails adjusting positions by adding or eliminating them in reaction to changes in the market or the price of the underlying stock. For instance, if the price of the underlying stock has increased and the trader thinks that the price may drop soon, they may sell part of their long call options.
4. ***Closing***: If the trader decides that the position is no longer lucrative or that the risk is too great, they must close out the entire option position.

It is significant to remember that any adjustment to an option strategy involves careful consideration, analysis, and evaluation of the market situation and prospective results. Before making any alterations to their option positions, traders should have a clear grasp of their objectives and risk tolerance. We are going to discuss several option strategies in various market scenarios, along with adjustment procedures, in the next chapters of this book.

❑

# Option Strategies for Bullish Market

A market that is projected to experience more price increases is said to be a bullish market. Investors in this market are enthusiastic about the prospects for the economy, their specific sector, or the asset they are trading in the future. In a bullish market, traders search for chances to purchase assets in the hope that their value will rise, then sell them at a higher price to profit. In the long run, they can decide to hold on to these assets in the hope that their value will increase.

A bullish market may have a rising trade volume, robust stock demand, and optimistic expectations for corporate earnings and economic development. Bullish markets may, however, also go through times of volatility and corrections, which traders need to be aware of and ready for.

There are several ways to identify a bullish market from a trader's perspective. Here are a few methods traders frequently employ: Candlestick patterns, volume, moving averages, price trends, option chain analysis, etc. It is advisable to pay attention to the option chain in order to determine the market trend as we will be trading in the derivative segment.

Let me present an option chain that depicts a very positive market sentiment. An option chain for the Bank Nifty index is shown in the image below.

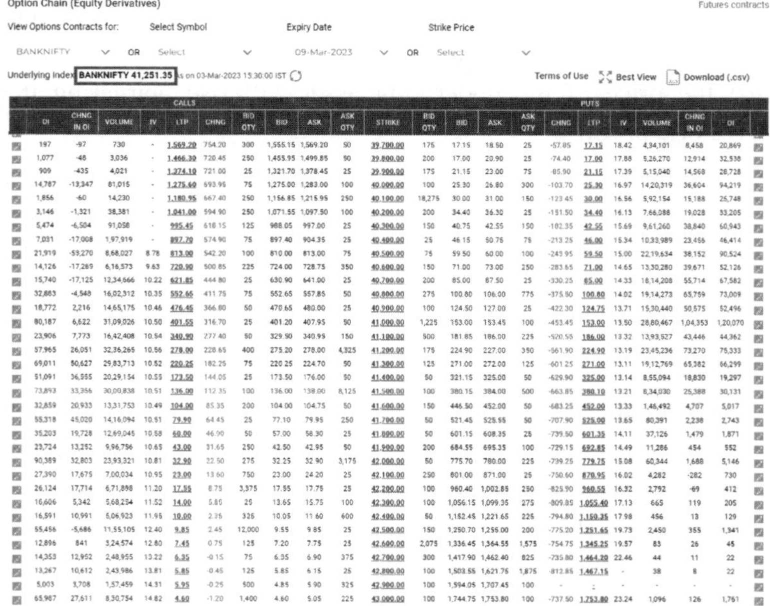

Option Chain (Equity Derivatives) Futures contracts

View Options Contracts for: BANKNIFTY OR Select Symbol: Select | Expiry Date: 09-Mar-2023 OR Strike Price: Select

Underlying Index: BANKNIFTY 41,251.35 As on 03-Mar-2023 15:30:00 IST | Terms of Use | Best View | Download (.csv)

| CALLS | | | | | | | | | | | PUTS | | | | | | | | | |
|---|---|---|---|---|---|---|---|---|---|---|---|---|---|---|---|---|---|---|---|---|
| OI | CHNG IN OI | VOLUME | IV | LTP | CHNG | BID QTY | BID | ASK | ASK QTY | STRIKE | BID QTY | BID | ASK | ASK QTY | CHNG | LTP | IV | VOLUME | CHNG IN OI | OI |
| 197 | -97 | 730 | - | 1,569.20 | 754.20 | 300 | 1,555.15 | 1,569.20 | 50 | 39,700.00 | 175 | 17.15 | 18.50 | 25 | -57.85 | 17.15 | 18.42 | 4,34,101 | 8,458 | 20,869 |
| 1,077 | -48 | 3,036 | - | 1,466.30 | 720.45 | 250 | 1,455.95 | 1,499.85 | 50 | 39,800.00 | 200 | 17.00 | 20.90 | 25 | -74.40 | 17.00 | 17.88 | 5,26,270 | 12,914 | 32,538 |
| 909 | -435 | 4,021 | - | 1,374.10 | 721.00 | 25 | 1,321.70 | 1,378.45 | 25 | 39,900.00 | 175 | 21.15 | 23.00 | 75 | -85.90 | 21.15 | 17.39 | 5,15,040 | 14,568 | 28,728 |
| 14,787 | -13,347 | 81,015 | - | 1,275.60 | 693.95 | 75 | 1,275.00 | 1,283.00 | 100 | 40,000.00 | 100 | 25.30 | 26.80 | 300 | -103.70 | 25.30 | 16.97 | 14,20,319 | 36,604 | 94,219 |
| 1,856 | -60 | 14,230 | - | 1,180.95 | 667.40 | 250 | 1,156.85 | 1,215.95 | 250 | 40,100.00 | 18,275 | 30.00 | 31.00 | 150 | -123.45 | 30.00 | 16.56 | 5,92,154 | 15,188 | 25,748 |
| 3,146 | -1,321 | 38,381 | - | 1,041.00 | 594.90 | 250 | 1,071.55 | 1,097.50 | 100 | 40,200.00 | 200 | 34.40 | 36.30 | 25 | -151.50 | 34.40 | 16.13 | 7,66,088 | 19,028 | 33,205 |
| 5,474 | -6,504 | 91,058 | - | 995.45 | 618.15 | 125 | 988.05 | 997.00 | 25 | 40,300.00 | 150 | 40.75 | 42.55 | 150 | -182.35 | 42.55 | 15.69 | 9,61,260 | 38,840 | 60,943 |
| 7,031 | -17,008 | 1,97,919 | - | 897.70 | 574.90 | 75 | 897.40 | 904.35 | 25 | 40,400.00 | 25 | 46.15 | 50.75 | 75 | -213.25 | 46.00 | 15.34 | 10,33,989 | 23,456 | 46,414 |
| 21,919 | -59,270 | 8,68,027 | 8.78 | 813.00 | 542.20 | 100 | 810.00 | 813.00 | 75 | 40,500.00 | 75 | 59.50 | 60.00 | 100 | -243.95 | 59.50 | 15.00 | 22,19,634 | 38,152 | 90,524 |
| 14,126 | -17,269 | 6,16,573 | 9.63 | 720.90 | 500.85 | 225 | 724.00 | 728.75 | 350 | 40,600.00 | 150 | 71.00 | 73.00 | 250 | -283.65 | 71.00 | 14.65 | 13,30,280 | 39,671 | 52,126 |
| 15,740 | -17,125 | 12,34,666 | 10.22 | 621.85 | 444.80 | 25 | 630.90 | 641.00 | 25 | 40,700.00 | 200 | 85.00 | 87.50 | 25 | -330.25 | 85.00 | 14.33 | 18,14,208 | 55,714 | 67,582 |
| 32,883 | -4,548 | 16,02,312 | 10.35 | 552.65 | 411.75 | 75 | 552.65 | 557.85 | 50 | 40,800.00 | 275 | 100.80 | 106.00 | 775 | -375.50 | 100.80 | 14.02 | 19,14,273 | 65,759 | 73,009 |
| 18,772 | 2,216 | 14,65,175 | 10.46 | 476.45 | 366.80 | 50 | 470.65 | 480.00 | 25 | 40,900.00 | 100 | 124.50 | 127.00 | 25 | -422.30 | 124.75 | 13.71 | 15,30,440 | 50,575 | 52,496 |
| 80,187 | 6,622 | 31,09,026 | 10.50 | 401.55 | 316.70 | 25 | 401.20 | 407.95 | 50 | 41,000.00 | 1,225 | 153.00 | 153.45 | 100 | -453.45 | 153.00 | 13.50 | 28,80,467 | 1,04,353 | 1,20,070 |
| 23,906 | 7,773 | 16,42,408 | 10.54 | 340.90 | 277.40 | 50 | 329.50 | 340.95 | 150 | 41,100.00 | 500 | 181.85 | 186.00 | 225 | -520.55 | 186.00 | 13.32 | 13,93,527 | 43,446 | 44,362 |
| 57,965 | 26,051 | 32,36,265 | 10.56 | 278.00 | 228.65 | 400 | 275.20 | 278.00 | 4,325 | 41,200.00 | 175 | 224.90 | 227.00 | 350 | -561.90 | 224.90 | 13.19 | 23,45,236 | 73,270 | 75,333 |
| 69,011 | 50,627 | 29,83,713 | 10.52 | 220.25 | 182.25 | 75 | 220.25 | 224.70 | 50 | 41,300.00 | 125 | 271.00 | 272.00 | 125 | -601.25 | 271.00 | 13.11 | 19,12,769 | 65,382 | 66,299 |
| 51,091 | 36,555 | 20,29,154 | 10.55 | 173.50 | 144.05 | 25 | 173.50 | 176.00 | 50 | 41,400.00 | 50 | 321.15 | 325.00 | 50 | -629.90 | 325.00 | 13.14 | 8,55,094 | 18,830 | 19,297 |
| 73,893 | 33,356 | 30,00,838 | 10.51 | 136.00 | 112.35 | 100 | 136.00 | 138.00 | 8,125 | 41,500.00 | 100 | 380.15 | 384.00 | 500 | -663.85 | 380.10 | 13.21 | 8,34,030 | 25,388 | 30,131 |
| 32,859 | 20,933 | 13,31,753 | 10.49 | 104.00 | 85.35 | 200 | 104.00 | 104.75 | 50 | 41,600.00 | 150 | 446.50 | 452.00 | 50 | -683.25 | 452.00 | 13.33 | 1,46,492 | 4,707 | 5,017 |
| 55,318 | 45,020 | 14,16,094 | 10.51 | 79.90 | 64.45 | 25 | 77.10 | 79.95 | 250 | 41,700.00 | 50 | 521.45 | 525.55 | 50 | -707.90 | 525.00 | 13.65 | 80,391 | 2,238 | 2,743 |
| 35,203 | 19,728 | 12,69,045 | 10.58 | 60.00 | 46.90 | 50 | 57.00 | 58.30 | 25 | 41,800.00 | 50 | 601.15 | 608.35 | 25 | -739.50 | 601.35 | 14.11 | 37,126 | 1,479 | 1,871 |
| 23,724 | 13,252 | 9,96,756 | 10.65 | 43.00 | 31.65 | 250 | 42.50 | 42.95 | 50 | 41,900.00 | 200 | 684.55 | 695.35 | 100 | -729.15 | 692.85 | 14.49 | 11,286 | 454 | 552 |
| 90,389 | 32,803 | 23,93,321 | 10.81 | 32.90 | 22.50 | 275 | 32.25 | 32.90 | 3,175 | 42,000.00 | 50 | 775.70 | 780.00 | 225 | -739.25 | 779.75 | 15.08 | 60,344 | 1,688 | 5,146 |
| 27,390 | 17,675 | 7,00,034 | 10.95 | 23.00 | 13.60 | 750 | 23.00 | 24.20 | 25 | 42,100.00 | 250 | 801.00 | 871.00 | 25 | -750.60 | 870.95 | 16.02 | 4,282 | -282 | 730 |
| 26,124 | 17,714 | 6,71,898 | 11.20 | 17.55 | 8.75 | 3,375 | 17.55 | 17.75 | 25 | 42,200.00 | 100 | 960.40 | 1,002.85 | 250 | -825.90 | 960.55 | 16.32 | 2,792 | -69 | 412 |
| 16,606 | 5,342 | 5,68,254 | 11.52 | 14.00 | 5.85 | 25 | 13.65 | 15.75 | 100 | 42,300.00 | 100 | 1,056.15 | 1,099.35 | 275 | -809.85 | 1,055.40 | 17.13 | 665 | 119 | 205 |
| 16,591 | 10,991 | 5,06,923 | 11.95 | 10.00 | 2.25 | 325 | 10.05 | 11.60 | 600 | 42,400.00 | 50 | 1,152.45 | 1,221.65 | 225 | -794.80 | 1,150.35 | 17.98 | 456 | 13 | 129 |
| 55,456 | -5,686 | 11,55,105 | 12.40 | 9.85 | 2.45 | 12,000 | 9.55 | 9.85 | 25 | 42,500.00 | 150 | 1,250.70 | 1,255.00 | 200 | -775.20 | 1,251.65 | 19.73 | 2,450 | 355 | 1,341 |
| 12,896 | 841 | 3,24,574 | 12.80 | 7.45 | 0.75 | 125 | 7.20 | 7.75 | 25 | 42,600.00 | 2,075 | 1,336.45 | 1,364.55 | 1,575 | -754.75 | 1,345.25 | 19.57 | 83 | 26 | 45 |
| 14,353 | 12,952 | 2,48,955 | 13.22 | 6.35 | -0.15 | 75 | 6.35 | 6.90 | 375 | 42,700.00 | 300 | 1,417.90 | 1,462.40 | 825 | -735.80 | 1,464.20 | 22.46 | 44 | 11 | 22 |
| 13,267 | 10,612 | 2,43,986 | 13.81 | 5.85 | -0.45 | 125 | 5.85 | 6.15 | 25 | 42,800.00 | 100 | 1,503.55 | 1,621.75 | 1,875 | -812.85 | 1,467.15 | - | 38 | 8 | 22 |
| 5,003 | 3,708 | 1,57,459 | 14.31 | 5.95 | -0.25 | 500 | 4.85 | 5.90 | 325 | 42,900.00 | 100 | 1,594.05 | 1,707.45 | 100 | - | - | - | - | - | - |
| 65,987 | 27,611 | 8,30,754 | 14.82 | 4.60 | -1.20 | 1,400 | 4.60 | 5.05 | 225 | 43,000.00 | 100 | 1,744.75 | 1,753.80 | 100 | -737.50 | 1,753.80 | 23.24 | 1,096 | 126 | 1,761 |

Out-of-the-money and near-in-the-money options on the call segment show long build-up while deep-in-the-money options show short covering. On the put side, however, both in-the-money and out-of-the-money options show a short build-up with high volume. So, the market ends up being quite positive, at least for a short period of time. In such market conditions, you can either write a naked put option or purchase a straightforward call option. Yet, there aren't many sophisticated spread approaches that may be used in this type of market condition. But I like to trade using a few basic techniques since they can be quickly altered if the market moves in the other direction to what we think it will. Hence, I'll either buy a straightforward call option or sell a put option. Let's examine each of these strategies in turn.

## CALL LONG STRATEGY

The call long strategy is a popular investment strategy used in the stock market. It involves buying a call option with the anticipation that the price of the underlying asset will rise, garnering the investor a profit.

A call option offers the buyer the right, but not the obligation, to buy a particular underlying asset at a fixed price (known as the strike price) within a predetermined time frame (known as the expiration date). The value of the call option rises along with the price of the underlying asset, enabling the buyer to sell it for more money than they paid for it and make a profit.

When an investor anticipates that the price of the underlying asset will increase in the future, they would often adopt the call long strategy. The option chain indicated above suggests that the price of the Bank Nifty index should rise during the next few days. Consequently, a trader may consider developing a call long strategy in order to make a profit in this move.

The choice of the strike price is a crucial factor in the success of any option strategy. Thus, attempt to choose a strike price that would produce the best results. At-the-money options, in my opinion, offer a respectable profit. The Bank Nifty spot is 41,251 in the option chain above. So, you have a choice between 41200CE (call option) and 41300CE. Consider that you picked up 41300CE.

## The strategy

**Buy** 41300CE

**Premium:** ₹220/- (rounded off)

**Total debit:** ₹220/-

**Maximum profit:** Uncapped

**Maximum loss:** Total debit times lot size = 220 × 25* = **₹5,500/-**

*(*25 is the lot size of Bank Nifty contract)*

**Breakeven point (BEP):** Strike price + Total debit = 41,300 + 220 = **41,520**

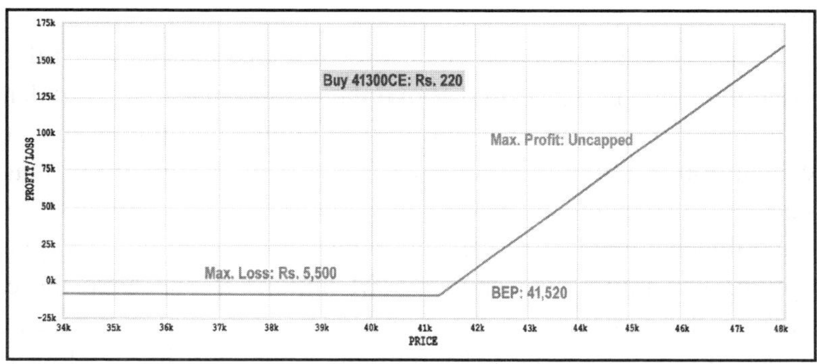


Since it is a straightforward buying strategy and your maximum loss is known, it doesn't need to be adjusted if the market isn't in your favour. In that situation, you can sell a call option to receive some credit. Nevertheless, in order to achieve that, you will need some more margin funds. If not, you can place a stop-loss order to safeguard your cash.

## PUT SHORT STRATEGY

Another well-liked stock market trading technique is the put short approach. It entails selling a put option with the hope that the price of the underlying asset will rise or hold steady, giving the trader a profit.

A put option offers the buyer the right, but not the responsibility, to sell a certain underlying asset at a predefined price, known as the strike price, within a given timeframe, known as the expiration date, while the option is open for trading. The value of the put option rises if the value of the underlying asset falls, enabling the buyer to sell the asset for more money than they paid for it and make a profit.

When an investor thinks that the price of the underlying asset will rise or stay stable in the future, they will often adopt the put short strategy. An investor might sell a put option on the stock of a certain company, for instance, if they think the stock price won't fall.

The Bank Nifty option chain shown above indicates that the price may either rise or hold above the 41,000 mark. So, a trader may think about writing a put option rather than purchasing a call option. Options trading gives you so much flexibility that you can also make a bullish trade by selling put options. To trade this sentiment, you can sell either an ATM or an OTM put option. You might also choose ITM options if you have more faith in the direction of the market. But if you're a beginner trader, it's best to write OTM options since they have a lower risk profile.

The fundamental drawback of writing options is that, while it theoretically allows for infinite risk exposure, the maximum profit potential is constrained to the premium collected. If the price of the underlying asset decreases, the put option's value will increase, and the investor may have to buy the underlying asset at a higher price than they sold the put option for. This can result in a loss, so investors should manage their risk by setting stop-loss orders or using other risk-management strategies like option strategy adjustments. Let's examine the strategy in more detail.

## The strategy

**Sell** 41200PE

**Premium**: ₹225/- (rounded off)

**Total credit:** ₹225/-

**Maximum profit:** Total credit times lot size = 225 × 25 = **₹5,625/-**

**Maximum loss:** Undefined

**Breakeven point:** Strike price – Premium received = 41,200 – 225 = **40,975**

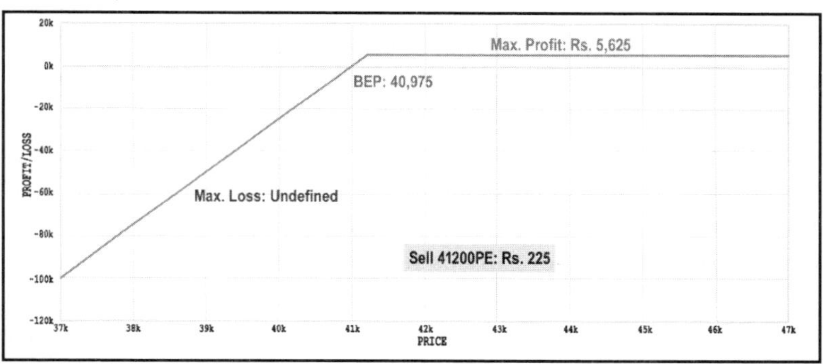


The payoff chart for this strategy shows that the highest profit you can get is ₹5,625/-, which you will receive in full if the index expires above the short strike level. Also, it demonstrates that you will make at least a profit above 40,975, which serves as the strategy's breakeven mark. But, if the index expires below it, you will lose money. If Bank Nifty keeps falling, the loss can be indefinite. You lose more money the further the index falls. As previously said, writing options offers the possibility of both restricted profit and unlimited loss.

## Adjustment

Markets occasionally don't move in the direction you think they should. Then, even when you are unable to generate a profit, you must manage your positions such that you do not lose money. To achieve this and balance the trading portfolio, you might need to create a few new positions. Adjustments of option strategy are what this is known as, and trust me, if you don't know how to fine-tune your positions, you can't be a good option trader. In any case, I'll show you how to manage your trades in the event of such bad luck.

Given that you had an optimistic outlook on the market, in this case, you sold 41200PE for ₹225/-. Sadly, if the market starts heading lower, your short positions would result in loss. If you believe that the market may find support at a lower level and reverse, you might consider rolling down (closing your current trade and starting a new trade at a lower strike) your positions in order to reduce the loss. What happens if the market doesn't turn around and break a crucial support? It might drop any lower, at which point your rolled position will start to lose money. Your initial trade resulted in a loss that you have booked, and this new trade will result in more losses for you. Is it not? Thus, maintain your current stance without changing it. Instead, sell a call option that has the same delta value as the put option. Consider that you began adjusting when the Bank Nifty tested the 41,200 mark, which would suggest that the sold put option is now an ATM option. You can sell a call option with the same strike and expiration because the value of the delta ATM option is almost equal to 0.50. Your current overall position is now a short straddle strategy with a neutral delta. Your holdings will start making you money if the market turns around or consolidates at that point.

Suppose,

The premium of **41200PE** has become **₹250/-** and

The premium of **41200CE** is **₹250/-**

Therefore,

**Total premium received** = 250 + 225 = **₹475/-**

**Lower breakeven point** = 41,200 – 475 = **40,725**

**Upper breakeven point** = 41,200 + 475 = **41,675**

**Maximum profit** = 475 × 25 = **₹11,875/-**

Now take a look at the updated payoff chart that is below. The new breakeven threshold is 40,725, which is 250 points below the previous breakeven point. But at the same time, you will acquire a breakeven threshold on the upside also. Your maximum earning potential has now increased to ₹11,875/-, which is a significant increase from your previous profit potential of ₹5,625/-. But the index must expire at 41,200 levels for you to realise the maximum profit. In the event that the market doesn't move in the way you expect, this is how the naked option position can be managed.

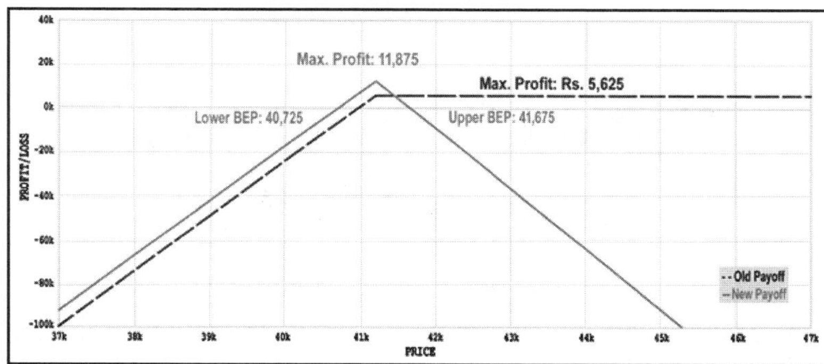


During this adjustment process, several questions may have arisen in your head. You can utilise some of the modification tactics we shall discuss later, so I am confident that these will allay your concerns. You can apply many adjusting techniques to one plan as well. Just continue reading.

❑

# Option Strategies for Bearish Market

A bearish market is one in which prices are dropping and are anticipated to do so in the near future from the viewpoint of a trader. Investors in this market are gloomy about the prospects for the economy, their sector, or the specific asset they are trading in the future.

In a negative market, traders search for chances to sell assets in expectation of a decline in value, then purchase them again at a discount to profit. To profit from the declining prices, they can also keep their cash on hand or short sell their assets. A bearish market may have a decline in trading volume, sluggish stock demand, and a pessimistic forecast for corporate earnings and economic growth.

Let's first look at an option chain for this market sentiment. This time, I'll demonstrate the option chain of the Nifty index.

The index's current market price is 17,310 (rounded off), as shown in the image below. The data for the 2 March 2023 expiry is shown in the option chain of the screenshot, which was taken on 27 February 2023. The option chain makes it very evident that the index will continue to trade negatively for at least a few days.

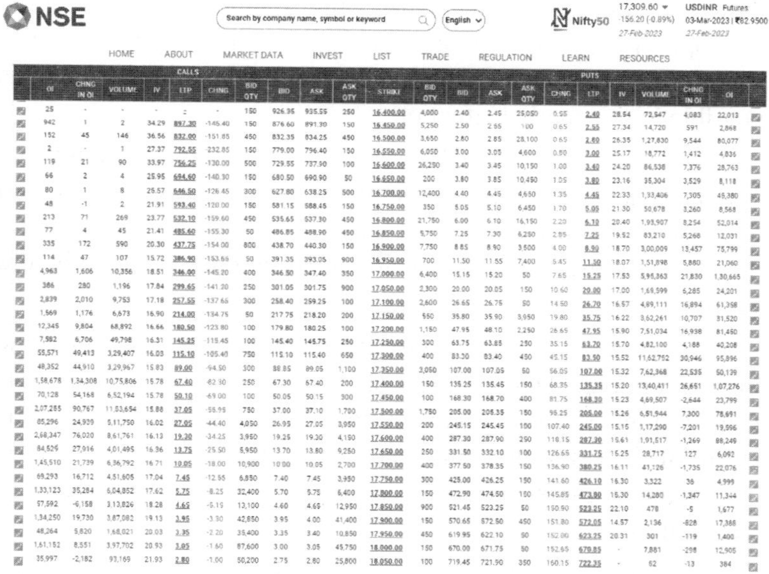

NSE

Search by company name, symbol or keyword

English

Nifty50 17,309.60 -156.20 (-0.89%) 27-Feb-2023

USDINR Futures 03-Mar-2023 | ₹82.9500 27-Feb-2023

HOME ABOUT MARKET DATA INVEST LIST TRADE REGULATION LEARN RESOURCES

| CALLS | | | | | | | | | | | | | | | | PUTS | | | | |
|---|---|---|---|---|---|---|---|---|---|---|---|---|---|---|---|---|---|---|---|---|
| OI | CHNG IN OI | VOLUME | IV | LTP | CHNG | BID QTY | BID | ASK | ASK QTY | STRIKE | BID QTY | BID | ASK | ASK QTY | CHNG | LTP | IV | VOLUME | CHNG IN OI | OI |
| 25 | - | - | - | - | - | 150 | 926.35 | 935.55 | 250 | 16,400.00 | 4,000 | 2.40 | 2.45 | 25,050 | 0.55 | 2.40 | 28.54 | 72,547 | 4,083 | 22,013 |
| 942 | 1 | 2 | 34.29 | 897.30 | -145.40 | 150 | 876.60 | 891.30 | 150 | 16,450.00 | 5,250 | 2.50 | 2.65 | 100 | 0.65 | 2.55 | 27.34 | 14,720 | 591 | 2,868 |
| 152 | 45 | 146 | 36.56 | 832.00 | -151.85 | 450 | 832.35 | 834.25 | 450 | 16,500.00 | 3,650 | 2.80 | 2.85 | 28,100 | 0.65 | 2.80 | 26.35 | 1,27,830 | 9,544 | 80,077 |
| 2 | - | 1 | 27.37 | 792.55 | -232.85 | 150 | 779.00 | 796.40 | 150 | 16,550.00 | 6,050 | 3.00 | 3.05 | 4,600 | 0.80 | 3.00 | 25.17 | 18,772 | 1,412 | 4,836 |
| 119 | 21 | 90 | 33.97 | 756.25 | -130.00 | 500 | 729.55 | 737.50 | 100 | 16,600.00 | 26,250 | 3.40 | 3.45 | 10,150 | 1.00 | 3.40 | 24.20 | 86,538 | 7,376 | 28,763 |
| 66 | 2 | 4 | 25.95 | 694.60 | -140.30 | 150 | 680.50 | 690.90 | 50 | 16,650.00 | 200 | 3.80 | 3.85 | 10,450 | 1.05 | 3.80 | 23.16 | 35,304 | 3,529 | 8,118 |
| 80 | 1 | 8 | 25.57 | 646.50 | -126.45 | 300 | 627.80 | 638.25 | 500 | 16,700.00 | 12,400 | 4.40 | 4.45 | 4,650 | 1.35 | 4.45 | 22.33 | 1,33,406 | 7,305 | 46,380 |
| 48 | -1 | 2 | 21.91 | 593.40 | -120.00 | 150 | 581.15 | 588.45 | 150 | 16,750.00 | 350 | 5.05 | 5.10 | 6,450 | 1.70 | 5.05 | 21.30 | 50,678 | 3,260 | 8,568 |
| 213 | 71 | 269 | 23.77 | 532.10 | -159.60 | 450 | 535.65 | 537.30 | 450 | 16,800.00 | 21,750 | 6.00 | 6.10 | 16,150 | 2.20 | 6.10 | 20.40 | 1,93,907 | 8,254 | 52,014 |
| 77 | 4 | 45 | 21.41 | 485.60 | -155.30 | 50 | 486.85 | 488.90 | 450 | 16,850.00 | 5,750 | 7.25 | 7.30 | 6,250 | 2.85 | 7.25 | 19.52 | 83,210 | 5,268 | 12,031 |
| 335 | 172 | 590 | 20.30 | 437.75 | -154.00 | 800 | 438.70 | 440.30 | 150 | 16,900.00 | 7,750 | 8.85 | 8.90 | 3,500 | 4.00 | 8.90 | 18.70 | 3,00,009 | 13,457 | 75,799 |
| 114 | 47 | 107 | 15.72 | 386.90 | -153.66 | 50 | 391.35 | 393.05 | 900 | 16,950.00 | 700 | 11.50 | 11.55 | 7,400 | 5.45 | 11.50 | 18.07 | 1,51,898 | 5,880 | 21,060 |
| 4,963 | 1,606 | 10,356 | 18.51 | 346.00 | -145.20 | 400 | 346.50 | 347.40 | 350 | 17,000.00 | 6,400 | 15.15 | 15.20 | 50 | 7.65 | 15.25 | 17.53 | 5,95,363 | 21,830 | 1,30,665 |
| 386 | 280 | 1,196 | 17.84 | 299.65 | -141.20 | 250 | 301.05 | 301.75 | 900 | 17,050.00 | 2,300 | 20.00 | 20.05 | 150 | 10.60 | 20.00 | 17.00 | 1,69,599 | 6,285 | 24,201 |
| 2,839 | 2,010 | 9,753 | 17.18 | 257.55 | -137.66 | 300 | 258.40 | 259.25 | 100 | 17,100.00 | 2,600 | 26.65 | 26.75 | 50 | 14.50 | 26.70 | 16.57 | 4,89,111 | 16,894 | 61,358 |
| 1,569 | 1,176 | 6,673 | 16.90 | 214.00 | -134.75 | 50 | 217.75 | 218.20 | 200 | 17,150.00 | 550 | 35.80 | 35.90 | 3,950 | 19.80 | 35.75 | 16.22 | 3,62,261 | 10,707 | 31,520 |
| 12,345 | 9,804 | 68,892 | 16.66 | 180.50 | -123.80 | 100 | 179.80 | 180.25 | 100 | 17,200.00 | 1,150 | 47.95 | 48.10 | 2,250 | 26.65 | 47.95 | 15.90 | 7,51,034 | 16,938 | 81,460 |
| 7,582 | 6,706 | 49,798 | 16.31 | 145.25 | -115.45 | 100 | 145.40 | 145.75 | 250 | 17,250.00 | 300 | 63.75 | 63.85 | 250 | 35.15 | 63.70 | 15.70 | 4,82,100 | 4,188 | 40,208 |
| 55,571 | 49,413 | 3,29,407 | 16.03 | 115.10 | -105.40 | 750 | 115.10 | 115.40 | 650 | 17,300.00 | 400 | 83.30 | 83.40 | 450 | 45.15 | 83.50 | 15.52 | 11,62,752 | 30,946 | 95,896 |
| 48,352 | 44,910 | 3,29,967 | 15.83 | 89.00 | -94.50 | 300 | 88.85 | 89.05 | 1,100 | 17,350.00 | 3,050 | 107.00 | 107.05 | 50 | 56.05 | 107.00 | 15.32 | 7,62,368 | 22,535 | 50,139 |
| 1,58,678 | 1,34,308 | 10,75,806 | 15.78 | 67.40 | -82.30 | 250 | 67.30 | 67.40 | 200 | 17,400.00 | 150 | 135.25 | 135.45 | 150 | 68.35 | 135.35 | 15.20 | 13,40,411 | 26,651 | 1,07,276 |
| 70,128 | 54,168 | 6,52,194 | 15.78 | 50.10 | -69.00 | 100 | 50.05 | 50.15 | 300 | 17,450.00 | 100 | 168.30 | 168.70 | 400 | 81.75 | 168.30 | 15.23 | 4,69,507 | -2,644 | 23,799 |
| 2,07,285 | 90,767 | 11,53,654 | 15.88 | 37.05 | -56.95 | 750 | 37.00 | 37.10 | 1,700 | 17,500.00 | 1,750 | 205.00 | 205.35 | 150 | 95.25 | 205.00 | 15.26 | 6,51,944 | 7,300 | 78,691 |
| 85,296 | 24,939 | 5,11,750 | 16.02 | 27.05 | -44.40 | 4,050 | 26.95 | 27.05 | 3,950 | 17,550.00 | 200 | 245.15 | 245.45 | 100 | 107.40 | 245.00 | 15.15 | 1,17,290 | -7,201 | 19,596 |
| 2,68,347 | 76,020 | 8,61,761 | 16.13 | 19.30 | -34.25 | 3,950 | 19.25 | 19.30 | 4,150 | 17,600.00 | 400 | 287.30 | 287.90 | 250 | 118.15 | 287.30 | 15.61 | 1,91,517 | -1,269 | 88,249 |
| 84,529 | 27,916 | 4,01,495 | 16.36 | 13.75 | -25.50 | 5,950 | 13.70 | 13.80 | 9,250 | 17,650.00 | 250 | 331.50 | 332.10 | 100 | 126.65 | 331.75 | 15.25 | 28,717 | 127 | 6,092 |
| 1,45,510 | 21,739 | 6,36,792 | 16.71 | 10.05 | -18.00 | 10,900 | 10.00 | 10.05 | 2,700 | 17,700.00 | 400 | 377.50 | 378.35 | 150 | 136.90 | 380.25 | 16.11 | 41,126 | -1,735 | 22,076 |
| 69,293 | 16,712 | 4,51,605 | 17.04 | 7.45 | -12.55 | 6,850 | 7.40 | 7.45 | 3,950 | 17,750.00 | 300 | 425.00 | 426.25 | 150 | 141.60 | 426.10 | 16.30 | 3,322 | 38 | 4,999 |
| 1,33,123 | 35,284 | 6,04,852 | 17.62 | 5.75 | -8.25 | 32,400 | 5.70 | 5.75 | 6,400 | 17,800.00 | 150 | 472.90 | 474.50 | 150 | 145.85 | 473.80 | 15.30 | 14,280 | -1,347 | 11,344 |
| 57,592 | -6,158 | 3,13,826 | 18.28 | 4.65 | -5.19 | 13,100 | 4.60 | 4.65 | 12,950 | 17,850.00 | 900 | 521.45 | 523.25 | 50 | 150.90 | 523.25 | 22.10 | 478 | -5 | 1,677 |
| 1,34,250 | 19,730 | 3,87,082 | 19.13 | 3.95 | -3.30 | 42,850 | 3.95 | 4.00 | 41,400 | 17,900.00 | 150 | 570.65 | 572.50 | 450 | 151.80 | 572.05 | 14.57 | 2,136 | -828 | 17,388 |
| 48,264 | 5,820 | 1,68,021 | 20.03 | 3.35 | -2.20 | 35,400 | 3.35 | 3.40 | 10,850 | 17,950.00 | 450 | 619.95 | 622.10 | 50 | 152.00 | 623.25 | 20.31 | 301 | -119 | 1,400 |
| 1,61,152 | 8,551 | 3,97,702 | 20.93 | 3.05 | -1.60 | 87,600 | 3.00 | 3.05 | 45,750 | 18,000.00 | 150 | 670.00 | 671.75 | 50 | 152.65 | 670.85 | - | 7,881 | -298 | 12,905 |
| 35,997 | -2,182 | 93,169 | 21.93 | 2.80 | -1.00 | 50,200 | 2.75 | 2.80 | 25,800 | 18,050.00 | 100 | 719.45 | 721.90 | 350 | 160.15 | 722.35 | - | 62 | -13 | 384 |

Buy a put option or sell a call option are the two simplest yet most profitable option strategies that can be employed in such market conditions. Let's go over each technique individually using payoff charts.

## PUT LONG STRATEGY

Another common stock market trading technique is the put long strategy. It consists of buying a put option in the hope that the price of the underlying asset will fall, registering the trader a profit.

A put option offers the buyer the right, but not the obligation, to sell a certain underlying asset at a predefined price, known as the strike price, within a given timeframe, known as the expiration date, while the option can be exercised for trading. The value of the put option appreciates if the value of the underlying asset falls, enabling the buyer to sell the asset for more money than they paid for it and make a profit.

Investors frequently employ the put long strategy when they anticipate a decline in the value of the underlying asset. The option chain shown above indicates that the price of Nifty should decrease soon. An implementation of a put long strategy is possible in this market situation.

Though it may seem like a low-risk approach, buying put options is actually a high-risk strategy, therefore investors should only use funds they can afford to lose. To reduce risk and increase possible returns, careful study and analysis must be done before adopting any investing strategy.

The time decay factor must also be taken into account while trading options. Due to their short lifespan, put options lose value as they get closer to expiration. Traders should therefore be aware of the expiration date and manage their risk appropriately by placing stop-loss orders or employing other risk-management techniques.

Right now, you know what a put long strategy is. So, let's formulate a plan. As was previously mentioned, trading at-the-money-option (ATM) is always recommended when buying options. So, I would rather purchase 17300PE, which bears a ₹83/- (rounded off) premium.

## The strategy

**Buy** 17300PE

**Premium:** ₹83/-

**Total debit:** ₹83/-

**Maximum profit:** Uncapped

**Maximum loss:** Total debit times lot size = 83 × 50 = **₹4,150/-**

**Breakeven point (BEP):** Strike price – Total debit = 17,300 – 83 = **17,217**

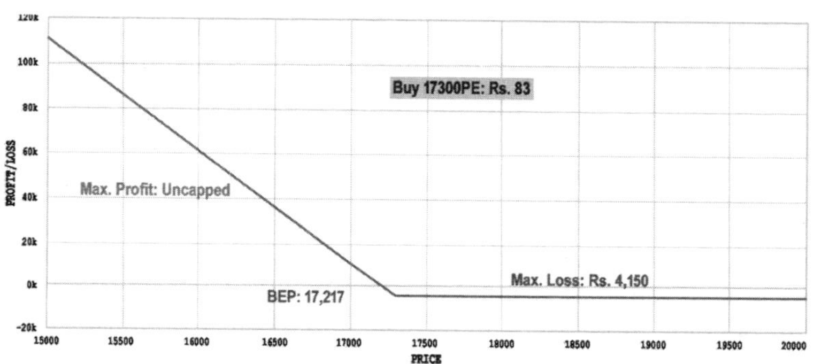


If the market doesn't move in your favour, this approach doesn't need to be adjusted because your maximum loss is limited to ₹4,150/-. You can short a put option at a lower level, as described in the call long technique, to gain some premium. If you want to protect your capital in any other case, you can set a stop loss. If the index moves against your expected direction, we will need to make adjustments to the strategy we will discuss next.

## CALL SHORT STRATEGY

Another prevalent stock market trading tactic is the call short method. It involves selling a call option with the hope that the price of the underlying asset will fall or stay steady while generating a profit for the trader. If the value of the underlying asset declines, so does the call option's value, enabling the seller to repurchase the asset at a profit by paying less than they originally asked for it.

When an investor expects that the price of the underlying asset will either decline or remain stable in the future, they would often adopt the call short strategy. However, if the value of the underlying asset rises, so will the call option's, and the seller might be forced to pay more for the underlying asset than they did for the call option. Investors must control their risk by employing stop-loss orders or other risk-management techniques because this could result in a loss.

In the aforementioned case of bearish market sentiment, you might sell a call option, instead of purchasing a put option. If you closely examine the option chain, the implied volatility (IV) is a bit high. As a result, the call premium of the options increases in cost. In this case, you should attempt to trade by selling call options because greater premiums can be earned this way. You have the option of selling call options at-the-money or out-of-the-money because, if the market moves in the desired direction, the theta will degrade more quickly. As was previously mentioned, theta decay is advantageous for option sellers. If you are a relatively inexperienced trader, it is best to stay away from selling in-the-money options as they carry some risk. To choose this approach:

**Sell** 17400CE

**Premium:** ₹67/- (rounded off)

**Total credit:** ₹67/-

**Maximum profit** = Total premium collected times lot size = 67 × 50 = **₹3,350**

**Maximum loss** = Undefined

**Breakeven point** = Strike price + Premium received = 17,400 + 67 = **17,467**

Let's examine this strategy's payoff chart.

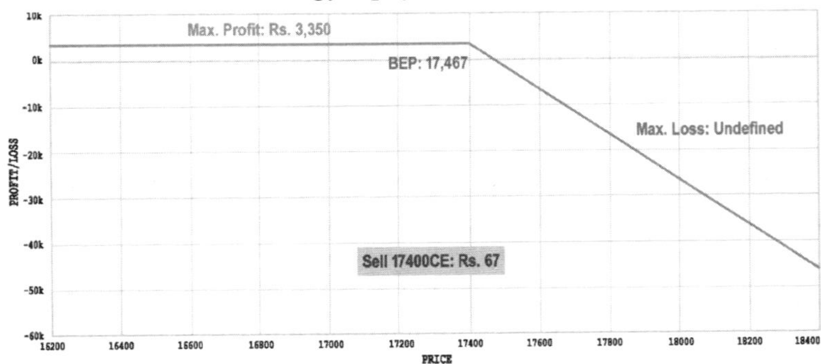

The payoff chart shows that if the index expires anywhere below 17,400, your maximum profit will be ₹3,350/-. Above that price, your profit will decrease, and at 17,467, the breakeven mark for this approach, your trade will result in a loss. As you are aware, selling options have an unlimited risk potential, and you will begin to lose money if the Nifty expires at a price higher than 17,467.

## Adjustment

In contrast to the earlier put short method covered in the section above, you can change your call short position if the index begins to move in the opposite direction of the one you predicted. You can manage your positions by making some adjustments in this situation as well. Here, all you have to do is sell a put option with a strike price of 17400 for the same expiration to execute a short straddle strategy. The fact that you can sell a put option at any other strike price now is important to note. Making a straddle while modifying the strategy is not at all required. The delta is very significant. You can choose a strike with a delta value that is nearly identical to the original strike's current delta value. The adjusted approach may occasionally turn into a short strangle or even an inverted short strangle in order to achieve the main goal of making it a delta neutral strategy. Take a peek at the new strategy now.

Suppose,

The premium of **17400CE** is **₹100/-** and

The premium of **17400PE** is **₹100/-**

Therefore,

**Total premium received** = 100 + 67 = **₹167**

**Lower breakeven point** = 17400 – 167 = **17,233**

**Upper breakeven point** = 17400 + 167 = **17,567**

**Maximum profit** = 167 × 50 = **₹8,350**

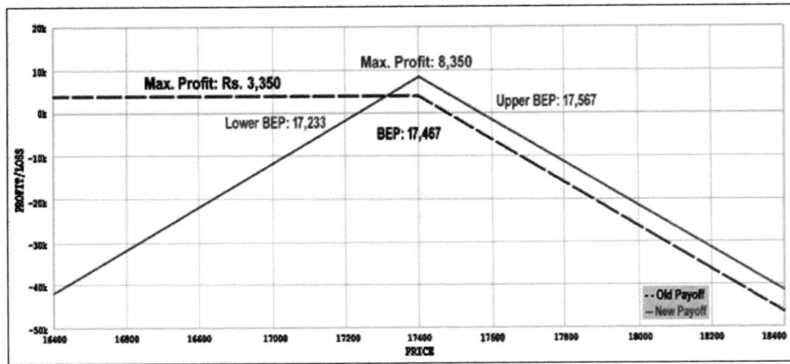


The breakeven point has moved from 17,467 levels before adjustment to 17,567 levels as can be seen in the payoff chart above. But you will also receive a lower breakeven point, which is at 17,233. Before, there was no lower breakeven point. Moreover, the maximum profit potential has risen from ₹3,350/- to ₹8,350/-. In case the market doesn't move in your favour, you can change your loss-making trade into a successful one with this method. Now, the topic of when to modify a plan of action can come up. When the price will challenge your breakeven is the solution. In this situation, you must execute a trade adjustment when the Nifty price reaches 17,467 or higher. You will undoubtedly incur a loss if you close the deal at that point. Your buffer on the upside will now be provided by the additional position. You can make a significant profit if the market turns around after a certain point and the contract expires around 17,400 level.

So, you might be wondering what would happen if the index continued to rise. In that case, you must close the extra position by realising a profit and opening a new one at a higher level. By doing this, you will receive an additional premium and raise the upper breakeven point to a new high. In this manner, you can turn a losing trade into a profit or greatly reduce the loss.

❑

# Option Strategy for Moderately Bullish Market

Prices are growing in a market that is moderately positive, but at a slower rate than in a very bullish market. Investors in this market are typically optimistic about the future prospects of the economy, their sector, or the specific asset they are trading, although they may also have a few concerns or worries.

Traders may search for chances to purchase assets that have the potential to increase in value in a moderately positive market, but they may do so carefully and with a more conservative investing plan. Instead of waiting for a significant increase, they can decide to capture some profits when the market increases.

From a trader's perspective, a somewhat optimistic market which has a firm support level beneath its current price and is predicted to see a small price increase soon is called a moderately bullish market or a sideways market with positive bias. More likely than decreasing is the possibility of the security's price increasing.

In a somewhat optimistic market, traders must be aware of possible dangers and have a clear trading strategy that takes into consideration the specifics of the market. If the market turns more bearish or bullish, they might need to modify their strategies. Several strategies, like the following, are suitable for such market conditions.

1. Bull put spread
2. Call debit spread
3. Long call calendar strategy
4. Covered call strategy
5. Call ratio back spread strategy
6. Stock repair strategy, etc.

Since I believe it's necessary to thoroughly understand a select number of strategies rather than knowing everything a little bit at a time, I'll just concentrate on three for current market trends. How many different tactics you are familiar with is not as significant as how well you are familiar with them. Now let's learn a few common methods and how to adjust them if the market isn't on our side.

## BULL PUT SPREAD STRATEGY

A bull put spread is an options trading strategy that involves selling put options at a higher strike price and buying put options at a lower strike price. Traders that are optimistic about the underlying asset and foresee an increase in price or stability utilise this method.

The bull put spread operates as follows:

***Sell a put option:*** The trader sells a put option with a higher strike price (generally ATM or OTM option), which indicates that if the option is exercised, they are required to purchase the underlying asset at that price.

***Purchase a put option***: When a trader purchases a put option, they can sell the underlying asset at a lower price if the option is exercised.

***Net credit:*** The trader obtains a net credit when they sell the put option with the higher strike price and buy the put option with the lower strike price, meaning that the premium from the sale of the higher strike put option is more than the premium for the lower strike put option.

***Maximum profit:*** The net credit received represents the maximum profit. This occurs when both put options expire worthless and the price of the underlying asset is higher than the higher strike price at expiration.

***Maximum loss:*** The maximum loss is capped at the difference between the strike prices less any net credit that was received. This happens when both put options are exercised and the value of the underlying asset is lower than the lowest strike price at expiration.

***Breakeven point:*** The breakeven point is the short strike price minus the net credit received. The trader will start making a profit if the price of the underlying asset rises above this point.

The bull put spread is a low-risk, low-reward trading technique that is appropriate for traders who are moderately bullish on the underlying asset. This method can be applied in a range of market situations, but it works best when the price of the underlying asset is anticipated to stay constant or rise. However, it carries risk, just like any trading method, and should only be employed by competent traders who are aware of the possible downsides.

You will understand the strategy well if you use an example. So that you can picture the strategy, let me show you an option chain for such a market perspective. This Bank of Baroda option chain was logged on 2 February 2021, at a stock price of ₹74/- (rounded off). The chain displays various options' component parts until the expiration on 25 February 2021.

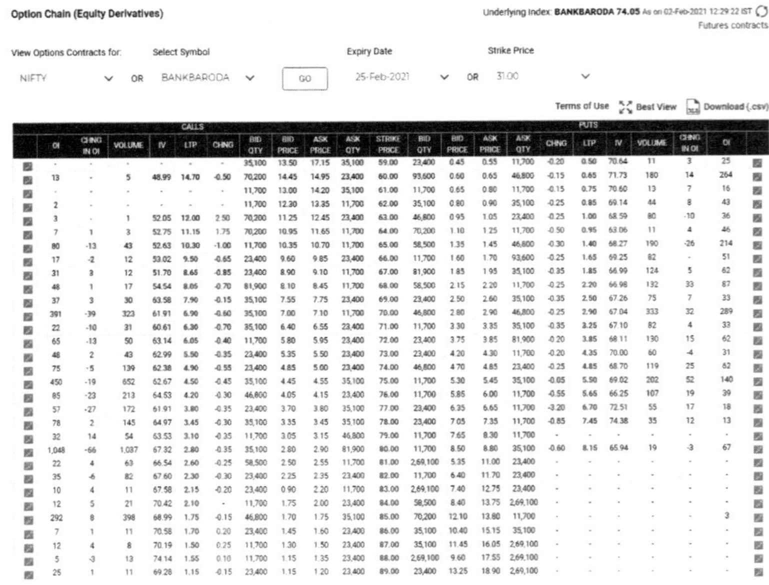

**Option Chain (Equity Derivatives)**

Underlying Index: **BANKBARODA 74.05** As on 02-Feb-2021 12:29:22 IST
Futures contracts

View Options Contracts for: NIFTY OR Select Symbol: BANKBARODA GO Expiry Date: 25-Feb-2021 OR Strike Price: 31.00

Terms of Use Best View Download (.csv)

| CALLS | | | | | | | | | | STRIKE | PUTS | | | | | | | | | |
|---|---|---|---|---|---|---|---|---|---|---|---|---|---|---|---|---|---|---|---|---|
| OI | CHNG IN OI | VOLUME | IV | LTP | CHNG | BID QTY | BID PRICE | ASK PRICE | ASK QTY | STRIKE PRICE | BID QTY | BID PRICE | ASK PRICE | ASK QTY | CHNG | LTP | IV | VOLUME | CHNG IN OI | OI |
| - | - | - | - | - | - | 35,100 | 13.50 | 17.15 | 35,100 | 59.00 | 23,400 | 0.45 | 0.55 | 11,700 | -0.20 | 0.50 | 70.64 | 11 | 3 | 25 |
| 13 | - | 5 | 48.99 | 14.70 | -0.50 | 70,200 | 14.45 | 14.95 | 23,400 | 60.00 | 93,600 | 0.60 | 0.65 | 46,800 | -0.15 | 0.65 | 71.73 | 180 | 14 | 264 |
| - | - | - | - | - | - | 11,700 | 13.00 | 14.20 | 35,100 | 61.00 | 11,700 | 0.65 | 0.80 | 11,700 | -0.15 | 0.75 | 70.60 | 13 | 7 | 16 |
| 2 | - | - | - | - | - | 11,700 | 12.30 | 13.35 | 11,700 | 62.00 | 35,100 | 0.80 | 0.90 | 35,100 | -0.25 | 0.85 | 69.14 | 44 | 8 | 43 |
| 3 | - | 1 | 52.05 | 12.00 | 2.50 | 70,200 | 11.25 | 12.45 | 23,400 | 63.00 | 46,800 | 0.95 | 1.05 | 23,400 | -0.25 | 1.00 | 68.59 | 80 | -10 | 36 |
| 7 | 1 | 3 | 52.75 | 11.15 | 1.75 | 70,200 | 10.95 | 11.65 | 11,700 | 64.00 | 70,200 | 1.10 | 1.25 | 11,700 | -0.50 | 0.95 | 63.06 | 11 | 4 | 46 |
| 80 | -13 | 43 | 52.63 | 10.30 | -1.00 | 11,700 | 10.35 | 10.70 | 11,700 | 65.00 | 58,500 | 1.35 | 1.45 | 46,800 | -0.30 | 1.40 | 68.27 | 190 | -26 | 214 |
| 17 | -2 | 12 | 53.02 | 9.50 | -0.65 | 23,400 | 9.60 | 9.85 | 23,400 | 66.00 | 11,700 | 1.60 | 1.70 | 93,600 | -0.25 | 1.65 | 69.25 | 82 | - | 51 |
| 31 | 3 | 12 | 51.70 | 8.65 | -0.85 | 23,400 | 8.90 | 9.10 | 11,700 | 67.00 | 81,900 | 1.85 | 1.95 | 35,100 | -0.35 | 1.85 | 66.99 | 124 | 5 | 62 |
| 48 | 1 | 17 | 54.54 | 8.05 | -0.70 | 81,900 | 8.10 | 8.45 | 11,700 | 68.00 | 58,500 | 2.15 | 2.20 | 11,700 | -0.25 | 2.20 | 66.98 | 132 | 33 | 87 |
| 37 | 3 | 30 | 63.58 | 7.90 | -0.15 | 35,100 | 7.55 | 7.75 | 23,400 | 69.00 | 23,400 | 2.50 | 2.60 | 35,100 | -0.35 | 2.50 | 67.26 | 75 | 7 | 33 |
| 391 | -39 | 323 | 61.91 | 6.90 | -0.60 | 35,100 | 7.00 | 7.10 | 11,700 | 70.00 | 46,800 | 2.80 | 2.90 | 46,800 | -0.25 | 2.90 | 67.04 | 333 | 32 | 289 |
| 22 | -10 | 31 | 60.61 | 6.30 | -0.70 | 35,100 | 6.40 | 6.55 | 23,400 | 71.00 | 11,700 | 3.30 | 3.35 | 35,100 | -0.35 | 3.25 | 67.10 | 82 | 4 | 33 |
| 65 | -13 | 50 | 63.14 | 6.05 | -0.40 | 11,700 | 5.80 | 5.95 | 23,400 | 72.00 | 23,400 | 3.75 | 3.85 | 81,900 | -0.20 | 3.85 | 68.11 | 130 | 15 | 62 |
| 48 | 2 | 43 | 62.99 | 5.50 | -0.35 | 23,400 | 5.35 | 5.50 | 23,400 | 73.00 | 23,400 | 4.20 | 4.30 | 11,700 | -0.20 | 4.35 | 70.00 | 60 | -4 | 31 |
| 75 | -5 | 139 | 62.38 | 4.90 | -0.55 | 23,400 | 4.85 | 5.00 | 23,400 | 74.00 | 46,800 | 4.70 | 4.85 | 23,400 | -0.25 | 4.85 | 68.70 | 119 | 25 | 62 |
| 450 | -19 | 652 | 62.67 | 4.50 | -0.45 | 35,100 | 4.45 | 4.55 | 35,100 | 75.00 | 11,700 | 5.30 | 5.45 | 35,100 | -0.05 | 5.50 | 69.02 | 202 | 52 | 140 |
| 85 | -23 | 213 | 64.53 | 4.20 | -0.30 | 46,800 | 4.05 | 4.15 | 23,400 | 76.00 | 11,700 | 5.85 | 6.00 | 11,700 | -0.55 | 5.65 | 66.25 | 107 | 19 | 39 |
| 57 | -27 | 172 | 61.91 | 3.80 | -0.35 | 23,400 | 3.70 | 3.80 | 35,100 | 77.00 | 23,400 | 6.35 | 6.65 | 11,700 | -3.20 | 6.70 | 72.51 | 55 | 17 | 18 |
| 78 | 2 | 145 | 64.97 | 3.45 | -0.30 | 35,100 | 3.35 | 3.45 | 35,100 | 78.00 | 23,400 | 7.05 | 7.35 | 11,700 | -0.85 | 7.45 | 74.38 | 35 | 12 | 13 |
| 32 | 14 | 54 | 63.53 | 3.10 | -0.35 | 11,700 | 3.05 | 3.15 | 46,800 | 79.00 | 11,700 | 7.65 | 8.30 | 11,700 | - | - | - | - | - | - |
| 1,048 | -66 | 1,037 | 67.32 | 2.80 | -0.35 | 35,100 | 2.80 | 2.90 | 81,900 | 80.00 | 11,700 | 8.50 | 8.80 | 35,100 | -0.60 | 8.15 | 65.94 | 19 | -3 | 67 |
| 22 | 4 | 63 | 66.54 | 2.60 | -0.25 | 58,500 | 2.50 | 2.55 | 11,700 | 81.00 | 2,69,100 | 5.35 | 11.00 | 23,400 | - | - | - | - | - | - |
| 35 | -6 | 82 | 67.60 | 2.30 | -0.30 | 23,400 | 2.25 | 2.35 | 23,400 | 82.00 | 11,700 | 6.40 | 11.70 | 23,400 | - | - | - | - | - | - |
| 10 | 4 | 11 | 67.58 | 2.15 | -0.20 | 23,400 | 0.90 | 2.20 | 11,700 | 83.00 | 2,69,100 | 7.40 | 12.75 | 23,400 | - | - | - | - | - | - |
| 12 | 5 | 21 | 70.42 | 2.10 | - | 11,700 | 1.75 | 2.00 | 23,400 | 84.00 | 58,500 | 8.40 | 13.75 | 2,69,100 | - | - | - | - | - | - |
| 292 | 8 | 398 | 68.99 | 1.75 | -0.15 | 46,800 | 1.70 | 1.75 | 35,100 | 85.00 | 70,200 | 12.10 | 13.80 | 11,700 | - | - | - | - | - | 3 |
| 7 | 1 | 11 | 70.58 | 1.70 | 0.20 | 23,400 | 1.45 | 1.60 | 23,400 | 86.00 | 35,100 | 10.40 | 15.15 | 35,100 | - | - | - | - | - | - |
| 12 | 4 | 8 | 70.19 | 1.50 | 0.25 | 11,700 | 1.30 | 1.50 | 23,400 | 87.00 | 35,100 | 11.45 | 16.05 | 2,69,100 | - | - | - | - | - | - |
| 5 | -3 | 13 | 74.14 | 1.55 | 0.10 | 11,700 | 1.15 | 1.35 | 23,400 | 88.00 | 2,69,100 | 9.60 | 17.55 | 2,69,100 | - | - | - | - | - | - |
| 25 | 1 | 11 | 69.28 | 1.15 | -0.15 | 23,400 | 1.15 | 1.20 | 23,400 | 89.00 | 23,400 | 13.25 | 18.90 | 2,69,100 | - | - | - | - | - | - |

## The strategy

Buy **70PE**; Premium: **₹2.90/-**

Sell **72PE**; Premium: **₹3.90/-** (Rounded off)

**Total credit** = 3.90 – 2.90 = ₹1.00/-

**Maximum profit** = Total premium collected times lot size = 1 × 11,700* = **₹11,700/-** (*11,700 being the lot size of the Bank of Baroda option contract)

**Maximum loss** = (Width of spread – Total credit) times lot size = (2.00 – 1.00) × 11,700 = **₹11,700/-**

**Breakeven point** = Short strike – Total credit = 72.00 – 1.00 = **71.00**

The payoff chart for this approach will appear as follows at expiration.

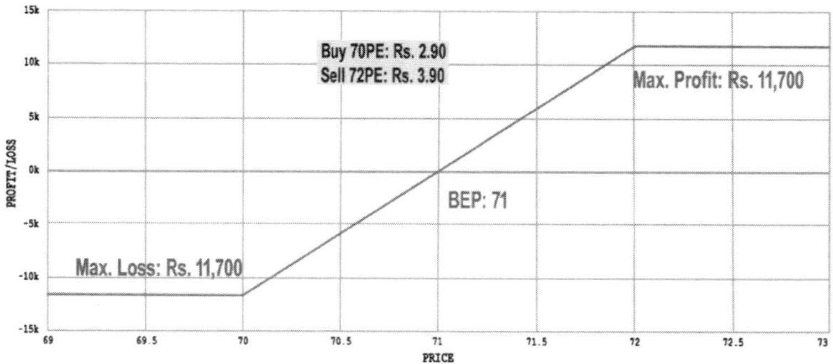


When the stock expires at a price above ₹72/-, the aforementioned chart predicts a maximum profit of ₹11,700/- and a maximum loss of ₹11,700/-. This approach will begin to pay off if the stock trades above the 71 mark and begins to lose below it. The breakeven point for this strategy is the stock price of 71/-.

## Adjustment

If the stock doesn't move in the desired direction, there are numerous modification strategies accessible. Many traders simply 'roll down', or close, their positions, using the same method but at a reduced cost. Your loss will increase if the stock price drops much more. In doing so, you would be contravening the adjustment ethos by recording a loss in the initial deal. The primary goal of adjustment is to turn your lost trade into a gainful one. And you would regret selling your earlier positions if the price turned around.

The best course of action is to create an additional credit spread on the opposing side in order to modify a bull put strategy. To lessen your loss, perform a call credit spread. Just keep in mind to maintain the spread the same on both sides. The call spread should be the same amount as the put spread in our case, which is ₹2.00. By doing this, you reduce the directional risk by putting the entire delta value near zero. If the stock price drops to the breakeven level, or ₹71, you can create a call credit spread by simultaneously selling 75CE and buying 77CE.

Let's suppose:

Premium of **77CE** is **₹2.80/-** (Buy) &

Premium of **75CE** is **₹3.40/-** (Sell)

**Credit received** = 3.40 – 2.80 = **₹0.60/-**

**Total credit** = Credit of put spread + Credit of call spread = 1.00 + 0.6 = **₹1.60/-**

**Lower breakeven** = 72.00 – 1.60 = **70.40**

**Upper breakeven** = 75.00 + 1.60 = **76.60**

**Maximum profit** = Total credit received times lot size = 1.60 × 11,700 = **₹18,720/-**

**Maximum loss** = Difference between long option and short option less credit received times lot size = (2.00 – 1.60) × 11,700 = **₹4,680/-**

Check out the payoff chart below now.

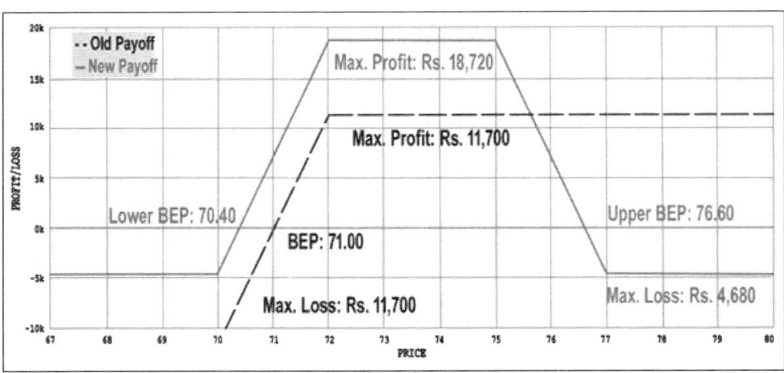


The modified strategy's payoff resembles a short iron condor strategy's payoff. As a result, the maximum loss potential, which was formerly ₹11,700/-, has been drastically reduced to ₹4,680/-. In addition, the lower breakeven has decreased to ₹70.40. But, after adjustment, you will also obtain an upper breakeven point.

But thanks to the new credit received, your maximum profit potential has now climbed to ₹18,720/-. You will be able to make a significant profit if the stock recovers at a specific point and expires between ₹70.40 and ₹76.60.

## CALL DEBIT SPREAD STRATEGY

A call debit spread is an option trading strategy that involves buying call options at a lower strike price and selling call options at a higher strike price. This strategy is used by traders who are moderately bullish on the underlying asset and expect the price to increase.

Here's how the call debit spread works:

***Purchase a call option:*** If the trader purchases a call option with a lower strike price and the option is exercised, they will have the right to purchase the underlying asset at that price.

***Sell a call option:*** The trader sells a call option with a higher strike price, which means they are obligated to sell the underlying asset at that price if the option is exercised.

***Net debit:*** The trader incurs a net debit when they purchase the lower strike call option (usually ITM or ATM) and sell the higher strike call option (usually OTM) since the premium for the lower strike call option was higher than the premium for the higher strike call option.

***Maximum profit:*** The difference between the strike prices less the net debit paid is the maximum profit. This happens when both call options are exercised and the value of the underlying asset is higher than the higher strike price at expiration.

***Maximum loss:*** The maximum loss is capped at the net debit that was actually paid. This happens when both call options expire worthless and the value of the underlying asset is below the lower strike price at expiration.

***Breakeven point:*** The breakeven point is calculated by adding the net debit paid to the lower strike price. If the price of the underlying asset increases over this level, the trader will begin to benefit.

The call debit spread is a low-risk, low-reward trading method that is appropriate for investors who are only somewhat positive on the underlying asset. This method can be applied in a range of market situations, but it works best when the predicted price rise of the underlying asset is expected to be moderate. This strategy is also known as the 'bull call spread'. Let's use an example to better grasp the method. To clarify it more, we'll use the identical Bank of Baroda option chain.

## The strategy

Buy **75CE**; Premium: **₹4.50/-**

Sell **80CE**; Premium: **₹2.80/-**

**Total debit** = 4.50 – 2.80 = **₹1.70/-**

**Maximum profit** = (Width of spread – Net debit) times the lot size = (5.00 – 1.70) × 11,700 = **₹38,610/-**

**Maximum loss** = Net debit times lot size = 1.70 × 11,700 = **₹19,890/-**

**Breakeven point** = Long call strike + Net debit = 75.00 + 1.70 = **76.70**

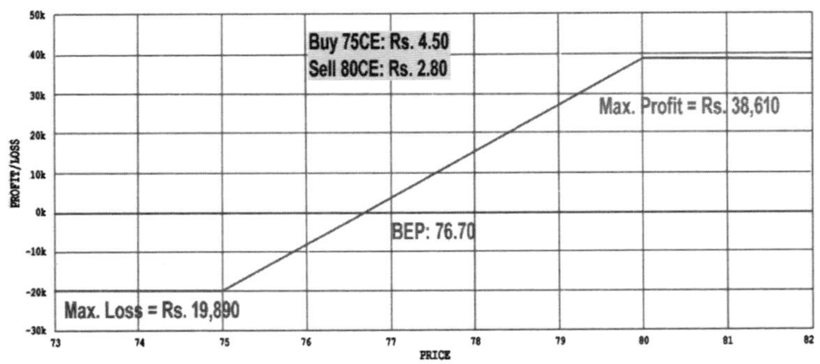


The payoff chart shows that if the stock price rises over the short strike, which is ₹80, a maximum profit of ₹38,610 can be realised. The profit is limited if the stock expires above that price. If the price drops below the long strike price of ₹75, you might lose up to ₹19,890/-. Your maximum loss is also specified because it is a net debit approach. The strategy's breakeven point is ₹76.70, below which your technique starts to lose money.

## Adjustment

In contrast to the earlier strategies, this one can be altered if the stock price starts to move against you. Also, you can build up a variety of strategies to reduce your losses here. Yet the simplest approach to get some more credit is to sell an additional call option. In this scenario, pick a strike so that it transforms your debit strategy into a zero (or almost zero) debit strategy. This indicates to choose a call option with a premium of about ₹1.70/-. Let us suppose that the price of Bank of Baroda's shares drops to ₹70, then the call option with a strike price of ₹76 will be worth a premium of ₹1.60/-.

## The new strategy

Sell **76CE**; Premium: **₹1.60/-**

**Net debit** = Previous debit – New credit = 1.70 – 1.60 = **₹0.10/-**

**Lower breakeven** = Earlier BEP – Additional credit received = 76.70 – 1.60 = **75.10**

**Upper breakeven** = Width of spread + New short strike – Net debit = 5 + 76.00 – 0.10 = **80.90**

**Maximum profit** = (New short strike – Long strike – Net debit) times lot size = (76.00 – 75.00 – 0.10) × 11,700 = **₹10,530/-**

**Maximum loss** = ₹1,700/- on downside and undefined on upside

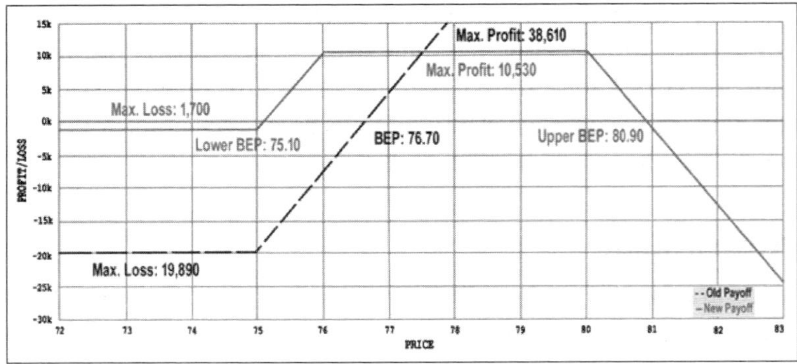


If you look at the payoff chart right now, the maximum downside risk has been greatly decreased from ₹19,890/- to just ₹1,700/- only. Additionally, the breakeven point decreases to ₹75.10 from ₹76.70 before adjustment. However, it results in a higher breakeven point of ₹80.90 and lowers the maximum profit potential to ₹10,530/- only. In this case, it's crucial for you to remember that protecting your cash should come first when a prediction goes wrong, with profit afterwards. Only when there is money in your trading account you do have a chance of recovering your wealth. Every adjustment has certain advantages as well as disadvantages.

You might be wondering what would happen if the stock price started to rise and challenged the upper breakeven point at this point. As you are aware, everything is possible in the stock market. The possibility exists that the stock will find support at the lower level and rebound from there. In that instance, simply square off the newly created second short position while modifying the strategy. By doing this, the call debit spread technique that you first used will now be considered a strategy. Therefore, even if the market doesn't work in your favour, you can still profit. At the very least, you'll be able to protect your capital.

## LONG CALL CALENDAR STRATEGY

The long call calendar spread is an options trading strategy that involves buying a call option at a later expiration date and selling a call option at an earlier expiration date. Traders who forecast a gradual, but not necessarily immediate, bullish or appreciative movement in the underlying asset use this method.

The long call calendar spread operates as follows:

***Buy a call option:*** If a call option with a later expiration date is purchased, it will grant the holder the right to purchase the underlying asset at the specified price.

***Sell a call option:*** If a call option with a sooner expiration date is sold, the trader will be required to sell the underlying asset at the price specified in the option if it is exercised.

***Different strike prices:*** The two call options should have similar or identical strike prices, but the premiums may vary based on the remaining time until expiration.

***Net debit:*** The trader incurs a net debit by purchasing the call option with the later expiration and selling the option with the earlier expiration.

***Maximum profit:*** The maximum profit is achieved when the price of the underlying asset is at the strike price of the sold call option at the time of its expiration. This is because the bought call option keeps its value and generates a profit while the sold call option expires worthless.

***Breakeven points:*** The breakeven points are calculated by adding and subtracting the net debit paid to the strike price of the bought call option. The trader will start making a profit if the price of the underlying asset rises above the lower breakeven point and sustains below the upper breakeven point.

The long call calendar spread is a low-risk, low-reward trading technique that is appropriate for investors who think that the underlying asset will become bullish moderately. This approach is adaptable to a range of market conditions, and it works best when the trader believes that the price of the underlying asset will be comparatively steady in the near future.

If you trade index options, you can also do so with weekly options. You can sell the current week's call option and buy the next week's call option on the same index, such as Nifty, Bank Nifty, or Fin Nifty.

We will use the identical Bank of Baroda option chain that was worked out in the preceding techniques to better show the calendar spread strategy. The stock may remain in this price range since the option chain suggests a mildly bullish sentiment and because there is moderate resistance at the ₹75.00 price level. Hence, if you want to choose a long call calendar spread, you might use this strike price.

## The strategy

Sell **75CE** (February series)

Premium: **₹4.50**/-

Buy **75CE** (March series)

Premium: **₹5.80/-** (say)

**Total debit** = 5.80 – 4.5 = ₹1.30/-

**Maximum profit** = Maximum profit is realised if it expires at ₹75.00 but the exact amount is undefined

**Maximum loss** = Net debit times lot size = 1.30 × 11,700 = **₹15,210/-**

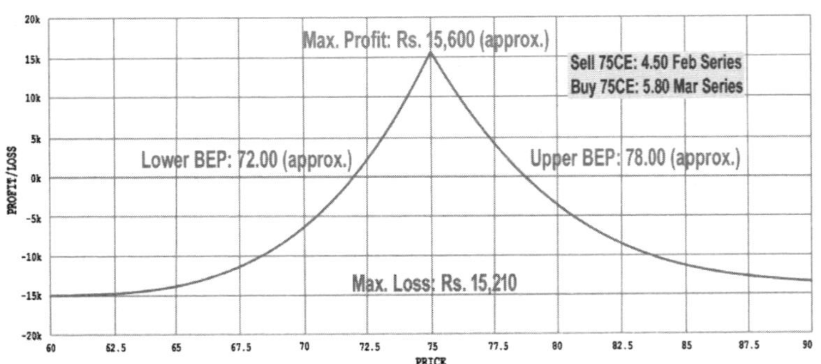


When the stock price on the expiration date equals the strike price of the call short option, the maximum profit is possible.

Because the long call has its greatest time value when the stock price reaches the strike price, this is the point of greatest profit. Again, the price disparity between the two options is at its biggest because the short call option expires worthless at expiration. It is important to note that it is impossible to predict the precise amount of the maximum profit because it depends on several elements, including the volatility of the price of the long call option. So, the payoff table above provides an approximation of the greatest earning possibilities.

Since this is a debit spread strategy, the maximum risk is equal to the cost of the spread, or the net debit amount. The money used to pay for the spread is lost if the stock price abruptly deviates from the strike price, as the difference between the two options approaches zero. Assume that if the stock price drops significantly, the cost of both call options approaches zero and their net difference equals zero. On the other hand, if the stock price rises quickly, both calls go deep-in-the-money, and their values eventually equalise, there will be no net difference.

Two breakeven marks are shown on the payoff chart, one above and one below the strike price of the spread. The stock prices on the expiration date of the short call at which the time value of the long call equals the strategy's actual cost are theoretically the breakeven points. As numerous factors affect the time value of the long call, it is impossible to predict with certainty where the breakeven point will be.

## Adjustments

Due to the fact that calendar spreads have two breakeven points, you must modify your strategy whenever the stock price approaches either the upper or lower breakeven point. I'll demonstrate each of the two adjustment methods separately. Let me reiterate that there are other procedures to modify a calendar spread in addition to these.

## *Adjustment 1*

First of all, as you were developing your strategy, your attitude towards the stock was either somewhat positive or neutral. Imagine that the stock price starts to fall and puts your lower breakeven point in jeopardy. In any case, pay close attention to the Greek values, especially the delta at that specific moment; if the delta value of any option reaches a level of 0.30 to 0.35, it's time for a change. The long call option will invite some loss at that point, while the short call option will provide some profit. In order to receive more credit, close the short position and take a profit off the table before opening a new short position close to the stock price. Theta decay will be minimal because the long call option is a far-month contract, allowing you to maintain the long position. If the stock price declines any lower, one can keep tweaking the strategy by following the same processes. It is not advised to change the strategy more than twice due to the growing gap between the delta values of two strikes. As the technique was initially delta neutral, the greater the difference between them, the more unbalanced the strategy will become, and if the stock price were to reverse for whatever reason, you might sustain a significant loss.

Consider closing the 75CE sold option for ₹3.20 and selling the 73CE at the same expiration for further credit. Suppose, the contract premium is ₹4.20. Thus, the sold option will have a booked profit of ₹1.30 (4.50 – 3.20). The chart below will now represent the adjusted payment.

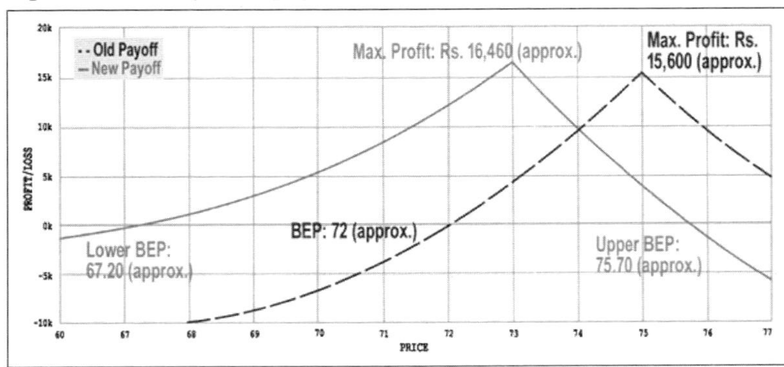

The lower breakeven mark, which was previously at ₹72.00, has been moved to around ₹67.20. This is a result of receiving the extra credit from selling 73CE. At ₹16,640, the maximum profit potential has now increased. Moreover, the upper breakeven mark has decreased from ₹78.00 to ₹75.70. In the event that the stock begins to decline, you can still manage your plan. Now, I'll let you know when the stock price approaches the higher breakeven point.

### *Adjustment 2*

Let's say the stock price is approaching the upper breakeven point, and you believe it will continue to rise. It's appropriate to consider making modifications at that point when both call options are in-the-money and the value of delta is between 0.65 and 0.70. You must manage your positions so that losing trades are turned into winning ones since you run the risk of losing a lot of money if the stock rises above ₹78.00. At a price level of ₹78.00, a long option with a March expiration will result in some profit, but a short option with a February expiration will result in some loss. Hence, you must sell a call option around the stock price for the March series (say 77CE) and terminate the short position (75CE Feb. series) by registering some loss. Choose the strike price so that the positions' mark to market (MTM) will be close to zero. Your total positions now represent a bull call spread for the stock, which means the upside risk is capped.

Suppose,

You have closed the **75CE** (short position) at **₹6/-**

The price of **75CE** (long position) is **₹7.40/-**

Price of **77CE** (Mar. series) is **₹6.50/-**

Therefore,

**Loss booked** = 4.50 – 6.00 = **– ₹1.50/-** per share

**Unrealised profit** = 7.40 – 5.80 = **₹1.60/-** per share

**MTM of the strategy** = 1.60 – 1.50 = **₹0.10/-** per share

## The new strategy

Sell **77CE**; Premium: **₹6.50/-**

Buy **75CE; Premium: ₹7.40/-** (existing position)

**Total debit** = Long premium + Loss booked – Short premium – MTM profit = 7.40 + 1.50 – 6.50 – 1.60 = **₹0.80/-**

**Maximum profit** = (Width of spread – Net debit) times the lot size = (2.00 – 0.80) × 11,700 = **₹14,040/-**

**Maximum loss** = Net debit times lot size = 0.80 × 11,700 = **₹9,360/-**

**Breakeven point** = Long call strike + Net debit = 75.00 + 0.80 = **75.80**

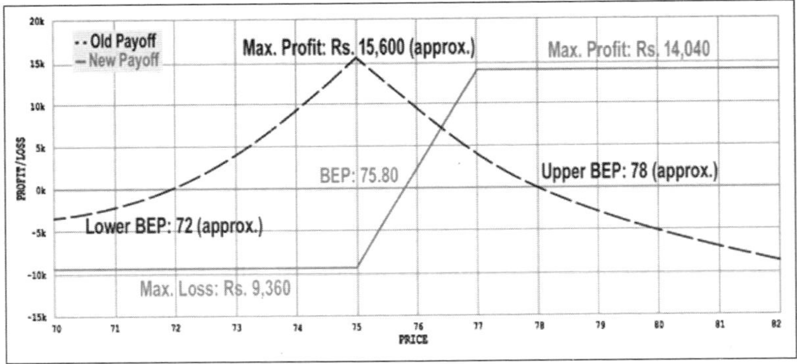


The benefit of calendar spread adjustment with bull call spread is that unlike in the past when it was at ₹78.00, there is no breakeven point on the upside. This means that if the stock price rises further, you would be able to make the maximum profit of ₹14,040/-. But at the same time, the lower breakeven point has moved to ₹75.80. However, the maximum risk potential has been decreased from a maximum loss of ₹15,210/- to only ₹9,360/-. If you believe the stock price will continue to rise, this is among the greatest calendar spread adjustment strategies.

❑

# Option Strategy for Moderately Bearish Market

A moderately bearish market is a market where prices are falling but at a slower pace than in a strongly bearish market. It is a market where investors may still have some hope or optimism despite having a generally pessimistic assessment of the future prospects of the economy, the sector, or the specific asset they are trading.

In a market that is only mildly negative, investors may hunt for chances to sell assets that will probably fall further, but they may proceed carefully and with a more conservative trading approach. In order to benefit from the declining prices, they can also try to hang onto cash or short sell assets.

Some of the characteristics of a moderately bearish market may include modest price declines, moderate trading volume, and a mix of negative and positive economic indicators. The market may experience some short-term rallies or pullbacks, but overall, the trend is downwards. So to speak, as opposed to a slightly positive market, it is range-bound and has a negative tilt. In this type of market situation, the market may drop at any time. In a sideways or downward market, the following strategies might be used:

1. Bear call spread
2. Put debit spread or bear put spread
3. Long put calendar strategy
4. Put ratio back spread strategy
5. Married put
6. Long put ladder strategy, etc.

Because simplicity is the greatest approach in options trading, we will just discuss three simple yet profitable strategies in a mildly bearish market. As we previously discussed, we don't need to be an expert in every strategy to earn from the market.

Let me first give you a general picture of an option chain in a somewhat negative market. The snapshot of the INDUSINDBK option chain shown below was obtained on 11 February 2021, when the spot price was ₹1,022.30. The option chain shows that there has been a call option short building and a put option long liquidation. As a result, the stock price may fluctuate in a limited area with a negative skew. In this case, we can use a bear call spread technique to trade in this trading environment. Let's talk about the plan:

**Option Chain (Equity Derivatives)** Futures contracts

View Options Contracts for: Select Symbol Expiry Date Strike Price

Select OR INDUSINDBK 25-Feb-2021 OR Select

Underlying Index: **INDUSINDBK 1,022.30** As on 11-Feb-2021 15:30:00 IST

Terms of Use Best View Download (.csv)

| CALLS | | | | | | | | | | | PUTS | | | | | | | | | |
|---|---|---|---|---|---|---|---|---|---|---|---|---|---|---|---|---|---|---|---|---|
| OI | CHNG IN OI | VOLUME | IV | LTP | CHNG | BID QTY | BID PRICE | ASK PRICE | ASK QTY | STRIKE PRICE | BID QTY | BID PRICE | ASK PRICE | ASK QTY | CHNG | LTP | IV | VOLUME | CHNG IN OI | OI |
| 4 | - | 1 | 99.15 | 270.50 | -33.50 | 4,500 | 247.70 | 289.00 | 4,500 | 760.00 | 1,800 | 1.35 | 1.70 | 900 | -0.25 | 1.65 | 78.71 | 19 | -5 | 199 |
| 6 | - | - | - | - | - | 4,500 | 240.00 | 250.10 | 900 | 780.00 | 1,800 | 1.80 | 2.50 | 2,700 | -0.90 | 2.10 | 79.19 | 38 | -11 | 138 |
| 57 | - | - | - | - | - | 900 | 227.40 | 232.70 | 4,500 | 800.00 | 900 | 2.45 | 3.00 | 900 | -0.30 | 2.95 | 78.06 | 103 | -9 | 701 |
| 137 | - | - | - | - | - | 3,600 | 191.65 | 212.50 | 900 | 820.00 | 900 | 2.60 | 3.35 | 900 | -0.55 | 3.35 | 73.65 | 37 | -7 | 262 |
| 273 | - | - | - | - | - | 2,700 | 189.15 | 191.90 | 900 | 840.00 | 900 | 3.90 | 4.10 | 900 | -1.10 | 4.05 | 70.19 | 53 | 7 | 336 |
| 202 | -7 | 10 | 55.89 | 168.70 | -3.40 | 13,500 | 171.10 | 173.95 | 900 | 860.00 | 900 | 5.10 | 6.00 | 4,500 | -1.10 | 5.70 | 69.38 | 139 | 3 | 446 |
| 89 | -2 | 4 | 63.91 | 152.70 | 5.05 | 1,800 | 149.25 | 157.15 | 2,700 | 880.00 | 900 | 7.00 | 7.65 | 1,800 | -1.45 | 7.30 | 67.04 | 88 | 9 | 230 |
| 555 | -4 | 43 | 60.13 | 134.00 | -5.30 | 5,400 | 120.05 | 138.75 | 900 | 900.00 | 1,800 | 9.50 | 9.85 | 900 | -1.60 | 9.70 | 65.59 | 434 | -15 | 1,175 |
| 199 | 1 | 9 | 61.35 | 118.00 | 1.00 | 900 | 116.35 | 120.55 | 900 | 920.00 | 900 | 10.00 | 12.75 | 900 | -2.00 | 12.60 | 63.87 | 237 | -37 | 362 |
| 245 | 5 | 25 | 63.06 | 104.00 | -3.35 | 900 | 102.85 | 105.30 | 900 | 940.00 | 1,800 | 16.30 | 17.45 | 900 | -2.10 | 16.80 | 63.14 | 323 | -7 | 396 |
| 155 | 1 | 23 | 59.96 | 87.20 | -7.85 | 1,800 | 87.00 | 90.75 | 900 | 960.00 | 900 | 21.50 | 22.60 | 900 | -2.30 | 21.55 | 61.90 | 493 | 4 | 332 |
| 364 | 4 | 139 | 61.22 | 75.10 | -3.70 | 900 | 73.40 | 77.10 | 900 | 980.00 | 900 | 27.40 | 28.80 | 900 | -1.95 | 28.20 | 61.57 | 468 | 5 | 240 |
| 1,245 | 1 | 438 | 60.64 | 63.50 | -2.60 | 900 | 62.60 | 63.60 | 1,800 | 1,000.00 | 900 | 35.50 | 36.00 | 1,800 | -2.10 | 35.85 | 60.94 | 1,190 | -71 | 974 |
| 303 | 75 | 812 | 62.67 | 52.45 | -2.85 | 900 | 52.75 | 53.45 | 900 | 1,020.00 | 900 | 39.50 | 45.65 | 1,800 | -1.95 | 45.05 | 60.91 | 504 | -40 | 240 |
| 846 | 238 | 1,693 | 62.60 | 44.15 | -2.30 | 1,800 | 44.15 | 44.65 | 900 | 1,040.00 | 1,800 | 55.10 | 57.35 | 900 | -0.40 | 57.40 | 63.07 | 263 | 5 | 712 |
| 730 | 52 | 893 | 63.32 | 37.10 | -1.50 | 900 | 36.20 | 37.35 | 900 | 1,060.00 | 900 | 67.50 | 70.50 | 900 | -2.05 | 69.30 | 63.14 | 78 | -4 | 154 |
| 682 | 91 | 730 | 63.42 | 30.30 | -2.00 | 900 | 29.65 | 30.75 | 1,800 | 1,080.00 | 900 | 80.30 | 93.95 | 900 | -2.15 | 79.85 | 59.87 | 20 | - | 54 |
| 1,490 | 137 | 1,199 | 64.92 | 25.00 | -1.40 | 900 | 24.80 | 25.20 | 900 | 1,100.00 | 900 | 96.05 | 98.85 | 900 | 1.80 | 99.00 | 66.82 | 18 | -12 | 48 |
| 280 | 9 | 355 | 65.43 | 20.50 | -1.45 | 900 | 20.30 | 24.90 | 900 | 1,120.00 | 900 | 110.10 | 124.45 | 1,800 | - | - | - | - | - | 4 |
| 257 | 26 | 304 | 66.13 | 16.95 | -0.65 | 900 | 16.55 | 19.00 | 900 | 1,140.00 | 1,800 | 117.05 | 133.65 | 900 | - | - | - | - | - | - |
| 470 | 5 | 276 | 67.17 | 13.70 | -1.20 | 900 | 13.65 | 13.85 | 900 | 1,160.00 | 1,800 | 142.50 | 157.20 | 2,700 | - | - | - | - | - | - |
| 525 | 4 | 246 | 68.39 | 11.40 | -0.95 | 900 | 11.15 | 11.40 | 900 | 1,180.00 | 1,800 | 149.80 | 173.70 | 1,800 | - | - | - | - | - | - |
| 485 | 39 | 407 | 69.58 | 9.50 | -1.00 | 900 | 9.30 | 9.50 | 3,600 | 1,200.00 | 1,800 | 159.55 | 193.05 | 1,800 | - | - | - | - | - | - |
| 113 | 3 | 61 | 70.42 | 7.80 | -0.45 | 900 | 7.55 | 7.90 | 900 | 1,220.00 | 2,700 | 178.50 | 209.90 | 1,800 | - | - | - | - | - | - |
| 282 | 8 | 158 | 71.52 | 6.50 | -0.90 | 900 | 6.45 | 6.55 | 900 | 1,240.00 | 20,700 | 191.00 | 241.60 | 20,700 | - | - | - | - | - | - |

# BEAR CALL SPREAD STRATEGY

The bear call spread is an options trading strategy in which a call option with a lower strike price is sold and a call option with a higher strike price is simultaneously purchased. Traders that are negative on the underlying asset and anticipate a decline in price employ this approach.

Here's how the bear call spread works:

***Sell a call option***: If the option is exercised, the trader must sell the underlying asset at the lower strike price specified in the call option they are selling.

***Purchase a call option***: The investor purchases a call option with a higher strike price, which entitles them to purchase the underlying asset at the higher price in the event that the option is executed.

***Expiration date***: The expiration dates for both call options should be the same.

***Net credit***: By selling the lower strike call option and buying the higher strike call option, the trader collects a net credit (*i.e.*, the premium collected from selling the lower strike call option is greater than the premium paid for buying the higher strike call option).

***Maximum profit:*** The highest profit is limited to be as much as the net credit taken in. This happens when both call options expire worthless and the value of the underlying asset is below the lower strike price at expiration.

***Maximum loss:*** The maximum loss is restricted to the difference between the strike prices minus the net credit collected. This happens when both call options are exercised and the value of the underlying asset is higher than the higher strike price at expiration.

***Breakeven point:*** The breakeven point is the short strike price plus the net credit collected. The trader will start making a profit if the price of the underlying asset falls below this point.

A limited-risk, limited-reward strategy, the bear call spread is appropriate for traders who are negative on the underlying asset. Due to the fact that this approach was developed for a net credit, it is also known as a 'bear call credit spread'. This strategy can be applied in a range of market circumstances, and it's particularly helpful when the trader anticipates that the price of the underlying asset will be largely unchanged or slightly declining in the near future.

We will take into account the option chain of INDUSINDBK as displayed above to construct the strategy.

## The strategy

You can sell 1040CE since it has a sizeable amount of open interest, which acts as a powerful resistance because the option chain suggests that the stock price of INDUSINDBK may decline in the near future. For the bear call spread to be built, you must simultaneously purchase 1100CE.

Sell **1040CE**; Premium: **₹44/-** (rounded off)

Buy **1100CE**; Premium: **₹25/-**

**Net credit** = 44.00 – 25.00 = **₹19/-**

**Maximum profit** = Total premium collected times lot size = 19 × 900 = **₹17,100/-**

**Maximum loss** = (Width of spread – Total credit) times lot size = (60.00 – 19.00) × 900 = **₹36,900/-**

**Breakeven point** = Short strike + Total credit = 1,040 + 19 = **1,059**

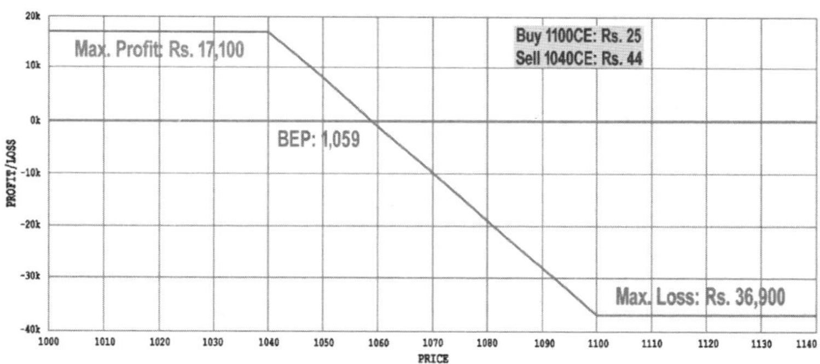


If the stock expires anyplace below the stock price of ₹1,040 or the sold strike, this method yields a maximum profit of ₹17,100/-. Above that price, the likelihood of profit decreases, and the strategy's breakeven point is at ₹1,059. Before reaching breakeven, the approach will begin allowing losses up to a maximum of ₹36,900/-. It is important to note at this time that the reward-to-risk ratio is greater than 1:2 and therefore starting the approach is not advised. But I'm merely demonstrating the trade to you for illustrative purposes. But you can make the trade if you are more certain about the downward movement.

## Adjustment

As no one can forecast market movement with 100 per cent accuracy, you must take precautions if the stock price tries to move in the opposite direction of what you projected. In that situation, you cannot remain motionless with your hands folded. To convert your loss into profit, you must do several actions. If the stock price crosses the breakeven point, you must intervene and make changes. I'll demonstrate how to leverage your holdings in this situation.

You must use a put option to create a credit spread if the stock price of INDUSINDBK increases and crosses ₹1,059 (the breakeven). Contrary to bull put adjustments, you must keep the same spread on both sides. The width of the put spread should be the same as the previous strategy's spread, which was ₹60. You can purchase 980CE and sell 1040PE simultaneously.

Let's say,

Premium of **940PE** is **₹9/-** (Buy) &

Premium of **1000PE is ₹20/-** (Sell)

**Credit received** = 20.00 – 9.00 = **₹11/-**

**Total credit** in the modified strategy is = Credit of put spread + Credit of call spread = 19.00 + 11.00 = **₹30/-**

**Lower breakeven** = 1000 – 30 = **970**

**Upper breakeven** = 1040 + 30 = **1070**

**Maximum profit** = Total credit received times lot size = 30 × 900 = **₹27,000/-**

**Maximum loss** = Difference between long option and short option less credit received; times lot size = (60.00 – 30.00) × 900 = **₹27,000/-**

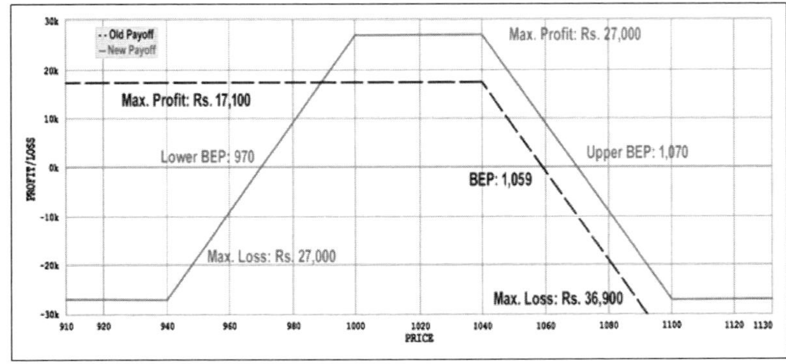

If you closely examine the payoff, you will see that it is nothing more than the payoff chart for a short iron condor approach. With some tweaking, the strategy has now evolved into a short iron condor. The payoff indicates that the breakeven point has changed from ₹1,059 to ₹1,070. On the downside, though, you will also reach breakeven at ₹970. Before modification, the greatest profit potential was just ₹17,100/-; now, it is ₹27,000/-. That is the key benefit of changing the strategy. Also, the maximum risk of the approach has dropped from ₹36,900/- to just ₹27,000/- as opposed to before the alteration. By opening a few more transactions, you can also reduce your maximum loss while increasing your possible return.

## BEAR PUT SPREAD

The bear put spread is an options trading strategy that involves buying a put option with a higher strike price (normally ITM or ATM option) and simultaneously selling a put option with a lower strike price (normally OTM option). This strategy is used by traders who are bearish on the underlying asset and expect the price to decrease.

The bear put spread operates as follows:

***Buy a put option:*** The trader buys a put option with a higher strike price, which gives them the right to sell the underlying asset at that price if the option is exercised.

***Sell a put option:*** The trader sells a put option with a lower strike price, which indicates that if the option is exercised, they are required to purchase the underlying asset at that price.

***Expiration date:*** The expiration dates for both put options should be the same.

***Net debit:*** The trader pays a net debit when they buy the higher strike put option and sell the lower strike put option since the premium for the higher strike put option was more than the premium for the lower strike put option they sold.

***Maximum profit:*** The maximum profit is limited to the difference between the strike prices minus the net debit paid. This occurs when both put options are exercised and the value of the underlying asset is lower than the lowest strike price at expiration.

***Maximum loss:*** The maximum loss will be limited to the net debit that was actually paid. This happens when both put options expire worthless and the value of the underlying asset is higher than the higher strike price at expiration.

***Breakeven point:*** The breakeven point is determined by subtracting the net debit from the higher strike price. If the value of the underlying asset drops below this level, the trader will begin to benefit.

The bear put spread is a limited-risk, limited-reward strategy, and it's suitable for traders who are bearish on the underlying asset. Due to the fact that this method requires the traders to pay for the trade, it is also known as a 'put debit spread'. This tactic can be applied in a range of market scenarios, and it's particularly helpful when the trader anticipates that the price of the underlying asset will be largely unchanged or slightly declining in the near future.

Let's use the same option chain for INDUSINDBK as an example to show how to use a bear put spread. As the stock's current market price is ₹1,022, it is possible to purchase a put option that is at-the-money, or 1020PE. The trader has the option to sell 960PE to obtain some credit in order to make the spread.

## The strategy

Buy **1020PE**; Premium: **₹45/-** (rounded off)

Sell **960PE**; Premium: **₹21/-** (rounded off)

**Total debit:** 45.00 – 21.00 = **₹24/-**

**Maximum profit** = (Width of spread – Net debit) times the lot size = (60.00 – 24.00) × 900 = **₹32,400/-**

**Maximum loss** = Net debit times lot size = 24.00 × 900 = **₹21,600/-**

**Breakeven point** = Long put strike – Net debit = 1020 – 24 = **996**

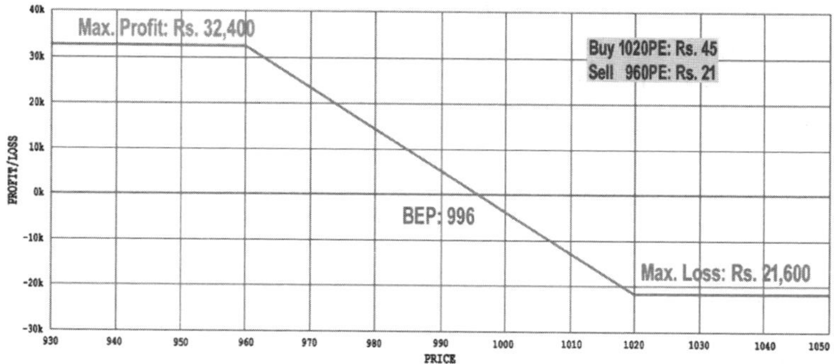


The aforementioned chart indicates a maximum loss of ₹21,600/- if INDUSINDBK's stock price rises to or above ₹1,020, the price at which the put option was sold. Yet regardless of how much the stock price rises, that is the worst loss a trader may sustain. If the stock price drops below ₹1,020, till ₹996, the strategy's breakeven threshold, the potential loss gradually decreases. If the stock declines even more from this price point, you will start to make money. Your maximum profit, however, is limited to ₹32,400 and may only be booked when the contract expires at or below ₹960. You have sold the put option at this price.

## Adjustment

If the stock turns out to be bearish, the above method will produce a respectable profit, and the risk-to-reward ratio is also acceptable. The difference between the long and short options' delta in the original approach is 0.20 if the long option has a delta value of roughly 0.50 and the short option has a value of roughly 0.30. This distinction will now serve as a benchmark for determining when to modify the approach. Imagine the difference has now decreased to half, or 0.10, suggesting that it is time to intervene with the primary method of loss elimination. Let's say the stock price at that time was ₹990. Although there are other options to prevent such a negative move, the ideal one is to sell a put option in order to obtain some extra credit. Selecting a put option results in a credit that is almost equal to the debit of the initial strategy, bringing the overall value of delta down to a range of 0.20. Suppose that the premium for 980PE is 23/- rupees, or almost the same as the net negative of the core strategy.

## The new strategy

Sell **980PE**; Premium: **₹23/-**

**Net debit** = Previous debit – New credit = 24.00 – 23.00 = **₹1/-**

**Upper breakeven** = Earlier BEP + New credit = 996 + 23 = **1,019**

**Lower breakeven** = New short strike – Width of spread + Net debit = 980 – 60 + 1 = **921**

**Maximum profit** = (New short strike – Long strike – Net debit) times lot size = (1020 – 980 – 1) × 900 = **₹35,100/-**

**Maximum loss** = Undefined

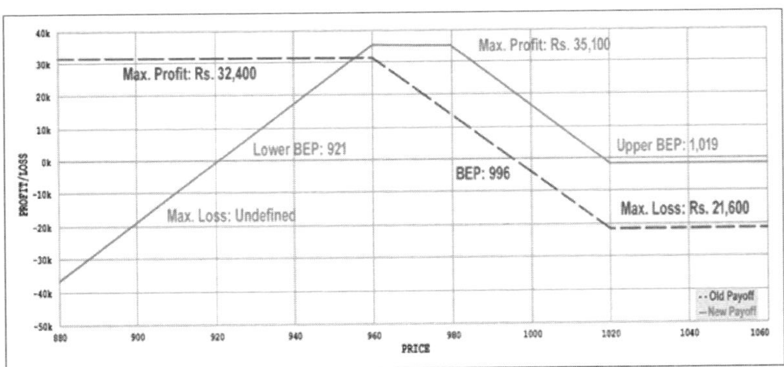


The customised strategy's payoff chart shows that the breakeven point has moved much upward from its previous value of ₹996 to ₹1,019, and the greatest part is that the maximum upside loss potential is limited to the amount of the debit paid or ₹900 only. However, if the share price of INDUSINDBK drops below ₹921, the maximum risk is unknown. The maximum profit potential was ₹32,400 before adjustment; it is now ₹35,100. Only when the option contract expires between the stock price range of ₹960 and ₹80 can the maximum profit be realised. If the bear put spread doesn't go your way, this is one of the finest adjusting strategies to use.

## LONG PUT CALENDAR SPREAD

The long put calendar spread is an options trading strategy that involves buying a put option with a longer-term expiration date and selling a put option with a shorter-term expiration date. This strategy is used by traders who expect the price of the underlying asset to decline in the short term or remain relatively stable.

Here's how the long put calendar spread works:

***Buy a put option:*** The trader buys a put option with a longer-term expiration date, which gives them the right to sell the underlying asset at a specific price if the option is exercised.

***Sell a put option:*** The trader sells a put option with a shorter expiration date. If the option is exercised, they are then required to purchase the underlying asset at that price.

***Underlying asset:*** The underlying asset for both put options should be the same.

***Net debit:*** The trader costs a net debit when they buy the longer-term put option and sell the shorter-term put option since the premium for the longer-term put option was higher than the premium for the shorter-term put option.

***Maximum profit:*** The maximum profit is achieved when the price of the underlying asset is at the strike price of the sold put option at the time of its expiration. This is due to the fact that the bought put option keeps its value and generates a profit while the sold put option expires worthless.

***Breakeven points:*** To get the breakeven points, add and subtract the net debit paid from the put option's strike price. If the price of the underlying asset falls below the upper breakeven point or stays above the lower breakeven point, the trader will begin to profit.

We'll use an example to help you grasp the concept a little better. The option chain as displayed in the aforementioned example indicates that INDUSINDBK is anticipated to trade range-bound or slightly bearish. So, a calendar spread with a put option can be created to profit from the stock. While developing the plan, make a note of the delta values for each strike so that you can make educated selections during the adjustment phase. If you select options that are out-of-the-money options, the delta values will vary from 0.40 to 0.60. Nonetheless, if adjustment is required, we shall discuss it later. Let's get acquainted with the technique first for the time being.

## The strategy

Sell **1000PE** (February series)

Premium: **₹36/-** (rounded off)

Buy **1000PE** (March series)

Premium: **₹55/-** (say)

**Total debit:** 55 – 36 = **₹19/-**

**Maximum profit** = Maximum profit is realised if it expires at ₹1,000 but the exact amount is undefined

**Maximum loss** = Net debit times lot size = 19 × 900 = **₹17,100/-**

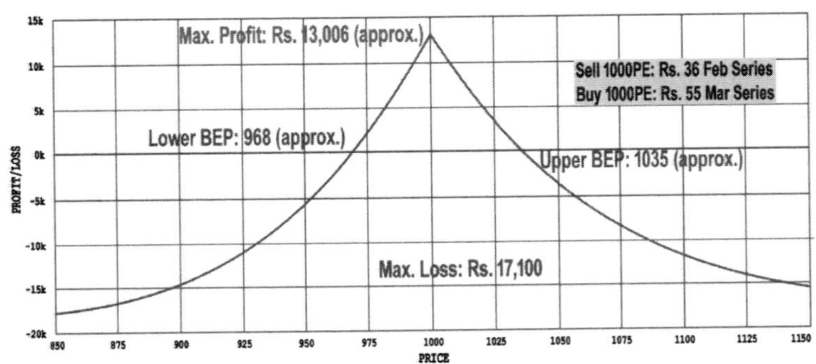

The highest profit is realised if the contract expires at the strike price where the put option was sold, according to the payoff chart. This is so that when the stock price and strike price coincide, the far-expiry put option has its highest time value. Nevertheless, because the premium of the long put option varies on a number of variables and the return is reliant on the long option as well, it is impossible to compute the precise profit.

The payoff also specifies that the strategy's cost, or a maximum loss of ₹17,100, is the maximum loss that could occur. Due to the fact that it is a debit strategy, the maximum loss is only capped at the net debit. In addition, it shows the approximate breakeven point on both the upside and downside. The long put option makes it hard to estimate the precise breakeven positions, as was stated in the call calendar spread.

## Adjustments

The long put calendar spread's payoff chart shows two breakeven points, which indicates that you should modify your strategy if any of them is challenged. Hence, in case any one side of the breakeven is tested, I'll demonstrate some potential management techniques.

### *Adjustment 1*

Let's assume that in the first scenario, the price of INDUSINDBK is rising and that any of the delta values reduce to approximately 0.20, triggering adjustment. If you want to keep things simple, consider controlling the technique when the stock price approaches your upper breakeven threshold. The near-term short option makes some money at that point, while the long-term long option suffers some losses. Close the short put option, taking a portion of the profit off the table, and then open a second short position of the same kind close to the stock price, where the delta is about 0.40. By doing this, you will earn some extra credit. Also, since the long put option is a far-month contract, there will be less premium decay, allowing the position to be held open.

Imagine that after a few days, the stock's spot price is ₹1,050 and the premium for 1000PE is ₹20. Hence, write off the sold option's profit of ₹16 (36 – 20) and start a new short position at the 1040 strike price.

## The Modified Strategy

Sell **1040PE** (Feb. expiry)

Premium: **₹35/-** (say)

Buy **1000PE** (Mar. expiry)

Premium: **₹55/-** (existing position)

**Total debit:** 35.00 – 55.00 + 16.00 = **₹4/-**

**Maximum profit** = Maximum profit is realised if it expires at ₹1,040 but the exact amount is undefined

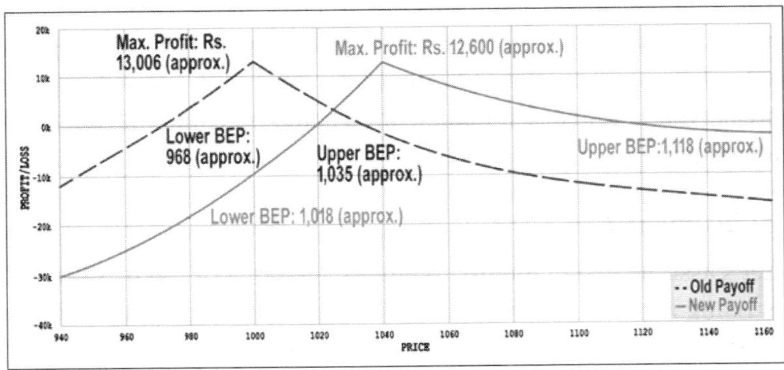


The payoff graph shows that the lower breakeven point has moved from ₹968 to ₹1,018. The upper breakeven has also significantly changed. With the adjustment, there has been a significant movement in breakeven points. Although the greatest profit potential in a calendar spread strategy cannot be predicted with precision, it will be close to ₹12,600/- assuming the volatility stays within the same range till expiration. The contract can expire at the short strike price of ₹1,040 to receive the highest profit. One crucial thing to keep in mind about the modified strategy is that, despite being a net debit strategy, the maximum risk has also increased on the downside. This is because, as you are aware, writing options entails an unknown risk potential and the short strike is above the long strike. Also, the risk of the maximum upside has significantly decreased. A put calendar spread can also be adjusted if it approaches the lower breakeven point.

### *Adjustment 2*

Greek delta values were almost 0.40 in the initial plan, and if any of the values rise near 0.70, it's appropriate to alter the strategy. Assume that the market begins to decline and that one of the delta values is 0.68. You must manage the approach such that the downside risk is limited if you believe the stock price will continue to fall. You can achieve this by changing the strategy into a bear put spread, which implies closing the short position in the near term and opening a short position with a put option in the March expiry. Hence, cut off trade 1000PE (Feb. series) by taking a loss and opening a new short position at a strike price close to the stock price. Choose a strike so that the modified strategy's MTM is as near to zero as possible. Assume that the premium for 980PE (March series) is ₹65.00, that of 1000PE (March series) is ₹70.00, and that of 1000PE (Feb. series) is ₹50/-.

Premium of **1000PE**: **₹50/-** (closed position)

Premium of **980PE** (Mar. series): **₹65/-**

Premium of **1000PE** (long position): **₹70/-**

Therefore,

**Loss booked** = 36 – 50 = – **₹14/-** per share

**Unrealised profit** = 70 – 55 = **₹15/-** per share

**MTM of the strategy** = 15 – 14 = **₹1/-** per share

**The new strategy**

Sell **960PE**; Premium: **₹65/-**

Buy **1000PE; ₹70/-** Premium: **₹70/-** (existing position)

**Total debit** = Long premium + Loss booked – Short premium – MTM profit = 55 + 14 – 65 – 1 = **₹3/-**

**Maximum profit** = (Width of spread – Net debit) times the lot size = (20 – 3) × 900 = **₹15,300/-**

**Maximum loss** = Net debit times lot size = 3 × 900 = **₹2,700/-**

**Breakeven point** = Long call strike – Net debit = 1000 – 3 = **₹997**

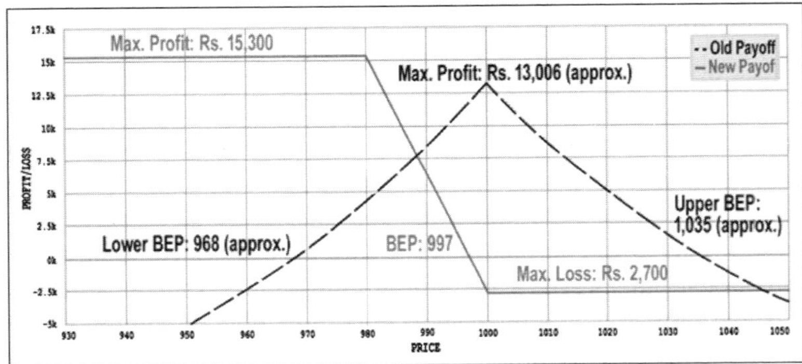


What makes changing calendar spread through debit spread so attractive is the downside breakeven, which was previously capped at ₹968. Now, there is no breakeven on the downside. But, as expected, the upside breakeven point has decreased to ₹997 which was earlier at ₹1,035. The maximum risk is now only ₹2,700 as opposed to ₹17,100 previously. The current maximum profit potential is a fixed sum of ₹15,300. Before, the highest profit was around ₹13,006 due to the long option contract premium's dependence on it. In this way, by following a few easy procedures, you can turn a losing trade into a gainful one.

❑

# Option Strategy for Sideways Market

A 'range-bound' or 'flat' market, often referred to as a sideways market, is one in which the price of a specific asset, such as a stock or index, stays within a very small range over time. With no discernible upward or downward movement, the price may swing back and forth between specific levels in a sideways market.

Investors' uncertainty regarding the price direction of the asset is a common feature of the market sentiment in a sideways market, which lacks direction or trend. Due to the lack of clarity regarding the market's direction, investors may be reluctant to purchase or sell, which can lead to low trading volumes and little price change.

When there is no significant news to move the market, it frequently trades in a range or a sideways fashion. Sometimes, following a sudden uptick or downtick, the market trades in a small area. It is merely a little pause for the market. You may refer to it as the period of breathing, and then the tendency might continue or perhaps change. This phase can, however, occasionally become very prolonged.

Traders can utilise a variety of methodologies, such as range trading or mean reversion, to benefit from a sideways market environment. Range trading is the practice of purchasing an item at the lower end of its trading range and selling it at the upper end to profit from price fluctuations within the range. Taking bets against the present price trend in the hope that the price would eventually return to its average value is known as mean reversion. Several option techniques may be used in this market situation. We will discuss a couple of them that are straightforward and simple to implement but quite powerful. Here are just a few of them:

1. Short strangle
2. Short straddle
3. Iron condor
4. Iron butterfly
5. Double calendar spread, etc.

Now, let's take a look at each of the techniques with adjustments individually.

## SHORT STRANGLE

Selling call and put options with the same expiration date but different strike prices is known as the 'short strangle' options trading strategy. The strike price of the put option is below the current value of the underlying asset, whereas the strike price of the call option is above the current value of the underlying asset.

The purpose of the short strangle strategy is to profit by accumulating the premiums from the selling of the call and put options while also benefitting from a sideways market sentiment, where the price of the underlying asset is anticipated to remain reasonably stable within a given range.

The price of the underlying asset must stay within the range specified by the call and put options' strike prices until the options' expiration date in order for a short strangle to maximise profit. In this case, the trader keeps the premiums received from the sale of the call and put options when both of them expire worthless.

However, there are pitfalls attached to this approach. The trader might have to sell the underlying asset at a loss if the price of the underlying asset increases noticeably over the call option's strike price. The trader may also be compelled to purchase the underlying asset at a price that is higher than the market price if the price of the underlying asset falls sharply below the strike price of the put option.

As the price of the underlying asset can move as high or as low as it wants, the potential loss of a short strangle is virtually limitless. The use of adjusting procedures is therefore necessary. The potential loss can be reduced by using stop-loss orders. However, if the stop-loss is activated, you lose the amount, but if the strategy is adjusted properly, the loss can be significantly decreased.

Let's use a real-world scenario to illustrate the method. The option chain below shows that the NIFTY index will move in a range. The option chain screenshot was taken on 3 April for an expiration date of 6 April 2023.

Option Chain (Equity Derivatives)

Futures contracts

View Options Contracts for: NIFTY OR Select Symbol: Select | Expiry Date: 06-Apr-2023 OR Strike Price: Select

Underlying Index: **NIFTY 17,348.05** As on 03-Apr-2023 13:11:52 IST

Terms of Use | Best View | Download (.csv)

| CALLS | | | | | | | | | | | PUTS | | | | | | | | | | |
|---|---|---|---|---|---|---|---|---|---|---|---|---|---|---|---|---|---|---|---|---|---|
| OI | CHNG IN OI | VOLUME | IV | LTP | CHNG | BID QTY | BID | ASK | ASK QTY | STRIKE | BID QTY | BID | ASK | ASK QTY | CHNG | LTP | IV | VOLUME | CHNG IN OI | OI |
| 11,392 | -1,060 | 2,590 | - | 860.30 | -1.25 | 500 | 851.65 | 853.15 | 400 | 16,500.00 | 39,450 | 1.30 | 1.35 | 1,39,600 | -2.90 | 1.35 | 24.60 | 2,57,364 | -9,637 | 1,00,563 |
| 186 | - | 2 | - | 790.20 | -55.30 | 200 | 798.55 | 804.60 | 200 | 16,550.00 | 18,150 | 1.25 | 1.30 | 15,900 | -3.25 | 1.30 | 23.21 | 69,636 | -3,289 | 10,324 |
| 486 | -66 | 140 | - | 770.05 | 10.10 | 500 | 751.95 | 753.30 | 100 | 16,600.00 | 23,000 | 1.40 | 1.45 | 46,050 | -3.65 | 1.40 | 22.16 | 1,99,908 | -5,381 | 47,691 |
| 181 | -25 | 187 | - | 714.65 | 7.90 | 500 | 701.65 | 703.00 | 100 | 16,650.00 | 8,000 | 1.55 | 1.60 | 20,800 | -4.20 | 1.55 | 21.08 | 1,15,695 | -10,311 | 16,461 |
| 2,577 | 22 | 307 | - | 662.05 | 1.10 | 500 | 651.95 | 653.15 | 500 | 16,700.00 | 49,500 | 1.80 | 1.85 | 7,650 | -4.60 | 1.85 | 20.29 | 2,46,022 | 21,125 | 63,257 |
| 162 | -3 | 19 | - | 605.80 | -10.40 | 50 | 601.45 | 605.00 | 150 | 16,750.00 | 8,250 | 2.20 | 2.25 | 23,900 | -5.25 | 2.25 | 19.47 | 2,12,774 | 8,557 | 35,619 |
| 1,335 | -327 | 1,513 | - | 558.00 | -5.40 | 100 | 553.05 | 554.95 | 100 | 16,800.00 | 19,900 | 2.65 | 2.70 | 25,350 | -5.85 | 2.70 | 18.54 | 4,48,677 | 7,709 | 82,088 |
| 356 | -44 | 423 | - | 506.65 | -11.75 | 500 | 504.20 | 505.25 | 500 | 16,850.00 | 17,650 | 3.35 | 3.40 | 8,800 | -6.70 | 3.40 | 17.85 | 2,63,088 | -221 | 33,898 |
| 4,210 | -266 | 2,621 | - | 457.80 | -13.15 | 50 | 454.15 | 455.70 | 550 | 16,900.00 | 4,600 | 4.10 | 4.15 | 13,500 | -8.05 | 4.15 | 16.91 | 6,18,638 | 20,666 | 79,696 |
| 1,418 | -198 | 908 | - | 413.15 | -15.75 | 500 | 406.45 | 407.55 | 500 | 16,950.00 | 11,950 | 5.50 | 5.55 | 6,200 | -9.60 | 5.55 | 16.28 | 4,25,834 | 16,822 | 48,009 |
| 52,480 | -3,370 | 41,485 | - | 359.30 | -15.90 | 400 | 358.30 | 359.35 | 200 | 17,000.00 | 1,000 | 7.75 | 7.80 | 13,650 | -11.20 | 7.75 | 15.77 | 10,05,730 | 20,315 | 1,82,581 |
| 6,485 | -1,029 | 6,931 | 11.52 | 315.75 | -11.80 | 250 | 311.70 | 312.70 | 200 | 17,050.00 | 4,750 | 10.70 | 10.75 | 550 | -12.85 | 10.75 | 15.17 | 4,30,424 | 5,834 | 40,835 |
| 24,902 | -2,240 | 83,518 | 12.34 | 269.55 | -20.10 | 400 | 266.70 | 267.40 | 250 | 17,100.00 | 50 | 15.30 | 15.35 | 4,700 | -14.60 | 15.30 | 14.77 | 8,89,600 | 26,194 | 1,18,523 |
| 8,293 | -794 | 45,472 | 12.52 | 224.00 | -21.95 | 300 | 223.05 | 223.50 | 50 | 17,150.00 | 6,900 | 21.70 | 21.80 | 4,650 | -15.65 | 21.75 | 14.39 | 6,31,776 | 8,186 | 41,763 |
| 50,270 | 4,900 | 3,23,560 | 12.39 | 182.50 | -25.56 | 200 | 182.05 | 182.35 | 100 | 17,200.00 | 100 | 30.80 | 30.85 | 1,950 | -16.75 | 30.80 | 14.09 | 12,36,386 | 15,969 | 1,40,745 |
| 21,866 | 4,245 | 2,52,666 | 12.32 | 143.85 | -26.80 | 550 | 143.95 | 144.20 | 100 | 17,250.00 | 300 | 42.75 | 42.80 | 1,750 | -17.55 | 42.80 | 13.71 | 8,73,244 | -2,149 | 77,171 |
| 1,04,903 | 35,823 | 13,55,911 | 12.24 | 110.25 | -25.75 | 100 | 110.10 | 110.30 | 400 | 17,300.00 | 500 | 58.85 | 58.90 | 850 | -16.65 | 58.85 | 13.44 | 20,94,706 | 17,104 | 1,47,274 |
| 1,14,704 | 63,208 | 15,00,144 | 12.04 | 80.75 | -24.35 | 550 | 80.65 | 80.75 | 1,150 | 17,350.00 | 1,550 | 79.45 | 79.60 | 500 | -15.75 | 79.55 | 13.19 | 15,35,637 | 41,312 | 77,949 |
| 2,12,201 | 1,18,062 | 24,09,345 | 11.89 | 56.55 | -22.20 | 900 | 56.45 | 56.60 | 3,250 | 17,400.00 | 600 | 105.05 | 105.25 | 150 | -13.60 | 105.20 | 13.04 | 18,56,951 | 58,473 | 89,974 |
| 1,03,078 | 60,714 | 10,83,440 | 11.72 | 37.70 | -19.15 | 2,400 | 37.60 | 37.70 | 1,950 | 17,450.00 | 200 | 136.55 | 136.90 | 200 | -11.05 | 136.40 | 12.97 | 3,58,273 | 10,247 | 25,447 |
| 1,94,418 | 81,417 | 17,79,862 | 11.63 | 24.00 | -14.00 | 200 | 24.00 | 24.05 | 400 | 17,500.00 | 150 | 172.90 | 173.00 | 250 | -6.75 | 172.50 | 13.09 | 4,87,242 | 5,621 | 42,068 |
| 80,686 | 18,094 | 8,73,094 | 11.46 | 14.30 | -11.35 | 1,750 | 14.30 | 14.35 | 5,150 | 17,550.00 | 50 | 213.00 | 219.55 | 100 | -3.46 | 212.00 | 13.16 | 74,551 | 217 | 4,109 |
| 1,22,059 | 18,496 | 11,63,475 | 11.51 | 8.40 | -7.80 | 4,700 | 8.40 | 8.45 | 5,450 | 17,600.00 | 500 | 257.05 | 257.65 | 100 | 0.40 | 257.00 | 13.80 | 73,978 | 1,328 | 5,934 |
| 1,13,353 | 46,629 | 6,47,027 | 11.63 | 4.95 | -4.65 | 13,150 | 4.90 | 4.95 | 7,500 | 17,650.00 | 150 | 303.50 | 304.15 | 100 | -9.60 | 295.95 | 14.29 | 9,021 | 53 | 32,731 |
| 1,88,750 | 60,187 | 8,34,032 | 12.17 | 3.45 | -3.00 | 9,450 | 3.40 | 3.45 | 12,900 | 17,700.00 | 250 | 351.90 | 352.90 | 50 | 5.55 | 352.00 | 15.35 | 10,484 | -50 | 35,416 |
| 45,126 | 14,173 | 3,95,145 | 12.70 | 2.40 | -1.30 | 49,750 | 2.35 | 2.40 | 33,800 | 17,750.00 | 50 | 400.25 | 401.35 | 50 | 2.70 | 396.55 | 18.88 | 1,387 | -3 | 6,052 |
| 1,31,904 | 48,124 | 6,63,465 | 13.36 | 1.80 | -0.95 | 1,21,050 | 1.75 | 1.80 | 76,000 | 17,800.00 | 500 | 449.50 | 450.55 | 100 | -5.80 | 444.35 | 18.56 | 3,510 | 140 | 16,624 |
| 55,601 | 13,241 | 2,06,070 | 14.10 | 1.40 | -0.65 | 48,450 | 1.40 | 1.45 | 16,300 | 17,850.00 | 100 | 499.25 | 501.25 | 100 | -1.70 | 496.05 | 16.39 | 2,658 | 143 | 20,287 |
| 66,916 | 9,897 | 2,45,746 | 14.99 | 1.15 | -0.45 | 71,250 | 1.15 | 1.20 | 63,200 | 17,900.00 | 550 | 548.70 | 549.80 | 500 | 3.85 | 536.60 | 15.09 | 2,454 | 56 | 21,637 |
| 13,300 | -3,585 | 1,13,096 | 15.88 | 1.00 | -0.40 | 41,450 | 1.00 | 1.05 | 31,950 | 17,950.00 | 300 | 596.80 | 600.65 | 300 | -2.05 | 593.00 | 25.69 | 22 | -6 | 125 |
| 95,587 | 11,419 | 2,83,830 | 16.94 | 0.95 | -0.40 | 1,26,900 | 0.95 | 1.00 | 1,08,200 | 18,000.00 | 50 | 648.10 | 650.40 | 100 | 5.70 | 643.00 | 25.01 | 4,519 | -1,576 | 6,048 |
| 10,106 | -934 | 52,566 | 17.70 | 0.80 | -0.40 | 28,450 | 0.80 | 0.85 | 21,850 | 18,050.00 | 100 | 696.65 | 701.50 | 250 | -62.50 | 718.85 | 37.99 | 16 | 9 | 9 |
| 25,074 | 2,201 | 1,14,873 | 18.67 | 0.80 | -0.30 | 1,20,150 | 0.75 | 0.80 | 45,100 | 18,100.00 | 300 | 745.80 | 751.55 | 100 | -1.30 | 745.65 | 31.76 | 91 | - | 151 |
| 4,159 | -1,930 | 36,384 | 19.92 | 0.85 | -0.25 | 19,990 | 0.80 | 0.85 | 12,900 | 18,150.00 | 100 | 788.75 | 807.75 | 4,300 | - | - | - | - | - | 48 |

The market price of Nifty is currently 17,348 and there is a large amount of open interest on both call and put options. Also, the option chain's ITM and OTM options have seen a significant amount of call writing. Significant put writing has occurred on the strikes 17000, 17100, 17200, and 17300 on the put side. Call option sellers will prevent the market from rising, while put option sellers will prevent the index from falling. As a result, the market is intended to trade in a specific area. You can concurrently sell 17500CE and 17200PE to create a short strangle strategy in this scenario. Although the 17400 strike has the largest call open interest, it is advised against selling such a close strike because it might be tested at any time.

## The strategy

Sell **17500CE**; Premium: **₹24/-** and

Sell **17200PE**; Premium: **₹31/-** (rounded off)

**Total premium received** = 24 + 31 = **₹55/-**

**Maximum profit** = Total credit times the lot size = 55 × 50 = **₹2,750/-**

**Maximum loss** = Undefined

**Lower breakeven point** = Lower strike – Total credit = 17,200 – 55 = **17,145**

**Upper breakeven point** = Upper strike + Total credit = 17,500 + 55 = **17,555**

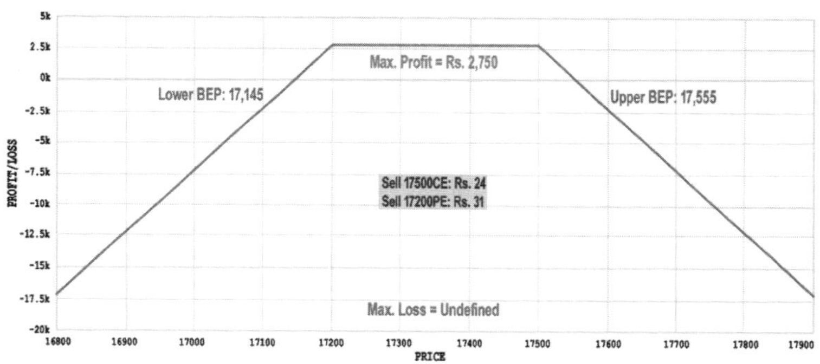


The preceding payoff graph makes it evident that even if the Nifty moves in the range of 17,145 to 17,555 before the expiration, you won't lose money using this approach. In fact, if the index expires inside the range of the strike prices you sold, the method will generate a maximum profit of ₹2,750/-. Beyond that, your profit will start to decline until it reaches breakeven, and if the price fluctuates further, you could lose money. Even though this technique has a modest maximum profit potential, the likelihood of achieving this profit is relatively high. Because of this, the strategy is one of the most often used within the community of option traders. It is important to note that if the index moves erratically outside of the range, there is an unlimited risk of loss. The adjustment strategy will be used in this situation. We will now study how to alter this technique if the market moves unpredictably outside the breakeven zone.

## Adjustment

In a short strangle, you must sell out-of-the-money options with a delta value that typically falls between 0.20 and 0.30. Since the overall value of the delta is near zero, it is a delta neutral strategy. The majority of tactics used in range-bound scenarios are delta neutral. As a result, you must adjust your strategy whenever the delta of any one of the strikes doubles. Also, if you are a conservative trader, you can change your strategy if one of the breakeven points is breached. Let's assume that when the method was developed, the delta of the two strikes was roughly 0.20 for each. When the delta of either 17200PE or 17500CE becomes 0.40, you must then make the necessary adjustments.

As you are aware, if the market rises, the delta of a call option will rise, and when the market falls, the value of a put option will rise. Consider a bullis3h market where the value of the delta for the 17500CE ticker is 0.40 in a short period of time. In that situation, you can take a small profit on the put option that you sold and start a new short position with a put option with a higher strike. You must choose a strike so that the total delta of the approach approaches zero. If all else fails, you can sell a put option that will pay you a premium equal to that of the call option.

Say, when Nifty price climbs up –

Premium of **17500CE** is **₹50/-**

Premium of **17200PE** is **₹10/-** and

Premium of **17400PE** is **₹48/-** (new option to be sold)

**Booked profit** = 31 – 10 = **₹21/-**

**MTM loss** = 50 – 24 = **₹26/-**

**New strategy**

Sell **17400PE**; Premium: **₹48/-**

Sell **17500CE**; Premium: **₹33/-** (existing position)

**Total premium received:** New short premium + Profit booked + Existing short premium – MTM loss = 48 + 21 + 24 – 26 = **₹67/-**

**Maximum profit** = Total credit times the lot size = 67 × 50 = **₹3,350/-**

**Maximum loss** = Undefined

**Lower breakeven point** = Lower strike – Total credit = 17,400 – 67 = **17,333**

**Upper breakeven point** = Upper strike + Total credit = 17,500 + 67 = **17,567**

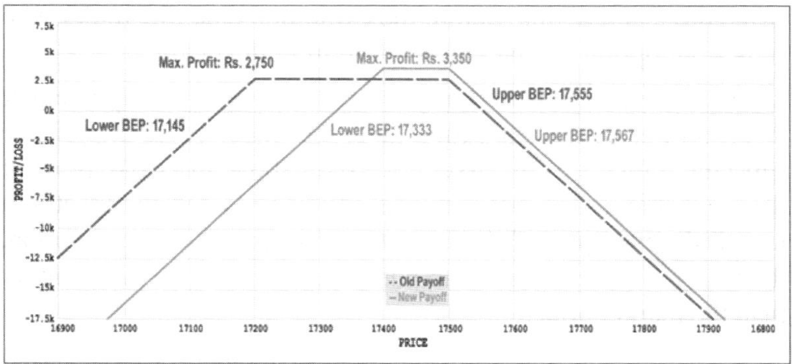


Looking at the payoff chart after modification, the top breakeven point has changed from 17,555 to 17,567. Due to maintaining the same open call option position, you would believe that the breakeven point hasn't changed significantly. Nonetheless, the maximum profit potential has expanded from ₹2,750/- to ₹3,350/-. Lower breakeven has moved from meaningfully 17,145 to 17,333 at the same time.

Your thoughts may have wandered to the following notion: what should you do if the price of the Nifty continues to rise? Simply move the put option higher in that event, and you can keep doing so until the short call strike. Thus, a short straddle will be the outcome of the strategy. Follow the short straddle modification stages, which will be covered in the book's later part, if the approach still requires adjustments.

# SHORT STRADDLE

A short straddle is an options trading strategy that involves simultaneously selling a call option and a put option at the same strike price, with the same expiration date, and on the same underlying asset. Because the trader is selling the options rather than buying them, the technique is known as a 'short'.

When a trader sells a call option, they receive a premium from the buyer of the option in exchange for the right to purchase the underlying asset at the strike price at any time before the expiration date. In exchange for the right to sell the underlying asset at the strike price at any time before the expiration date, the trader who sells a put option receives a premium from the buyer.

However, if the underlying asset moves significantly in either direction before the expiration date, the trader could experience substantial losses. If the asset price rises above the strike price of the call option, the trader may be obligated to sell the asset at a loss. If the asset price falls below the strike price of the put option, the trader may be obligated to purchase the asset at a price higher than the market price.

Generally, the short straddle strategy includes a large risk if the asset price fluctuates significantly in either direction but can be beneficial if the underlying asset is relatively steady. When using a short straddle, as with any trading technique, it's crucial to carefully weigh the risks and potential profits.

In contrast to short strangle, where options could be sold on two separate strikes, short straddle requires that all options be sold at the same strike price. The other terms, which include the same underlying and expiration dates, will not change. When the market appears to trade in a constrained area, this practice is used. The amount of credit obtained determines the highest profit potential and the possible loss is limitless because writing options carry unlimited risk.

To determine the short straddle approach, let's use the same option chain as before. The current price of the Nifty is 17,348.

This is quite close to the 17350-strike price and carries nearly the same premium. Hence, to create a short straddle, we can simultaneously sell 17350 call and put options, which is also an ATM strike.

## The strategy

Sell **17350CE**; Premium: **₹81/-** (rounded off)

Sell **17350PE**; Premium: **₹80/-** (rounded off)

**Total premium received:** 81 + 80 = **₹161/-**

**Maximum profit** = Total credit times the lot size = 161 × 50 = **₹8,050/-**

**Maximum loss** = Undefined

**Lower breakeven point** = Sold strike – Total credit = 17,350 – 161 = **17,189**

**Upper breakeven point** = Sold strike + Total credit = 17,350 + 161 = **17,511**

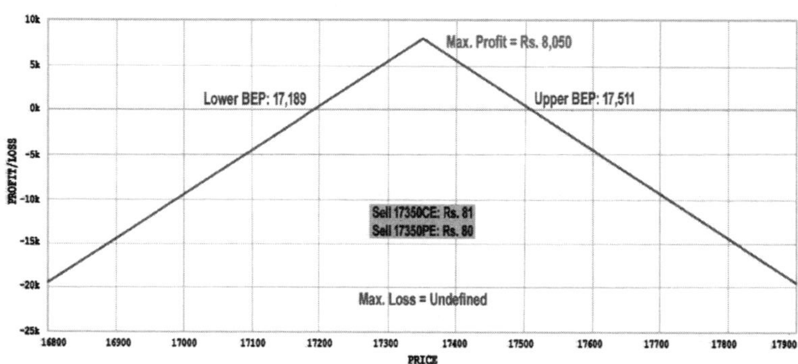


According to the graph above, if the index matures at 17,350, the price at which the options were sold, a maximum profit of ₹8,050/- can be made. As the price moves further from the sold strike price, the turnover gradually falls. On the downside, the approach begins to lose money around 17,189, while on the upside, it is 17,511. You will earn if Nifty expires anywhere between these two breakeven areas. Beyond these two stages, the technique is exposed to unrestricted risk. It is evident from this payoff chart that the approach only produces a profit when the market moves within the range. What happens if the index crosses one of the breakeven points and makes a significant move? In this situation, you must make certain changes to the plan in order to justify your defeat. The adjustment approach listed below can help you safeguard your capital in such a bad situation.

## Adjustment

Typically, options bearing a delta value in the range of 0.50 were sold at-the-money when using the short straddle method. So, you only need to keep the strategy in place when the delta of any one of the options dramatically increases. As a general rule, the adjustment procedure begins when the value of delta for any one of the strikes rises from 0.75 to 0.80. If not, the trader can wait until one of the breakeven is contested. The delta value for 17350PE will rise if the Nifty price declines since the strike becomes an in-the-money option at this point. Let's assume that the value of the 17350PE's delta when the index declines is 0.75. This is the time you should step into the strategy for alteration. In this scenario, the short put option will result in some losses while the short call option will provide some profits. So, you have to book some profit off the table and sell one call option with the value of delta almost equal to 0.75.

Now imagine that the Nifty has fallen to 17,200 levels; at that point, the premium for 17350PE becomes ₹180/- and the premium for 17350CE is ₹20/-, while the premium and delta for 17100CE are ₹260/- and 0.75 respectively. Then, in order to earn more premium, book a profit on the 17350CE option and establish an additional short position on 17100CE.

Now,

Premium of **17350CE** is **₹20/-**

Premium of **17350PE** is **₹180/-** and

Premium of **17100CE** is **₹260/-** (new option to be sold)

**Booked profit** = 81 – 20 = **₹61/-**

**MTM loss** = 80 – 180 = **– ₹100/-**

**New strategy**

Sell **17100CE**; Premium: **₹260/-**

Sell **17350PE**; Premium: **₹80/-** (existing position)

The adjusted strategy has now become an inverted strangle, meaning both options are now in-the-money options. This is a crucial thing to note. As a result, even if you obtained a credit for ₹340/(260 + 80), the amount of intrinsic values must be subtracted from the real credit.

Therefore,

**Net credit** = Credit received – Width of the spread = 340 – 250 = **₹90/-**

**Maximum profit** = Net credit times the lot size = 90 × 50 = **₹4,500/-**

**Maximum loss** = Undefined

**Lower breakeven point** = Put strike – Net credit = 17,100 – 90 = **17,010**

**Upper breakeven point** = Call strike + Net credit = 17,350 + 90 = **17,440**

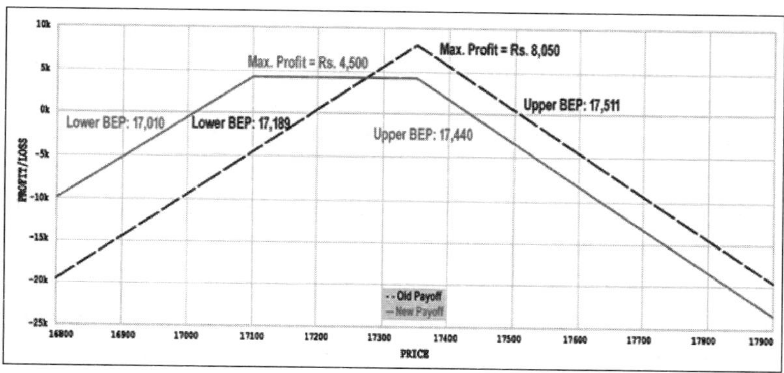

The lower breakeven, which was earlier at 17,189, has been drastically reduced to 17,010 with the aid of this adjustment process. At the same time, the upper breakeven also dropped down by 71 points. Previously, the maximum profit possibility was ₹8,050/-; however, the likely amount is ₹4,500/- only. Also, over a 250-point range, the likelihood of receiving the maximum profit has increased. You will be able to harvest the most if the index expires at any point between 17,100 and 17,350 levels. Likewise, if the short straddle approach fails, you can change to the lower breakeven level. You can close the short call trade and start a new short at a lower level if the Nifty plunges even further. But keep in mind to consider the delta value of the other option (*i.e.,* put option in this case). You must abandon the technique whenever the value reaches a level close to 1, at which point the option will function as a futures contract.

So, here's a thought that might cross your mind: how can the straddle be adjusted if it tests the upper breakeven? The solution is straightforward: try modifying your put option strategy by taking the same actions. Close the short put option that is making you some money and start a new short position but with a higher strike, like we just did.

## SHORT IRON CONDOR STRATEGY

The short iron condor is a popular options trading strategy used by traders who expect the price of an underlying asset to remain stable within a certain range. It combines the short call spread with the short put spread, two vertical spreads. It is a four-legged strategy consisting of a bull put spread and a bear call spread. With this approach, all options should have the same expiration date and the short put's strike price should be lower than the short call's strike price. A hedged variation of the short strangle technique is the short iron condor spread.

In order to execute a short iron condor, a trader must simultaneously sell a put option with a strike price lower than the current value of the underlying asset and a call option with a strike price higher than the value of the asset. As a result, a price range is created in which the trader anticipates the underlying item will stay.

A put option with a strike price even lower than the put option sold and a call option with a strike price even higher than the call option sold are likewise purchased by the trader. In the event that the price of the underlying asset swings outside of the expected range, this is done to reduce the greatest loss that the trader could sustain.

This tactic generates a credit as its final outcome, which is equal to the discrepancy between the premiums obtained from selling the call and put options and the premiums paid for the higher and lower strike options.

The trader will maintain the credit earned through the strategy if the price of the underlying asset stays inside the band indicated by the short call and put options. However, if the price of the underlying asset moves beyond the range, the trader could face losses that are limited to the difference between the strike prices of the higher and lower strike options and the net credit received.

Overall, using the short iron condor technique can help traders produce profits in a steady market while reducing their risk of loss. To reduce risks, traders must, however, carefully watch the market and modify their positions as needed.

The four legs of the iron condor approach will be as follows, using the same strangle as in the preceding method:

Sell **17500CE**; Premium: **₹24/-** and

Sell **17200PE**; Premium: **₹31/-** (rounded off)

Buy **17700CE**; Premium: **₹3/-** (rounded off)

Buy **17000PE**; Premium: **₹8/-** (rounded off)

**Net credit** = (24 + 31 – 3 – 8) = **₹44/-**

**Maximum profit** = Total credit times the lot size i.e. 44 × 50 = **₹2,200/-**

**Maximum loss** = Difference between the strike prices of either spread less the premium received at initiation times; the contract size = (200 – 44) × 50 = **₹7,800/-**

**Lower breakeven point** = Sold lower strike – Total credit = 17,200 – 44 = **17,156**

**Upper breakeven point** = Sold upper strike + Total credit = 17,500 + 44 = **17,544**

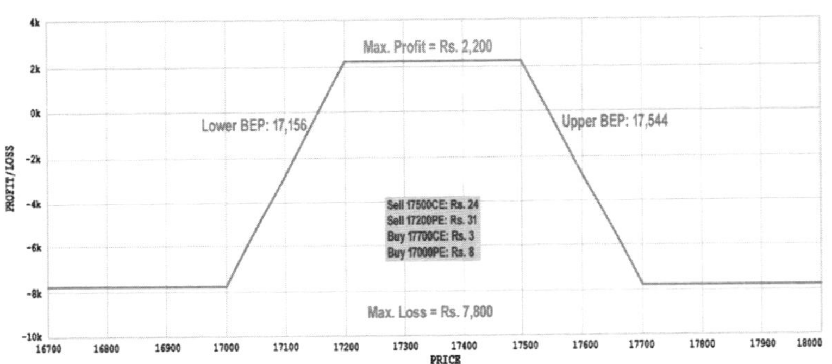


The maximum risk in the short strangle strategy was not specified, but as it is a hedged strategy, the maximum loss is limited to ₹7,800/- only. Both the far out-of-the-money bought call option and the far out-of-the-money put option will hedge against risk on the upside and downside, respectively. Hedging has also resulted in a maximum profit potential that is now only ₹2,200/- as opposed to ₹2,750/- in a pure short strangle. Iron condor, in contrast to short strangle, is used in a range-bound market. But what if the market suddenly begins to move intermittently? The best thing about option trading is that you can adjust any strategies if the market deviates from what you had anticipated. So, you can adjust the iron condor spread in the event of adverse movement to cut your losses or turn it into a profit.

## Adjustment

In contrast to the short strangle, the short iron condor is likewise a delta neutral strategy, which means that its overall delta value is close to zero. When there is a significant imbalance in the value of the strategy's delta, the correction operation is started in the short strangle strategy. When the difference between the delta values of any option combination, such as a bull put spread or a bear call spread, is twice, you must modify an iron condor. Alternatively, you can wait until the market reaches one of the breakeven points and use the identical steps as the short strangle adjustment.

Imagine that you have chosen a weekly option strategy and the Nifty price is falling and the overall delta doubled. Close the pair of call options in that situation as it will generate some profit and create a new bear call spread with lower strikes. Attempt to keep the spread's width constant with the initial approach.

Say, back then

Premium of **17500CE** is **₹6/-**

Premium of **17700CE** is **₹1/-**

Premium of **17200PE** is **₹48/-**

Premium of **17000PE** is **₹18/-** and

Premium of **17250CE** is **₹70/-** (new option to be sold)

Premium of **17450CE** is **₹10/-** (new option to be bought)

**Booked profit** = (24 – 3) – (6 – 1) = **₹16/-**

**MTM loss** = (24 - 3) – (48 – 18) = – **₹9/-**

**New strategy**

Sell **17250CE**; Premium: **₹70/-**

Buy **17450CE;** Premium: **₹10/-**

Sell **17200PE;** Premium: **₹31/-** (existing position)

Buy **17000PE**; Premium: **₹8/-** (existing position)

**Total premium received:** New short premium + Profit booked + Existing short premium – MTM loss = (70 – 10) + 16 + (31 – 8) – 9 = **₹90/-**

**Maximum profit** = Total credit times the lot size = 90 × 50 = **₹4,500/-**

**Maximum loss** = Difference between the strike prices of either spread less the premium received at initiation; times the contract size = (200 – 90) × 50 = **₹5,500/-**

**Lower breakeven point** = Lower sold strike – Total credit = 17,200 – 90 = **17,110**

**Upper breakeven point** = Upper sold strike + Total credit = 17,250 + 90 = **17,340**

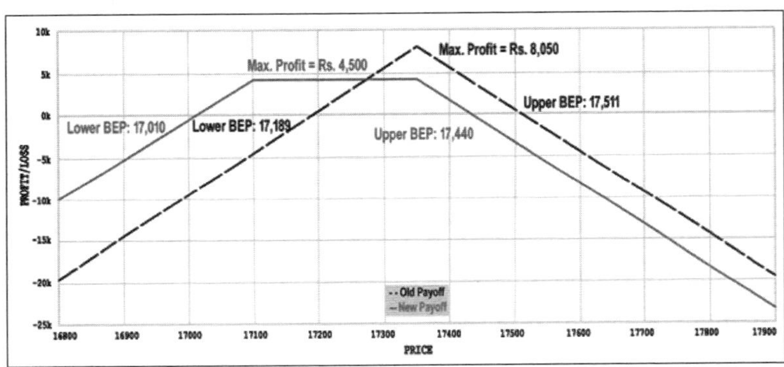


The payoff shows that after adjustment, the highest profit potential has grown by two times. Moreover, the maximum risk has been decreased significantly from ₹7,800/- to ₹5,500/. The upper breakeven is now 17,340 and the lower breakeven has moved to 17,110. At this stage, if the breakeven does not drastically decrease, it appears pointless to change the strategy. Is it not? However, shifting the breakeven is not the only goal of option strategy adjustment; you also need to consider other factors, such as maximum risk and reward. After adjustment, the risk-to-reward ratio in this situation works to your advantage. You will be able to maximise the strategy's benefits if the market bounces in any way and expires in your profitable zone.

## Short iron butterfly strategy

Another option trading method called the short iron butterfly is employed to profit from a range-bound market with little volatility. When traders foresee that the price of the underlying asset will remain largely steady inside a given range, they utilise this technique. The short iron butterfly entails selling two option contracts with identical strike prices and buying two additional option contracts with different strike prices. This method is nothing more than the short straddle technique with hedges.

The short iron butterfly functions as follows:

- ✓ Sell an at-the-money (ATM) call option: This means that the strike price of the call option should be equal to the current market price of the underlying asset.
- ✓ Sell an at-the-money (ATM) put option: This means that the strike price of the put option should be equal to the current market price of the underlying asset.
- ✓ Buy an out-of-the-money (OTM) call option: This means that the strike price of the call option should be higher than the current market price of the underlying asset.
- ✓ Buy an out-of-the-money (OTM) put option: This means that the strike price of the put option should be lower than the current market price of the underlying asset.

All four option contracts should have the same expiration date.

A profit zone is formed around the two sold strike prices using the short iron butterfly strategy. When the underlying asset's strike price coincides with the sold options' expiration price, the maximum profit is realised. The underlying asset must go above the strike price of the purchased options for the maximum loss to occur at expiration. The strike prices of the sold options plus or minus the premium received are where the breakeven points occur.

In low-volatility markets, the short iron butterfly strategy is a low-risk, low-reward trading method. The trading expenses for this technique can be substantial because it calls for using four different options contracts. The losses may also be considerable if the underlying asset goes through a significant price change. Consequently, before employing this method, traders should carefully weigh the risks.

To show the iron butterfly spread, we'll once more use the identical short straddle approach that was previously described.

## The strategy

Sell **17350CE**; Premium: **₹81/-** (rounded off)

Sell **17350PE;** Premium: **₹80/-** (rounded off)

Buy **17650CE**; Premium: **₹5/-** (rounded off)

Buy **17050PE**; Premium: **₹11/-** (rounded off)

**Net credit** = 81 + 80 – 5 – 11 = **₹145/-**

Hence,

**Maximum profit** = Total credit times the lot size = 145 × 50 = **₹7,250/-**

**Maximum loss** = Difference between the lowest and middle strike prices less the net credit received at initiation; times the contract size = (300 – 145) × 50 = **₹7,750/-**

**Lower breakeven** = Centre strike – Total credit = 17,350 – 145 = **17,205**

**Upper breakeven** = Centre strike + Total credit = 17350 + 145 = **17,495**

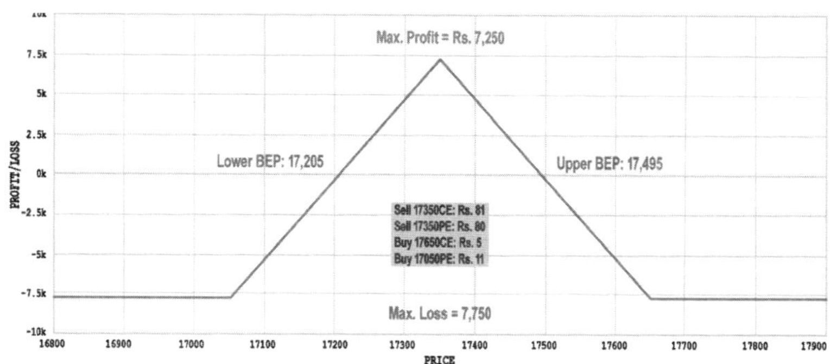


The payoff chart makes it evident that if the option expires at the short strike price of 17,350, the highest profit might be ₹7,250/-. If the price of the Nifty goes away from the centre strike, the profit potential gradually decreases. When the price of the index crosses 17,495 on the upside and 17,205 on the downside, the strategy begins to produce negative returns. Only when it expires above the call long strike or below the put long strike is the maximum risk constrained to ₹7,750/-. This is one of the most straightforward option strategies for range-bound markets. The biggest difficulties arise whenever the underlying exhibits a strong movement in any direction. In this case, the trader might manage the approach to cut the loss as much as possible. To learn the adjusting methods to use when the Nifty experiences a sudden movement, keep reading.

## Adjustment

Since the short iron butterfly is also a delta neutral approach, you can make modifications as soon as the delta's value starts to deviate. Some traders will think about making adjustments if the call or put spread's value doubles. To be honest, though, there isn't any set amount of time for an exact adjustment. Many people wait until one of the breakeven points has been violated in order to keep things simple. Nevertheless, let's learn the method.

The short iron butterfly strategy's adjustment resembles a straightforward short straddle in many ways. The only distinction is that you must combine either the put option pair or the call option pair. Consider a scenario in which the index turns bullish and attempts to test the upper breakeven mark. When you build a bull put spread at a point where you can get a net premium equivalent to the bear call spread, you should book profit on the put option pair. This will offer you some profit. Suppose that the call option pair and the 17350PE and 17050PE option pair each have a net credit that is almost identical.

Say,

Premium of **17350CE** is **₹160/-**

Premium of **17650CE** is **₹35/-**

Premium of **17350PE** is **₹36/-**

Premium of **17050PE** is **₹4/-**

And

Premium of **17550PE** is **₹190/-** (new option to be sold)

Premium of **17250PE** is **₹26/-** (new option to be bought)

Now,

**Booked profit** = (80 – 11) – (26 – 4) = **₹47/-**

**MTM loss** = (81 – 5) – (160 – 35) = – **₹49/-**

**New strategy**

Sell **17550PE**; Premium: **₹190/-**

Buy **17250PE**; Premium: **₹26/-**

Sell **17350CE**; Premium: **₹81/-** (existing position)

Buy **17650CE**; Premium: **₹5/-** (existing position)

Both the options are now in-the-money because the strategy has changed to an inverted strangle strategy. Because of this, even though you have a total credit of ₹240/[(190 – 26) + (81 – 5)], the intrinsic values must be subtracted from the actual credit.

Therefore,

**Net credit** = Credit received – Width of the spread = 240 – 200= **₹40/-**

**Maximum profit** = Net credit times the lot size = 40 × 50 = **₹2,000/-**

**Maximum loss** = Difference between the strike prices of either spread less width of the spread, less the premium received at initiation; times the contract size = (300 – 200 – 40) × 50 = **₹3,000/-**

**Lower breakeven point** = Sold call strike – Net credit = 17,350 – 40 = **17,310**

**Upper breakeven point** = Sold put strike + Net credit = 17,550 + 40 = **17,590**

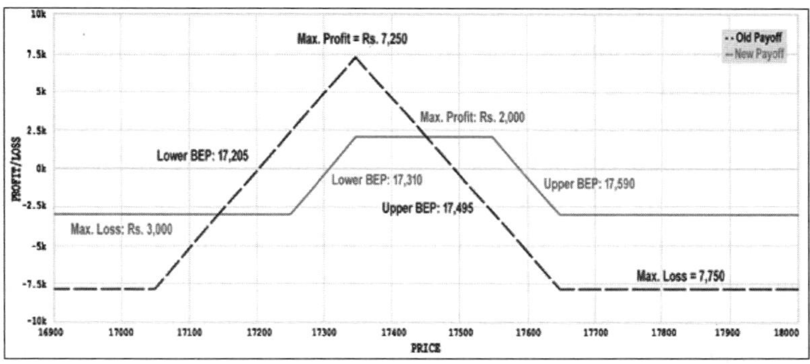


Look at the payoff chart's upper breakeven point first; after modification, it has moved to 17,590 from 17,495. The lower breakeven point has also shifted upward at the same time. You may have observed that the greatest profit potential is now only ₹2,000/- instead of the previous ₹7,250/-. Here, the maximum risk is now just ₹3,000/- instead of ₹7,750/- as it was before the modification. Above all, you have got a wider range of 200 points for the maximum reward. On the other hand, in the past, it was a certain price (*i.e.,* 17,350) that was extremely challenging to really reach. This is one of the biggest benefits that may be attained with a short butterfly adjustment. You can take a chance and alter your strategy one more time if the market keeps rising. Only twice may the short straddle or short iron butterfly be modified. No matter how successful the approach is, it is always advisable to stop using it after two tries because each option will have a delta value that is approximately equivalent to one. Always keep in mind that modifications have a cost, and making extreme adjustments can hurt your trading portfolio.

## Double calendar spread

The double calendar spread is simply an expansion of the calendar spread technique. Combining a long call calendar spread with a long put calendar spread is the approach. Hence, four option legs are traded concurrently in a double calendar spread. The strategy can be described as the deployment of a short strangle strategy in the near-term expiry along with the purchase of a pair of long-term call and put options in order to hedge it. One has the choice to buy the option at the same strike in near-expiry as the option sold at the current expiry. But, buying and selling at the same strike is not at all essential. You have the opportunity to purchase a near-expiry option bearing the same premium as a sold current option.

The goal of this strategy is to take advantage of time decay and benefit from the difference between the premiums received from the sale of the near-term options and the premiums paid for the longer-term options. The largest profit is only permissible to be the difference between the two calendar spreads less the net debit used to open the position. If the underlying asset price is at or close to the strike price at the time the near-term options expire, the maximum loss is confined to the net debit used to open the position. The breakeven point is the strike price of the near-term options plus the net debit paid for the position.

When the market appears to be in a calm situation but the volatility is anticipated to rise soon, a long double calendar spread is used. This approach works well when the market appears to trade in a range yet has excessive volatility. It is not advisable to establish a strategy when there might be a contraction in volatility. Let's know the strategy better with an example.

**Option Chain (Equity Derivatives)**

Futures contracts

View Options Contracts for: NIFTY OR Select Symbol: Select | Expiry Date: 06-Apr-2023 OR Strike Price: Select

Underlying Index: **NIFTY 17,348.05** As on 03-Apr-2023 13:11:52 IST

Terms of Use | Best View | Download (.csv)

| CALLS | | | | | | | | | | | PUTS | | | | | | | | | |
|---|---|---|---|---|---|---|---|---|---|---|---|---|---|---|---|---|---|---|---|---|
| OI | CHNG IN OI | VOLUME | IV | LTP | CHNG | BID QTY | BID | ASK | ASK QTY | STRIKE | BID QTY | BID | ASK | ASK QTY | CHNG | LTP | IV | VOLUME | CHNG IN OI | OI |
| 11,392 | -1,060 | 2,590 | - | 860.30 | -1.25 | 500 | 851.65 | 853.15 | 400 | 16,500.00 | 39,450 | 1.30 | 1.35 | 1,39,600 | -2.90 | 1.35 | 24.60 | 2,57,364 | -9,637 | 1,00,563 |
| 186 | - | 2 | - | 790.20 | -55.30 | 200 | 798.55 | 804.60 | 200 | 16,550.00 | 18,150 | 1.25 | 1.30 | 15,900 | -3.25 | 1.30 | 23.21 | 69,636 | -3,289 | 10,324 |
| 486 | -66 | 140 | - | 770.05 | 10.10 | 500 | 751.95 | 753.30 | 100 | 16,600.00 | 23,000 | 1.40 | 1.45 | 46,050 | -3.65 | 1.40 | 22.16 | 1,99,908 | -5,381 | 47,691 |
| 181 | -25 | 187 | - | 714.65 | 7.90 | 500 | 701.65 | 703.00 | 100 | 16,650.00 | 8,000 | 1.55 | 1.60 | 20,800 | -4.20 | 1.55 | 21.08 | 1,15,695 | -10,311 | 15,461 |
| 2,577 | 22 | 307 | - | 662.05 | 1.10 | 500 | 651.95 | 653.15 | 500 | 16,700.00 | 49,500 | 1.80 | 1.85 | 7,650 | -4.60 | 1.85 | 20.29 | 2,46,022 | 21,125 | 63,257 |
| 162 | -3 | 19 | - | 605.80 | -10.40 | 50 | 601.45 | 605.00 | 150 | 16,750.00 | 8,250 | 2.20 | 2.25 | 23,900 | -5.25 | 2.25 | 19.47 | 2,12,774 | 8,557 | 35,619 |
| 1,335 | -327 | 1,513 | - | 558.00 | -5.40 | 100 | 553.05 | 554.95 | 100 | 16,800.00 | 19,900 | 2.65 | 2.70 | 25,350 | -5.85 | 2.70 | 18.54 | 4,48,677 | 7,709 | 82,088 |
| 356 | -44 | 423 | - | 506.65 | -11.75 | 500 | 504.20 | 505.25 | 500 | 16,850.00 | 17,550 | 3.35 | 3.40 | 8,800 | -6.70 | 3.40 | 17.85 | 3,53,088 | -221 | 33,898 |
| 4,210 | -266 | 2,621 | - | 457.80 | -13.15 | 50 | 454.15 | 455.70 | 550 | 16,900.00 | 4,600 | 4.10 | 4.15 | 13,500 | -8.05 | 4.15 | 16.91 | 6,18,638 | 20,666 | 79,696 |
| 1,418 | -198 | 908 | - | 413.15 | -15.75 | 500 | 406.45 | 407.55 | 500 | 16,950.00 | 11,950 | 5.50 | 5.55 | 6,200 | -9.60 | 5.55 | 16.28 | 4,25,834 | 16,822 | 48,009 |
| 52,480 | -3,370 | 41,485 | - | 359.30 | -15.90 | 400 | 358.30 | 359.35 | 200 | 17,000.00 | 1,000 | 7.75 | 7.80 | 13,650 | -11.20 | 7.75 | 15.77 | 10,05,730 | 20,315 | 1,82,581 |
| 6,485 | -1,029 | 6,931 | 11.52 | 315.75 | -11.80 | 250 | 311.70 | 312.70 | 200 | 17,050.00 | 4,750 | 10.70 | 10.75 | 550 | -12.85 | 10.75 | 15.17 | 4,30,424 | 5,834 | 40,835 |
| 24,902 | -2,240 | 83,518 | 12.34 | 269.55 | -20.10 | 400 | 266.70 | 267.40 | 250 | 17,100.00 | 50 | 15.30 | 15.35 | 4,700 | -14.60 | 15.30 | 14.77 | 8,89,600 | 26,194 | 1,18,523 |
| 8,293 | -794 | 45,472 | 12.52 | 224.00 | -21.95 | 300 | 223.05 | 223.50 | 50 | 17,150.00 | 6,900 | 21.70 | 21.80 | 4,650 | -15.65 | 21.75 | 14.39 | 6,31,776 | 8,186 | 41,763 |
| 50,270 | 4,900 | 3,23,550 | 12.39 | 182.50 | -25.55 | 200 | 182.05 | 182.35 | 100 | 17,200.00 | 100 | 30.80 | 30.85 | 1,950 | -16.75 | 30.80 | 14.09 | 12,36,386 | 15,969 | 1,40,745 |
| 21,866 | 4,245 | 2,52,666 | 12.32 | 143.85 | -26.80 | 550 | 143.95 | 144.20 | 100 | 17,250.00 | 300 | 42.75 | 42.80 | 1,750 | -17.55 | 42.80 | 13.71 | 8,73,244 | -2,149 | 77,171 |
| 1,04,903 | 35,823 | 13,55,911 | 12.24 | 110.25 | -25.75 | 100 | 110.10 | 110.30 | 400 | 17,300.00 | 500 | 58.85 | 58.90 | 850 | -16.65 | 58.85 | 13.44 | 20,94,706 | 17,104 | 1,47,274 |
| 1,14,704 | 63,208 | 15,00,144 | 12.04 | 80.75 | -24.35 | 550 | 80.65 | 80.75 | 1,150 | 17,350.00 | 1,550 | 79.45 | 79.60 | 500 | -15.75 | 79.55 | 13.19 | 15,35,637 | 41,312 | 77,949 |
| 2,12,201 | 1,18,062 | 24,09,345 | 11.89 | 56.55 | -22.20 | 900 | 56.45 | 56.60 | 3,250 | 17,400.00 | 600 | 105.05 | 105.25 | 150 | -13.60 | 105.20 | 13.04 | 18,56,951 | 58,473 | 89,974 |
| 1,03,078 | 60,714 | 10,83,440 | 11.72 | 37.70 | -19.15 | 2,400 | 37.60 | 37.70 | 1,950 | 17,450.00 | 200 | 136.55 | 136.90 | 200 | -11.05 | 136.40 | 12.97 | 3,58,273 | 10,247 | 25,447 |
| 1,94,418 | 81,417 | 17,79,862 | 11.63 | 24.00 | -14.80 | 200 | 24.00 | 24.05 | 400 | 17,500.00 | 150 | 172.90 | 173.00 | 250 | -6.75 | 172.50 | 13.09 | 4,87,242 | 5,621 | 42,068 |
| 80,686 | 18,034 | 8,73,034 | 11.46 | 14.30 | -11.35 | 1,750 | 14.30 | 14.35 | 5,150 | 17,550.00 | 50 | 213.00 | 213.55 | 100 | -3.45 | 212.00 | 13.15 | 74,551 | 217 | 4,109 |
| 1,22,059 | 18,496 | 11,53,475 | 11.51 | 8.40 | -7.80 | 4,700 | 8.40 | 8.45 | 5,450 | 17,600.00 | 500 | 257.05 | 257.65 | 100 | 0.40 | 257.00 | 13.80 | 73,978 | 1,328 | 5,934 |
| 1,13,353 | 46,629 | 6,47,027 | 11.63 | 4.95 | -4.65 | 13,150 | 4.90 | 4.95 | 7,500 | 17,650.00 | 150 | 303.50 | 304.15 | 100 | -9.60 | 295.95 | 14.29 | 9,021 | 53 | 32,731 |
| 1,88,750 | 60,187 | 8,34,032 | 12.17 | 3.45 | -3.00 | 9,450 | 3.40 | 3.45 | 12,900 | 17,700.00 | 250 | 351.90 | 352.90 | 50 | 5.55 | 352.00 | 15.35 | 10,484 | -50 | 35,416 |
| 45,126 | 14,173 | 3,95,145 | 12.70 | 2.40 | -1.30 | 49,750 | 2.35 | 2.40 | 33,800 | 17,750.00 | 50 | 400.25 | 401.35 | 50 | 2.70 | 396.55 | 18.88 | 1,387 | -3 | 6,052 |
| 1,31,904 | 48,124 | 6,63,465 | 13.36 | 1.80 | -0.95 | 1,21,050 | 1.75 | 1.80 | 76,000 | 17,800.00 | 500 | 449.50 | 450.55 | 100 | -5.80 | 444.35 | 18.56 | 3,510 | 140 | 16,624 |
| 55,601 | 13,241 | 2,06,070 | 14.10 | 1.40 | -0.65 | 48,450 | 1.40 | 1.45 | 16,300 | 17,850.00 | 100 | 499.25 | 501.25 | 100 | -1.70 | 496.05 | 16.39 | 2,658 | 143 | 20,287 |
| 66,916 | 9,897 | 2,45,746 | 14.99 | 1.15 | -0.45 | 71,250 | 1.15 | 1.20 | 63,200 | 17,900.00 | 550 | 548.70 | 549.80 | 500 | 3.85 | 536.60 | 15.09 | 2,454 | 56 | 21,637 |
| 13,300 | -3,585 | 1,13,096 | 15.88 | 1.00 | -0.40 | 41,450 | 1.00 | 1.05 | 31,950 | 17,950.00 | 300 | 596.80 | 600.65 | 300 | -2.05 | 593.00 | 25.69 | 22 | -6 | 125 |
| 95,587 | 11,419 | 2,83,830 | 16.94 | 0.95 | -0.40 | 1,26,900 | 0.95 | 1.00 | 1,08,200 | 18,000.00 | 50 | 648.10 | 650.40 | 100 | 5.70 | 643.00 | 25.01 | 4,519 | -1,576 | 6,048 |
| 10,106 | -934 | 52,566 | 17.70 | 0.80 | -0.40 | 28,450 | 0.80 | 0.85 | 21,850 | 18,050.00 | 100 | 696.65 | 701.50 | 250 | -62.50 | 718.85 | 37.99 | 16 | 9 | 9 |
| 25,074 | 2,201 | 1,14,873 | 18.67 | 0.80 | -0.30 | 1,20,150 | 0.75 | 0.80 | 45,100 | 18,100.00 | 300 | 745.80 | 751.55 | 100 | -1.30 | 745.65 | 31.76 | 91 | - | 151 |
| 4,159 | -1,930 | 36,384 | 19.92 | 0.85 | -0.25 | 19,950 | 0.80 | 0.85 | 12,900 | 18,150.00 | 100 | 788.75 | 807.75 | 4,300 | - | - | - | - | - | 48 |

The Nifty index's option chain on 3 April 2023, when it was trading at 17,348, is shown in the image above. The option chain illustrates the open interest build-up for 6 April expiry and it indicates that the index may remain sideways till the option expires. Hence, for this expiry, a sideways strategy like a double calendar can be established. Due to the fact that the double calendar is a horizontal spread strategy, you also need to buy options in the long-term expiry. Let's examine the option chain for the upcoming expiration, which is the 13 April expiry (below image). On 3 April 2023, both screenshots of the options were taken simultaneously.

**Option Chain (Equity Derivatives)**

Futures contracts

View Options Contracts for: NIFTY OR Select Symbol: Select | Expiry Date: 13-Apr-2023 OR Strike Price: Select

Underlying Index: **NIFTY 17,348.05** As on 03-Apr-2023 13:11:52 IST

Terms of Use | Best View | Download (.csv)

| CALLS | | | | | | | | | | | PUTS | | | | | | | | | |
|---|---|---|---|---|---|---|---|---|---|---|---|---|---|---|---|---|---|---|---|---|
| OI | CHNG IN OI | VOLUME | IV | LTP | CHNG | BID QTY | BID | ASK | ASK QTY | STRIKE | BID QTY | BID | ASK | ASK QTY | CHNG | LTP | IV | VOLUME | CHNG IN OI | OI |
| 421 | -4 | 21 | - | 895.00 | 7.65 | 500 | 872.85 | 883.75 | 200 | 16,500.00 | 1,050 | 5.60 | 5.65 | 250 | -5.40 | 5.65 | 17.11 | 12,414 | 422 | 5,623 |
| 78 | 4 | 18 | - | 820.00 | -6.10 | 600 | 811.10 | 848.75 | 50 | 16,550.00 | 4,550 | 6.30 | 6.40 | 250 | -6.00 | 6.35 | 16.71 | 2,632 | 454 | 946 |
| 216 | -2 | 7 | - | 752.15 | -39.25 | 4,050 | 765.40 | 800.80 | 250 | 16,600.00 | 5,150 | 7.35 | 7.45 | 150 | -6.60 | 7.45 | 16.27 | 9,016 | 359 | 3,959 |
| 37 | - | - | - | - | - | 150 | 716.00 | 766.85 | 6,250 | 16,650.00 | 4,050 | 8.35 | 8.45 | 50 | -7.10 | 8.40 | 15.74 | 4,728 | -197 | 3,756 |
| 235 | 5 | 19 | - | 685.00 | -1.85 | 150 | 673.55 | 683.55 | 150 | 16,700.00 | 4,900 | 10.15 | 10.25 | 200 | -8.05 | 10.20 | 15.46 | 10,643 | 1,612 | 5,091 |
| 113 | - | 4 | - | 643.90 | 4.30 | 300 | 628.80 | 635.70 | 150 | 16,750.00 | 3,050 | 12.15 | 12.30 | 5,500 | -9.20 | 12.00 | 15.15 | 4,428 | 656 | 1,812 |
| 330 | 3 | 83 | - | 600.00 | 3.00 | 200 | 581.80 | 583.60 | 200 | 16,800.00 | 5,150 | 14.55 | 14.70 | 6,750 | -9.95 | 14.45 | 14.80 | 24,914 | 2,680 | 8,862 |
| 85 | 3 | 8 | - | 534.85 | -68.55 | 450 | 530.90 | 541.40 | 650 | 16,850.00 | 2,800 | 17.55 | 17.70 | 4,250 | -11.10 | 17.35 | 14.52 | 8,762 | 1,080 | 2,594 |
| 532 | 2 | 143 | - | 491.05 | -15.95 | 200 | 488.75 | 489.90 | 200 | 16,900.00 | 650 | 21.50 | 21.60 | 800 | -11.45 | 21.55 | 14.21 | 21,298 | 2,310 | 8,405 |
| 166 | -2 | 25 | - | 423.15 | -37.15 | 50 | 439.95 | 448.85 | 450 | 16,950.00 | 2,500 | 26.20 | 26.40 | 4,650 | -12.50 | 26.10 | 14.19 | 8,470 | 1,312 | 3,042 |
| 2,451 | -121 | 3,018 | 8.75 | 405.00 | -15.55 | 200 | 400.50 | 401.50 | 200 | 17,000.00 | 5,000 | 32.20 | 32.40 | 6,600 | -13.40 | 32.00 | 13.80 | 35,019 | 2,981 | 12,355 |
| 349 | -15 | 94 | 9.72 | 366.90 | -10.80 | 200 | 358.70 | 359.70 | 200 | 17,050.00 | 4,400 | 39.60 | 39.85 | 50 | -13.75 | 39.20 | 13.55 | 9,161 | 1,644 | 2,981 |
| 1,948 | 1,090 | 2,418 | 8.45 | 322.60 | -18.20 | 250 | 316.95 | 318.00 | 50 | 17,100.00 | 950 | 48.05 | 48.30 | 1,400 | -14.20 | 47.85 | 13.30 | 30,580 | 3,190 | 10,763 |
| 766 | -90 | 935 | 9.85 | 282.00 | -16.90 | 50 | 277.85 | 278.90 | 50 | 17,150.00 | 1,100 | 59.00 | 59.20 | 850 | -14.75 | 58.25 | 13.13 | 11,488 | 1,138 | 3,166 |
| 5,516 | 193 | 7,922 | 10.75 | 244.00 | -19.70 | 50 | 242.00 | 242.75 | 500 | 17,200.00 | 1,550 | 71.55 | 71.80 | 50 | -14.65 | 71.30 | 12.97 | 41,690 | 1,682 | 12,280 |
| 1,162 | 193 | 3,559 | 10.79 | 209.10 | -19.20 | 300 | 206.65 | 207.35 | 150 | 17,250.00 | 550 | 86.90 | 87.20 | 1,000 | -15.20 | 86.10 | 12.84 | 12,290 | 404 | 2,789 |
| 8,144 | 1,756 | 31,864 | 10.75 | 175.00 | -20.30 | 400 | 174.15 | 174.80 | 1,600 | 17,300.00 | 500 | 104.95 | 105.15 | 500 | -13.75 | 105.20 | 12.74 | 42,286 | 3,051 | 10,196 |
| 4,194 | 2,439 | 20,562 | 10.73 | 146.90 | -19.25 | 50 | 145.50 | 146.00 | 250 | 17,350.00 | 500 | 124.95 | 125.35 | 100 | -14.40 | 123.95 | 12.65 | 18,191 | 1,969 | 3,391 |
| 12,887 | 6,686 | 51,119 | 10.66 | 118.80 | -18.95 | 150 | 118.70 | 119.00 | 350 | 17,400.00 | 400 | 149.05 | 149.40 | 250 | -11.15 | 149.15 | 12.59 | 37,724 | 3,273 | 6,723 |
| 3,609 | 1,626 | 13,055 | 10.61 | 97.45 | -16.55 | 1,250 | 95.45 | 95.85 | 750 | 17,450.00 | 650 | 175.10 | 175.85 | 400 | -9.90 | 175.00 | 12.52 | 4,291 | 319 | 727 |
| 15,634 | 6,258 | 56,949 | 10.52 | 75.90 | -14.95 | 50 | 75.60 | 75.80 | 1,250 | 17,500.00 | 100 | 205.10 | 205.75 | 800 | -7.45 | 204.05 | 12.64 | 13,577 | 477 | 2,759 |
| 5,097 | 1,284 | 14,590 | 10.46 | 58.50 | -12.45 | 150 | 58.05 | 58.30 | 200 | 17,550.00 | 150 | 237.65 | 238.70 | 250 | -5.05 | 234.45 | 11.77 | 1,250 | 142 | 472 |
| 20,538 | 6,787 | 62,796 | 10.40 | 44.75 | -11.40 | 250 | 44.50 | 44.60 | 100 | 17,600.00 | 100 | 272.85 | 273.60 | 250 | -5.90 | 272.00 | 12.63 | 5,579 | 1,191 | 2,321 |
| 4,509 | 2,060 | 19,518 | 10.30 | 33.50 | -9.55 | 2,000 | 32.90 | 33.05 | 50 | 17,650.00 | 200 | 310.55 | 311.80 | 50 | -0.95 | 310.60 | 13.43 | 139 | 31 | 159 |
| 13,985 | 5,904 | 39,534 | 10.31 | 24.40 | -8.70 | 500 | 24.30 | 24.45 | 2,950 | 17,700.00 | 200 | 353.30 | 354.30 | 200 | -20.30 | 332.75 | 11.98 | 904 | 120 | 391 |
| 7,404 | 3,188 | 20,149 | 10.45 | 18.70 | -6.90 | 3,800 | 18.25 | 18.40 | 2,300 | 17,750.00 | 100 | 394.70 | 399.20 | 50 | 8.10 | 396.30 | 14.86 | 93 | 65 | 101 |
| 8,982 | 3,577 | 32,484 | 10.53 | 13.50 | -5.55 | 1,950 | 13.45 | 13.60 | 3,850 | 17,800.00 | 200 | 440.75 | 441.85 | 200 | -2.75 | 439.55 | 15.25 | 372 | 52 | 347 |
| 1,525 | 746 | 5,826 | 10.65 | 10.30 | -3.95 | 100 | 10.05 | 10.20 | 1,350 | 17,850.00 | 450 | 485.45 | 494.50 | 450 | 14.85 | 498.55 | 17.59 | 43 | 34 | 34 |
| 7,194 | 1,610 | 15,703 | 10.87 | 7.85 | -3.55 | 4,500 | 7.80 | 7.90 | 1,850 | 17,900.00 | 1,000 | 533.25 | 537.00 | 550 | -0.60 | 536.00 | 17.08 | 23 | 6 | 51 |
| 1,241 | 334 | 4,629 | 11.12 | 6.15 | -2.80 | 750 | 6.10 | 6.25 | 4,450 | 17,950.00 | 650 | 579.35 | 600.85 | 5,450 | 62.15 | 603.70 | 20.61 | 4 | 2 | 2 |
| 10,252 | 1,484 | 23,726 | 11.54 | 5.15 | -2.15 | 400 | 5.10 | 5.15 | 6,500 | 18,000.00 | 150 | 625.95 | 639.15 | 100 | -16.35 | 620.00 | 16.68 | 177 | 100 | 241 |
| 602 | 150 | 1,852 | 11.85 | 4.25 | -1.70 | 50 | 4.15 | 4.25 | 3,500 | 18,050.00 | 150 | 656.90 | 690.65 | 150 | 80.30 | 683.35 | 19.95 | 7 | 1 | 1 |
| 2,642 | 1,244 | 8,038 | 12.33 | 3.55 | -1.20 | 1,100 | 3.55 | 3.60 | 10,550 | 18,100.00 | 500 | 704.00 | 743.45 | 500 | - | - | - | - | - | 1 |
| 269 | -58 | 794 | 12.66 | 3.10 | -0.90 | 1,550 | 3.00 | 3.15 | 100 | 18,150.00 | 1,000 | 775.75 | 788.40 | 150 | - | - | - | - | - | - |

In a double calendar spread, one has the choice to buy the option at the same strike in long-term expiry as the option sold at the near-term expiry. But, buying and selling at the same strike is not at all essential. You have the opportunity to purchase a long-term option bearing the same premium as a sold near-term option. Thus, you can set up a double calendar spread on this underlying in the manner shown below.

## The strategy

Sell **17500CE** (6 Apr. series)

Premium: **₹24/-**

Sell **17200PE** (6 Apr. series)

Premium: **₹31/-** (rounded off)

Buy **17500CE** (13 Apr. series)

Premium: **₹76/-** (rounded off)

Buy **17200PE** (13 Apr. series)

Premium: **₹71/-** (rounded off)

**Net debit** = 76 + 71 – 24 – 31 = **₹92/-**

**Maximum loss** = 92 × 50 = ₹4,600/- (approx.)

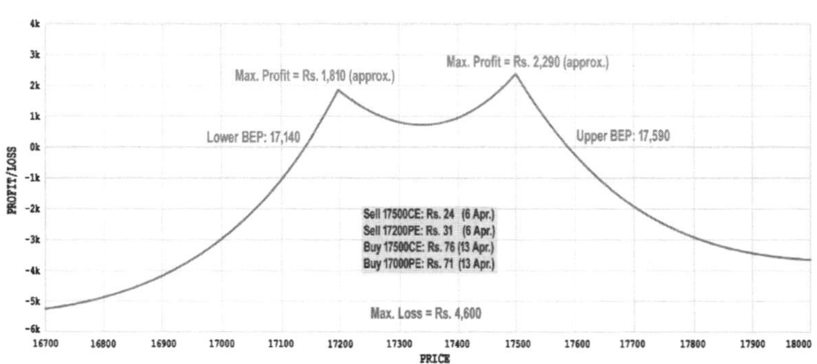


The maximum profit potential and breakeven points in a calendar spread cannot be determined with any degree of accuracy since they depend on the premium of long options with a far expiration. But, because one of the short options expires worthless and the trader receives all of the premium, the maximum profit can be made at either ₹1,810/- or ₹2,290/-, which is where the short positions were established. Additionally, the long option will have maximum time value and the difference in price between the long and short option is the greatest. The greatest risk associated with this technique is nearly equal to the cost of the trade. This is because the net difference in option premium between each option pair approaches zero when the price of the underlying moves sharply in any direction. The highest loss in this illustration is roughly ₹4,600/- only.

## Adjustment

Double calendar spread adjustments are quite similar to short iron condor modifications. If you design a strategy with an overall delta value close to zero, you will need to make adjustments if the delta value suddenly changes. When the delta difference reaches ± (20 to 25), you can start making adjustments. Otherwise, you can watch for the index to test a particular breakeven threshold. Suppose that in a few days, the price of the Nifty would rise substantially to 17,500 and touches the upper breakeven. Sometimes, even though the upper breakeven is far from the spot price, you can make minor adjustments to the approach if you believe that the underlying will continue to rise in the near future, particularly if it has been maintaining above the important psychological level.

In this case, you can simply roll up your put option pair for some more credit to take some cash off the table. This implies closing out a pair of 17200PE options and opening new positions using the same type of options on the 17450 strike.

Suppose, at that time

Premium of **17500CE** (6 Apr. series): **₹52/-**

Premium of **17500CE** (13 Apr. series): **₹117/-**

Premium of **17200PE** (6 Apr. series): **₹6/-**

Premium of **17200PE** (13 Apr. series): **₹35/-**

Premium of **17450PE** (6 Apr. series): **₹47/-** (new option to be sold)

Premium of **17450PE** (13 Apr. series): **₹101/-** (new option to be bought)

**Booked loss** = (30 – 6) – (71 – 35) = – **₹12/-** (per share)

**MTM Profit** = (117 – 76) – (52 – 24) = **₹13/-** (per share)

## New strategy

Sell **17450PE** (6 Apr. series): **₹47/-**

Buy **17450PE** (13 Apr. series): **₹101/-**

Sell **17500CE** (6 Apr. series): **₹24/-** (existing position)

Buy **17500CE** (13 Apr. series): **₹76/-** (existing position)

**Total debit** = Net debit + Booked loss – MTM profit = {(101 – 47) + (76 – 24)} – 12 + 13 = **₹107/-**

**Maximum loss** = Net debit times lot size = 107 × 50 = **₹5,350/-**

**Maximum profit** = Maximum profit can be realised at the short strikes

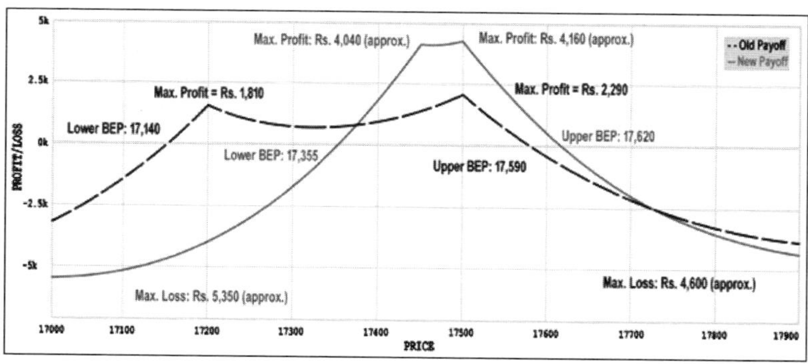


Although the amount is approximative, the maximum earning potential has grown to ₹4,160/- from ₹2,290/-. The two strikes where the short bets were established are where the maximum profit can be made. The potential profit is higher for the call short strike in this instance than the put short strike. The lower breakeven point has also shifted somewhat, from 17,140 to 17,355, while the higher breakeven point has risen from 17,590 to 17,620. Nevertheless, because long option holdings are involved, it is difficult to figure out the precise breakeven points. The strategy's net debit, or ₹5,350/-, which was ₹4,600/- before the alteration, limits the maximum loss potential. This has caused not just the upper breakeven point to go upward but also the profit potential. Yet, as I previously stated, any modification also has certain drawbacks. The potential for maximum risk has also marginally increased after modification.

❑

# Option Buying Vs. Option Selling

Let's start by learning some fundamental information about the options market. There are four different categories of market participants in the options market, as we previously learnt at the beginning of the book. They are put buyers, put sellers, call writers, and call buyers. On the flip side of every option transaction, someone is selling it and vice versa. When purchasing a call option, you anticipate that the premium and underlying price will rise. You will sell your call option at a higher price and earn the difference amount. The call writer simultaneously hopes that the underlying will expire below the strike price and lose all of its value so that they may keep the entire premium. Who is going to win between the buyers and sellers in the current situation? To understand it, you must be aware of the variables influencing the option's pricing.

The price of the option is influenced by several variables, but the three main variables that have the most impact are price movement of the underlying, implied volatility, and time before expiration. Let's now go over the benefits and drawbacks of purchasing and selling options while taking each component individually into account.

1. ***Price movement*:** As we have covered in the early chapters of the book, five different market perspectives can be indicated by a security's price: bullish, bearish, sideways positive, sideways negative, and range-bound. When does an option buyer now make money? Only when the price of the underlying becomes significantly bullish will a call option buyer benefit, and only when the price of the underlying drops sharply would a put option buyer profit. On the other hand, the call writer won't lose money unless the security has a sharp uptrend. In the remaining four market conditions, the seller will prevail. Therefore, an option seller's chance of winning a trade is 80%.

Let's use a payoff chart to illustrate the differences. We will consider the call long and put short payoff charts as described in a very bullish market.

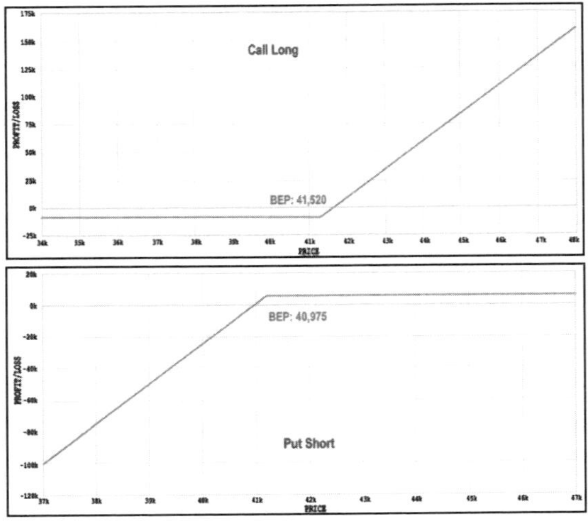

Look at both strategies' breakeven points (BEP). Option writers benefit greatly from the BEP reduction of 545 points that occurs when selling put options as opposed to purchasing call options.

2. ***Time to expiry:*** Option is a decaying asset. With time, the option premium fades away. Even if the other variables that influence option pricing, such as the security's price and volatility, are the same, the option will be worthless when it expires. Time decay is the biggest enemy of option holders, commonly known as theta decay. However, it is an option seller's best friend.

Only if the option is in-the-money at expiration will the option buyers earn. Because of this, the price of an option and its remaining time are always associated. The more the time left to expiry, the more the chances for an option to be in-the-money. Options having a longer expiration date are more lucrative. However, as time goes on, it loses value because the likelihood of being successful decreases day by day. In the above example, time decay will allow the put writer to collect the premium even if the Bank Nifty price remains unchanged.

3. ***Volatility***: Implied volatility (IV) is a fairly complicated subject, so we won't get into it in great length in this book. Volatility, put simply, describes how a security's price might vary from its typical value. The price of an option is directly proportionate to the implied volatility, making it a measure of implied volatility. When IV rises, the price of the option rises as well, and vice versa. This is true for both call as well as put options.

When purchasing an option, the buyer wants to sell it for more money than they paid for it. This will occur if the option's implied volatility is initially low and then rises. Option writers, on the other hand, prefer to sell options when prices are high and then repurchase them when prices decline. This happens if the option's implied volatility is high and then starts to decline. However, based on what we have observed, implied volatility tends to decrease over time. IV behaves in a manner that is comparable to elastic. Stretching it tends to cause it to return to its original position. Rarely, however, can a low IV over time have the opposite effect. Thus, if you can write the option when your IV is high and square off your position when it returns to normal, you should do so. Additionally, since there is less chance of an increase in IV than a decrease, there is also less chance that an option seller will lose money as a result of an increase in IV.

The best way to write options is to pledge the shares and mutual funds that are currently in your demat account. Additionally, you have the option of mortgaging your bank fixed deposits to obtain margin from your broker. These long-term investment assets in your accounts will be dormant. There may not be a better use for these assets if you can utilise them to write options for additional revenue. This, in my opinion, is the greatest benefit that selling options can provide. You are using the same capital for trading and investing. What more can the derivatives market provide?

The majority of the approaches presented here are option writing strategies since writing options has several advantages and risk may be greatly minimised when selling options. However, adjustment knowledge is a prerequisite for earning money through option writing. I encourage you to trade options by writing if you are competent at adjustments. You must be familiar with option selling if you want to profit from the derivatives market. Buying options successfully requires tremendous expertise, which most traders lack. To survive in the options market, you must understand option writing.

Now, you might be wondering why doesn't everyone sell options if there are so many benefits to doing so and every circumstance favour option writers. The answer is risk. When selling an option, the writer assumes all possible risks. Option writing is more complicated than it immediately appears. If you write an option expecting to get the entire premium upon expiration, you could occasionally be proven wrong. If the news is unfavourable or there is a lot of volatility, you might lose everything. Option writing occasionally requires adjustment if the market doesn't move in your favour. As was covered earlier in the book, an option writer must modify their strategy as needed.

❑

# Conclusion

In *The Gita of Option Trading: Trading Options With Purpose*, we looked at the fundamentals of option trading and demonstrated how to spot short-term trends using information from FII, DII, and professional traders. Along with real-world examples and adjusting methods for each strategy, we also covered several noteworthy trading strategies for each market condition.

Through this learning process, we have discovered that trading options involves a greater understanding of market movements and the underlying assets than just buying and selling options. We now know that trading options with a purpose entails having a defined strategy in place as well as the flexibility to adjust it as necessary to adapt to changing market conditions.

One of the most important lessons from this book is that trading options is a long-term investing strategy that takes patience, discipline, and an openness to learning rather than a quick method for getting rich. The ability to recognise market patterns, have a well-thought-out trading strategy, and have a firm grasp of option trading's fundamentals are all necessary for success, as I have shown.

There is a plethora of strategies accessible to reap the rewards from option trading, but it is not required to be familiar with them all, which is another crucial lesson we have learnt. Choose a couple of them, and become an expert in those tactics. Before trading with real money, thoroughly understand them and back-test them. Let me share with you a crucial fact about trading options: understanding the technique by itself is not enough to generate income. How successfully you manage the strategy when the market is not on your side is more essential. The key component to successful option trading is the adjustment of the option strategy.

It looks quite simple and exciting to learn an option strategy and adjustment approach by reading a book or watching a YouTube video. But there will be many difficulties you must overcome in real life. Don't be discouraged then; simply read the plan again and see if you missed anything. If so, repeat the process correctly this time. As I stated, the most crucial quality for a successful option trader is self-control. Since no one can foresee the market with absolute certainty, self-discipline is the only formula for success in trading. You may occasionally need to take losses as well and book them. That is an inherent aspect of trading. But over the long run, your profit should outweigh your losses, and you can do so by exercising self-control.

The majority of strategies in this book are illustrated with the help of weekly option chains. However, the same techniques are also applicable to weekly and monthly options. Trading in long-term expiries is advised for tenderfoot traders so that they have adequate time to make adjustments.

Another important lesson we have learnt is the importance of data. We have emphasised the value of using data to make wise trading decisions throughout the whole book. As we've seen, we can spot short-term trends and make better informed trading decisions by looking at the option chain and monitoring the trading activity of FII, DII, and Pro traders.

Overall, *The Gita of Option Trading: Trading Options With Purpose* is a thorough introduction to option trading that covers the fundamentals, advanced strategies, and adjustment methods. Whether they are novice or experienced traders, it is a must-read for anybody interested in option trading. Readers will be well-equipped to handle the complicated world of option trading and make wise trading decisions with this book as their guide.

Last but not least, if you think the book is worth reading, don't be shy to express your thoughts in the review area so that your fellow traders may be inspired to do the same. Let's educate every retail trader and turn them into professional traders.

❑

# Disclaimer

The option approaches covered in this book are solely meant to be informative and educative; they shouldn't be interpreted as trading or investing advice. None of the information presented here should be interpreted as a recommendation that a certain trading strategy is suited for a given individual. This book's analytical techniques, suggested strategies and adjustment techniques are founded on past price trends and data. Nothing in this book's lessons is implied or guaranteed to bring a profit by the author. Trading options carries risk and is not suited for all investors.

The author is NOT a SEBI registered adviser, to sum up. Each strategy or adjustment method mentioned in this book comes directly from the author's own experience. The author recommends everyone to be aware of potential risks associated with trading stocks and options. All opinions and trade mentions in this book are the author's own. Before executing a trade, he advises every trader to conduct independent research and ensure that they are aware of all the threats. He is in no way promising that these trades will be profitable.